A PEDAGOGY OF BECOMING

VIBS

Volume 116

Robert Ginsberg
Executive Editor

A volume in
Philosophy of Education
PHED
George David Miller, Editor

A PEDAGOGY OF BECOMING

Edited by

Jon Mills

Amsterdam – New York, NY 2002

The paper on which this book is printed meets the requirements of "ISO 9706:1994, Information and documentation - Paper for documents - Requirements for permanence".

ISBN: 90-420-1507-1
©Editions Rodopi B.V., Amsterdam – New York, NY 2002
Printed in The Netherlands

For my grandfather, Foster Keagle,
whom I never knew but feel is a part of this.

CONTENTS

EDITORIAL FOREWORD

Jon Mills has edited a timely volume of studies speaking to the heart of perennial and contemporary issues facing education including: the role of wisdom, the value of virtue, the urgency of empathy, the effectiveness of dialogue, the mysticism of spirituality, and the impact of technology. These sharply written essays, anchored solidly in theory but offering plenty of practical advice, crystallize many of the concerns in higher education today.

The distinct voices in this volume are the voices of the new century. They confront scientism and reduction, and in both oblique and explicit terms return to *paideia*—excellence, how it is acquired and transmitted. This theme could not be more appropriate for a shrinking world and the wisdom and virtue needed to live together in such a world.

This volume is the seventh in the Philosophy of Education Special Series of the Value Inquiry Book Series. It is our first collective volume. Although by no means the product of design, the essays in this anthology represent a synthesis of many of the ideas in earlier volumes. These works include studies in phenomenology (Michael Kazanjian, *Phenomenology and Education*); Whitehead studies (Malcolm D. Evans, *Whitehead and Philosophy of Education: The Seamless Coat of Learning*; and Foster N. Walker, *Enjoyment and the Activity of the Mind: Dialogues on Whitehead and Education*); a Heideggerian critique of teaching poetry (Haim Gordon, *Dwelling Poetically: Educational Challenges in Heidegger's Thinking on Poetry*); and post-Freirean studies (in Conrad Pritscher and George David Miller, *On Education and Values: In Praise Pariahs and Nomads*; and my, *Negotiating Toward Truth: The Extinction of Teachers and Students*). What a boon for this volume to appear at this juncture of the special series.

This volume can function as a centerpiece of a philosophy of education course or could even spin off into a course of its own—so rich and varied are its contents. At the very least, this text is due to the thoughtful consideration of all of us who are wary of allowing the means of enlightenment to become tools of ignorance.

George David Miller
Editor
Philosophy of Education Special Series

ACKNOWLEDGMENTS

When I was a graduate student at twenty-two years of age, I remember discussing my interests and future career possibilities with my advisor who, with sensitivity to a young man's ambitions, said pleasurably: "You should consider being a professor, it's not a bad life." This simple aphorism left a lasting impression on me. Besides my parents, the people who have had the most memorable impact on my development were a few remarkable teachers. An inspiring high school English teacher who kindled my imagination, an undergraduate psychology professor who gently pointed me to the correct answer on a multiple-choice test when I was lost, and the cynical declaration of a criminologist who told me that I would never publish until I had a Ph.D.—these are but a few events that influenced my desire to teach. It was in graduate school, however, where I was fortunate enough to receive personal mentorship from a few exceptional human beings who, in their encouragement and concern, moved me as a student aspiring to follow in their footsteps.

I am afforded the rare opportunity to show my gratitude to three such men who represent the true spirit of the profession, and thus have graciously offered their contributions to this volume. To Frank Gruba-McCallister I owe the privilege of knowing a truly compassionate human being who personifies what it means to be a psychologist. To George David Miller I am indebted for his inspiration and encouragement to pursue philosophy which I have made my life's passion. To John Lachs I am beholden to his personal kindness, investment, and commitment to my development who, in his wisdom, broaches a way of being few teachers could ever aspire to surpass.

I wish to extend my deepest appreciation to Andrew MacRae and The Research Institute at Lakeridge Health for awarding me a grant, which has helped make this project possible. I further thank Shafik Nanji and Brian Gilbert from the Ontario Institute for Studies in Education (OISE) of the University of Toronto for their informal contributions and discussions. Sections from a previous article, "Better Teaching Through Provocation," *College Teaching*, 46:1 (1998), pp. 21-25, were adapted for Chapter Five, and I extend my appreciation to Heldref Publications for copyright permission. Finally, I thank my wife Nadine Gorsky for her editorial suggestions.

No one deserves greater acknowledgment for my development than my parents who, in their distinctive ways, have always provided the hope, validation, and love that only the best teachers could give. My mother, who herself is a teacher, and her mother and father before that, is fond of saying, "Never quit." It is this type of acquired faith in oneself that truly makes me appreciate how a mother is the pinnacle of education.

ACKNOWLEDGMENTS

When I was a graduate student at twenty-two years of age, I remember discussing my interests and future career possibilities with my advisor who, with sensitivity to a young man's ambitions, said pleasurably: "You should consider being a professor, it's not a bad life." This simple aphorism left a lasting impression on me. Besides my parents, the people who have had the most memorable impact on my development were a few remarkable teachers. An inspiring high school English teacher who kindled my imagination, an undergraduate psychology professor who gently pointed me to the correct answer on a multiple-choice test when I was lost, and the cynical declaration of a criminologist who told me that I would never publish until I had a Ph.D.—these are but a few events that influenced my desire to teach. It was in graduate school, however, where I was fortunate enough to receive personal mentorship from a few exceptional human beings who, in their encouragement and concern, moved me as a student aspiring to follow in their footsteps.

I am afforded the rare opportunity to show my gratitude to three such men who represent the true spirit of the profession, and thus have graciously offered their contributions to this volume. To Frank Gruba-McCallister I owe the privilege of knowing a truly compassionate human being who personifies what it means to be a psychologist. To George David Miller I am indebted for his inspiration and encouragement to pursue philosophy which I have made my life's passion. To John Lachs I am beholden to his personal kindness, investment, and commitment to my development who, in his wisdom, broaches a way of being few teachers could ever aspire to surpass.

I wish to extend my deepest appreciation to Andrew MacRae and The Research Institute at Lakeridge Health for awarding me a grant, which has helped make this project possible. I further thank Shafik Nanji and Brian Gilbert from the Ontario Institute for Studies in Education (OISE) of the University of Toronto for their informal contributions and discussions. Sections from a previous article, "Better Teaching Through Provocation," *College Teaching*, 46:1 (1998), pp. 21-25, were adapted for Chapter Five, and I extend my appreciation to Heldref Publications for copyright permission. Finally, I thank my wife Nadine Gorsky for her editorial suggestions.

No one deserves greater acknowledgment for my development than my parents who, in their distinctive ways, have always provided the hope, validation, and love that only the best teachers could give. My mother, who herself is a teacher, and her mother and father before that, is fond of saying, "Never quit." It is this type of acquired faith in oneself that truly makes me appreciate how a mother is the pinnacle of education.

INTRODUCTION: *PAIDEIA* RECONSIDERED

Jon Mills

Education is a being, a being that constantly stands in opposition to itself. It is precisely through such opposition that it comes to understand itself by confronting its own process, the process of its own becoming. And with any system that confronts its own being, change becomes the language of life. Whether fertile or sterile, progressive or stagnant, revolutionary or mundane, education finds itself as the coming-to-presence of self-consciousness. Like Hegel's articulation of *Geist*, education educates itself as it passes through its various dialectical configurations on its ascendence toward self-understanding. Education as self-consciousness may be said to be a being that analyzes its own being, a purposive activity that transmutes itself with each appraisal. Never fully content with its appearance, it remains in a perpetual state of unrest, dissecting its own anatomy, examining and reevaluating its own nature, until "in utter dismemberment, it finds itself."[1]

1. Education as Process

In today's ever-increasing pluralistic and multicultural societies, the political-ization of education has come under siege.[2] Many progressive academics call for a radical reform in educational paradigms, adopting pedagogical practices from postmodern, critical, feminist, and anti-colonial sectors[3] that challenge conservative, academic rationalism.[4] Under the rubric of cultural and value pluralism,[5] there has been a trend in theory to embrace the concepts of community, unity, developmentalism, interdisciplinary cooperation, and value interdependence leading to a holistic paradigm.[6]

From this standpoint, teaching is viewed as a process of becoming which involves a holistic commitment to methodological, curricular, and pedagogical development. The trend toward holism is reflected in the appearance of moral education, spiritualism, and an emphasis on the cultivation and integration of intellectual, psychological, and social development that transcends the mere academic focus on skill acquisition.[7]

Yet the challenge of pluralism has led to ideological clashes over curricular, pedagogical, and institutional value practices.[8] The question of pluralistic education is thought to either subjugate individuality and cultural difference to universal prescriptivism or to banish ties of commonality and unity to the black hole of relativism. It becomes a social challenge to weigh the merits and limitations of tolerance and acceptance of opposing pluralist, separatist, and individualist platforms that espouse divergent values. While many scholars advocate the politicalization of educational reform, the question of directionality and the problem of balance become contestable topics.

There is often a chasm between educational theory and practice, that is, between the real structure of education and the abstract principles that inform an ideology. Perhaps a way to bridge the chasm between theory and application lies in our personal invested interest in the spirit of the profession, for teaching is a way of being. In reality, academic departments are as isolated and more compartmentalized than ever before. With the prevalence and growth of academic and scientific specialization, demands for interdisciplinary unification have often resulted in an obstinate stalemate. Yet with such a multiplicity of approaches, educational reform is far from being stagnant. In the words of John Dewey, "Only diversity makes change and progress."[9]

Education can never stand outside of evolutionary forces that inform its concrete relations. In fact, it is through its own self-evolution that education appears as the concrete universals which occupy space. Historically within Western civilization, we may see that the coming into being of education has gone through many appearances bringing the ever increasingly complex instantiation of consciousness into relation with the actual. From the ancients' focus on educational holism and citizenry, to scholasticism's dogmatic demands for obedient submission to religious authority only to be shattered by the Enlightenment, to the rising spirit of Individualism that captivated the Romantic movement and modern political-social reform which has further trickled into the very fabric of post-industrial, technological society—every generation is concerned with fostering and transmitting its culture and ideology. What becomes the locus of education is inevitably embedded within our social ontology and reflects the contextual reality of human desire. What we desire becomes the edifice of our values.

In history as in nature, the only aspect of education that has remained constant is change. Whether we accept Heraclitus' dictum: "Everything flows" (*panta hrei*), Hegel's dialectic of Spirit, or Whitehead's process reality, change has a concrete realization in time. The time has come for a change in our conception of the role of teaching and the values it purports to engender through the classroom experience.

Teacher education today, whether preservice or in-service, administrative or classroom based, has strayed away from the ancients' pursuit of human excellence to concentrate instead on the acquisition of specialized knowledge and applied skills. While present-day education may be said to nourish the intellect, it is far from nourishing the soul as exemplified by Plato's theory of *paideia*. For Plato, the essence of education is most simply and elegantly expressed in the idea of "nurture."[10] As the unity of the mind (*nous*) or intellect, morality (*ethos*), and desire (*eros*), the process of nurturing the soul was the essential aim of Greek education.

From my perspective, few college and university teachers are concerned with the overall personal development of their students. Even fewer are concerned with forming teacher-student mentoring relationships. Instead, they mainly concentrate on providing knowledge and help develop technical abilities through instruction. While there are many thoughtful, humanistic, and talented teachers who bring their creative imagination and conscience to bear upon their classroom aims, there are many teachers, I would argue even more, who are more concerned about their personal academic pursuits rather than their responsibility to educate the young.

How often does a professor come to class, give a lecture, then leave; who keeps minimal office hours with the door shut in order to deter interruption, thus giving the impression that he or she does not wish to be disturbed? This is the type of teacher who is not likely to go out of the way to form a relationship with students, the type who is more concerned about his or her next book or getting tenured, publishing over teaching, and perhaps the type that uses the same old yellow lecture notes and teaches the same outdated material just reeling in the years until retirement.

Perhaps this is the nature of the educational beast—publish or perish, obtain grants and patents, secure professional recognition. From this standpoint, the intrinsic need to provide quality teaching and foster close student involvement is simply less of a priority. As a result, the personal mentorship and concernful solicitude that is embodied in the Platonic concept of nurturing students to become and fulfill their possibilities seems to be either impractical, overly idealistic, or merely a wishful fantasy.

2. Valuation and the Question of Human Excellence

Higher education is in need of a radical transformation, a reconstitution that will address the wider subject of the overall development of the human being. This has been a perennial concern since antiquity but today remains only a peripheral footnote on education's agenda. In fact, in our global market economy, education has been reduced to the status of a commodity, a commodity that is nonetheless very much in demand. Scientific, technological, and medical advancements have ensured that educational and research institutions will continue to be the boon of social progress. However, such progress is primarily measured by a dollar sign instead of the greater well-being of our societies at large and the individual characters of its citizens.

Perhaps this is simply a product of our historicity; we participate in a social ontology that can neither be refused nor annulled.[11] And in order to flourish and prosper, education must serve a social purpose and provide a useful product based in accordance with community value-judgments. Today this often amounts to highly specialized knowledge and applied technical abilities that arise out of social and market demands. What a community values ultimately becomes the foundation of its educational structures, and it is through the dissemination of its value practices that education is understood as a socially controlled experience.[12]

Within our increasingly competitive consumer and multicultural societies, the role of education is of vital importance to the future of individual and collective development. Beyond the more generalized aims of education that seek to cultivate intellectual and occupational achievement, we may notice that in certain spectrums of educational philosophy and pedagogy, education is gradually taking on a new appearance as it moves toward a curriculum for being that elevates human values and ideals over mere knowledge and skill acquisition.[13] This phenomena is made possible by educators who place primacy on the significance of nurturing the overall development of students' pursuits of human excellence in accordance with an intelligible principle of value. Student development is advanced by teachers who sincerely seek to perfect their craft,[14] and this is often initiated by those who see teaching as a calling.[15] From this vantage point, education is gradually evolving into a more reflective and caring being, one that values students' personhoods and the interpersonal and cultural sensitivities that inform our world consciousness.

Albeit slowly, we are beginning to see the actualization of an interdisciplinary trend toward education emphasizing an integrative and multidimensional approach to curricular and pedagogical holism. Resulting from this interdisciplinary current, there has also been a move to incorporate contemporary perspectives within academic programs and preexisting curriculum structures without necessarily displacing tradition. These movements may be said to reflect the coming into being of a new education.

Yet despite this recent fashion in education, there is still a firm antithesis between the educational goals of skill and knowledge acquisition versus that of personal and moral development. Democratic education draws a distinction between the promulgation of academic excellence versus that of personal values, arguing that such values are individually and culturally selective, subjective, and contextual, hence beyond the confines of general education.

To teach subjective valuation practices over others is to presuppose, at least theoretically, that certain values are superior to others or contain universal truths which possess the attributes of objectivity, and therefore should be pursued. While the nature of teaching is by definition the expression of value, the question of the epistemology of value and the negative encroachment on students' rights is often a concern when considering the type of values that are professed over others. We may all agree that murder should be condemned and kindness toward our fellow human beings engendered, but we draw the line when it comes to which God(s) to worship, which political party or social system to espouse, and which ways we want to live our personal and private lives.

When these issues are considered critically, what right does education have in foisting certain values upon students over others? Can it under any circumstance justify its positions? Perhaps this is self-evident: *Yes*, it can and it does. Education can justify and does teach certain values over others in many contexts, particularly when they adhere to objective facts, custom, scientific and logical authority, and collective agreement or social consensus. But in other contexts it falls short, particularly when it comes to values that are subjectively based on choices governed by personal liberty, preference, and ethnic or cultural differences that stand in opposition to those of others. From this viewpoint, the holistic instruction of human excellence appears to be curtailed by the multitude of life experiences that serve to impact on identity and personal growth.

While academic excellence is fostered within socially organized educational systems, it is argued that the teaching of personal excellence is a matter which more appropriately belongs to the family, community, and private or religious institutions. As a result, the question and teaching of universal valuation may be said to be foreclosed from the mainstream of educational objectives and is thus abandoned to the abyss of relativism. If formal education is barred from inculcating universal value practices, then personal values are ultimately relative to a particular individual or group regardless of whether we agree with them or not.

Due to the potential for personal and moral lassitude, can a case be made for the teaching of values within our proper educational systems? One might immediately conclude, yes. But this is further confounded by ambiguity over what actually constitutes value. From the dialogue, *Meno*, Plato poses many difficult questions about the nature of virtue including its ability to be taught. Meno asks:

> Can you tell me, Socrates—is virtue something that can be taught? Or does it come by practice? Or is it neither teaching nor practice that gives it to a man but natural aptitude or something else?[16]

To which Socrates replies: "The fact is that far from knowing whether it can be taught, I have no idea what virtue is."[17]

Despite Socrates' dubious conclusion, he still contends that virtue or human excellence can be attained—presumably through dialectic. Yet the teaching of values within education also poses other problems because not only does it raise the equivocal question of what kinds of values *will* be taught, but more importantly, what values *should* be taught. Of course the dark shadow of relativism always trails us when we attempt to foster values that are by definition subjective, even if such values are collectively shared.

On the other hand, should an educational system and its pedagogical aims continue to produce graduates who only possess skills but no excellences? Is not psychological, emotional, interpersonal, and ethical development that promotes social conscientiousness and a virtuous life just as important as intellectual achievement? When we look at the aims of our academic institutions, the latter is always preferred to the former. Within this context, formal education at best may expand the minds of students and provide skills, but it remains almost impotent when attempting to cultivate the overall excellence of the human being.

3. A Return to *Paideia*

For the Greeks, the purpose of education or *paideia* concerned the acquisition and transmission of human excellence (*arete*), what we typically refer to today as "virtue." But education within our contemporary societies is far from inculcating a holistic worldview based on psycho-social, intellectual, and moral virtues and instead focuses on the specific skills, abilities, trades, and knowledge that are field dependent and thus designed to provide students with resources necessary to obtain and sustain an occupation. While this is a necessary and pragmatic motivation, it is far from a sufficient condition, for the question of human excellence is often overshadowed by rigid conceptions that demarcate the range and scope of education.

For Aristotle, education is a teleological activity, an activity of the soul.[18] As such, it strives toward an end, toward the actualization of its potential, the completion of its process. Because the art and science of education is an expression of the soul, we can hardly speak of education without evoking the highest aspirations of human consciousness, namely, the virtuous and ethical life. In the *Nicomachean Ethics*, Aristotle equates the good with happiness and believes that through political science (which includes education), the virtue of human happiness or "living well" (*eudaimonia*) may be attained as the best ends.

> [T]he main concern of politics is to engender a certain character in the citizens and to make them good and disposed to perform noble actions.[19]

Human excellence is not a specific experience, feeling, activity, or action, but rather it is what Aristotle calls a *hexis* and what Dewey refers to as a "habit."[20] A *hexis* is not just a skill, capability, or an answer that may be retrieved from a fund of knowledge at any given moment, instead it is a disposition which may be said to be always present. As dispositional attitudes or tendencies of personality, the acquisition of virtue becomes the subjective ground of one's character, a fundamental perspective one takes toward the world at large. Therefore, human excellence is not just a state one is in, it is a way of being, a way of being virtuous.

While Kant was against the formation of habits because he thought they led to a loss of freedom and independence,[21] he was, like Aristotle and John Stuart Mill, concerned with the instruction of the good in the formation of dispositional character traits. In *Education*, Kant informs us that,

> Education . . . must be the moralization of man. He is to acquire not merely the skills needed for all sorts of ends, but also the disposition to choose only good ends.[22]

Kant's practical philosophy is grounded in reason which forms the sediment of character as the "disposition of the will."[23] But the acquisition of virtuous traits that become the foundation of character need not be restricted to the powers of reason alone. One's way of being is more sociologically, psychologically, emotionally, and spiritually integrative and holistic than the mere appeal to reason.

Unlike the distinction between theoretical and practical philosophy in both Aristotle and Kant, Dewey focuses on the practical function of thought and its implication for the philosophy of education. Following the American tradition and evolutionary theory, Dewey maintains that philosophy arises out of interpersonal conflicts within a social matrix and is primarily concerned with pragmatic demands and solutions. Thus, for Dewey, the proper function and ontological status of philosophy is education.

> If we are willing to conceive education as the process of forming fundamental dispositions, intellectual and emotional, toward nature and fellow men, philosophy may even be defined as *the general theory of education*.[24]

While there are systematic variations in the structure and purpose of education for Aristotle, Kant, and Dewey, all three theorists underscore the importance of fostering dispositional character traits within an educational environment that nurtures a holistic approach to the development of human excellence.

This brings us back to the question of whether or not education should include among its objectives the instruction of human excellence. Perhaps this should be its primary aim. We become what we desire, and what we desire is always imbued with value. Our desires or values form our orientation toward living and thus become the foundation for our thoughts, feelings, and actions. This is why the Greeks revered *eros* as the supreme aim of education.[25] They further thought that *eros* should be educated to desire the supreme object of desire, namely, the good. In essence, education is a process of becoming that results in practical wisdom (*phronesis*); for if education would merely remain within the realm of thought devoid of any application, then education would be vacuous. Through the reflective capacity to differentiate immediate desire from what is truly desirable, we come to authentically recognize and value what is good for ourselves and others.

While we may receive little opposition to the assertion that virtue and the good should be pursued in order to live a full and desirable life, the question of what constitutes the good and henceforth what constitutes human excellence needs to be addressed within the context of education. As these issues are explored in the following chapters, we may see a unified teleological and pedagogical thread that seeks to promote the habituation of value. In the words of Bertrand Russell:

> Education . . . may be defined as the *formation, by means of instruction, of certain mental habits and a certain outlook on life and the world.*[26]

Should the habituation of dispositional traits of excellence be broadly focused to include a philosophy of living that broaches a virtuous worldview? Like many of my colleagues in this book, I believe that this is indeed the proper role of teaching.

This brings us to the role of the pedagogue in the formation and instruction of human excellence. Should individual teachers and educational infrastructures take a more active function in the propagation and development of virtue among students? Are not the values of authenticity, wisdom, justice, moral intentionality, ethical comportment, empathy, compassion, and love just as important as academic skill acquisition? And what could be a more appropriate environment to instill such ideals than in institutions of higher learning where the faculty and administration are thought to have embraced such values for themselves?

Yet the formal instruction of valuation has barely seen the light of day within our educational institutions, and when it has, it has largely become marginalized to the private sectors or religious schools where a few outstanding faculty members have adopted the instruction of human excellence as their overall mission. When academia is hard pressed to justify requiring the teaching of introductory philosophy courses to all undergraduates, it is no surprise that we see a dearth of colleges and universities that stress the importance of a mandatory class on ethics.

4. Toward a Pedagogy of Becoming

The collection of essays in this volume may be said to advocate a return to the spirit of the Greek notion of *paideia* emphasizing a pedagogy of becoming. Most of these essays stress a holistic approach to education that transcends the school of thought that education should remain focused on the pursuit of knowledge and applied skill acquisition. Instead, education should aspire toward the inclusion, promotion, and nurturance of human virtue and valuation as a fundamental goal. In order to expand the scope and range of desirable education, the cultivation of virtue and good character amplifies academic excellence. These distinguished scholars are from diverse academic and inter-disciplinary backgrounds who espouse humanistic and unorthodox approaches to teaching and educational theory. Topics range from the purely conceptual to applied methodology including teaching strategies, techniques, and classroom examples. Chapters address several key issues and contemporary trends in education exploring the values of wisdom, morality, compassion, empathy, spirituality, teacher-student interdependence, authenticity, and self-understand-ing as well as provide reinterpretations of conventional teaching, changing teacher roles, and alternative approaches to pedagogy. We share the fundamental presumption that the role of the teacher, and education in general, should embrace the broader obligation of the pursuit of human excellence. In short, teachers should personally value and care for the lives of their students.

In Chapter One, David A. Jopling addresses the question of whether or not wisdom can be taught. He outlines three robust philosophical models of wisdom: the Socratic, the Stoic, and the Spinozaic. Taken together, these yield a picture of the wise person who is deeply life-affirming, open to a reality greater than one's own, attuned to the meaningful importance of what is most fundamental to human life, aware of self-limitations, self-knowledgeable and self-restrained, and profoundly connected to reality.

Jopling argues that the first step in teaching wisdom must be to convince non-philosophers (that is, people who do not love wisdom) of the importance of these virtues. But this presents an unusual hermeneutic challenge: how can wisdom be taught to someone who has never before encountered it, desired it, or thought about it? Often, the unwise hold unwise beliefs about the value of wisdom, which display varying degrees of immunity to rational argument and compelling evidence. This appears to be a pedagogical Catch-22. Superficially, this problem seems to support the view that wisdom cannot be taught: the most that can be done is to remind the unwise of certain facts whose significance they should realize—but the realization must ultimately be theirs. This view, however, makes it a mystery how anyone acquires wisdom.

A more plausible response to the pedagogical Catch-22—one modelled on a wide range of other successful pedagogies, therapies, and psycho-technologies—involves pressing into service certain universal cognitive and behavioral capabilities: behavioral rehabituation and molding, suggestibility and auto-suggestibility, and mimesis. Jopling ultimately advocates that wisdom—or its adaptive surrogate—can be taught using sub-rational and extra-philosophical means: for instance, with the help of rhetoric, persuasion, simplification, vivid imaging, metaphors, self-fulfilling maxims, role modelling, daily exercises, and psychological techniques. Examples of these are found in Stoic pedagogy, and in Spinoza's philosophical psychology. Jopling recognizes that wisdom is a process imbued with personal value that necessarily informs and transforms itself, hence it is achieved through struggle in contemplation and action.

Next, Janusz A. Polanowski tackles the issue of moral teaching in Chapter Two. In reevaluating moral education in academia, Polanowski argues that most ethics courses inadequately prepare students to address real life moral dilemmas because they fail to provide the appropriate skills that make them better moral agents. He focuses on three major limitations to current ethics instruction. The first shortcoming lies in the gap between theory and practice. Value education is mainly concerned with exploring and imparting theoretical knowledge to its students rather than on providing concrete practical life decisions and skills. By failing to address the existential complexities of moral responsibility, choice, and action as they relate to everyday life experiences, current approaches that inundate students with theory and no action fall short of their objectives. This is why he claims students are often in no better a position to know how to behave ethically than they were before taking the class.

The second limitation to teaching ethics based solely on theory has to do with the logical incompatibilities of various philosophical moral traditions, thus leaving students with the impression that there is no moral knowledge but only theories whose applicability to real life remains dubious. Thirdly, current moral education provides students with no practical skills in dealing with their own personal moral conundrums. As a solution to these pitfalls, Polanowski proposes that we concentrate our efforts on fostering in students analytical skills that will help them deal more efficiently with personal moral experiences. By exposing students to rational discourse about concrete moral issues that have personal meaning based in experience, we may foster appreciation for the clear moral thinking that is so rare in our modern world. Polanowski shows us how moral teaching is a personal commitment to how we should live our lives as ethical beings. As in Jopling's chapter, he ultimately demonstrates that moral actual-ization is a process of becoming.

In Chapter Three, Frank Gruba-McCallister explores the role of compassion and spirituality in education. Utilizing a perspective informed by the mystical tradition to understand the educational process, he sees the goal of education as the cultivation of an innate mystical vocation possessed by every human being. In order to achieve this goal, students must learn how to negotiate various life paradoxes inherent to the human condition. Gruba-McCallister asserts that true education is precipitating a crisis based upon one's encounter with these paradoxes and using this crisis as an opportunity for growth.

The mystical tradition's understanding of existence as the harmonious embracing of all paradoxes involved in the educational process are discussed. The first set of paradoxes involve confronting two ways of knowing structured in human experience, namely, discursive and direct knowledge. The second concerns two fundamental roles that are involved in living out one's mystical vocation—the mystic as contemplative and the mystic as prophet. Methods for cultivating the mystical vocation are explored with a strong emphasis on the central attitude of compassion. As a deeply engaging inquiry into the nature of the spiritual, Gruba-McCallister reminds us that teaching is about care.

George David Miller in Chapter Four advocates a pedagogy based on student-teacher interdependency through mutual classroom dialogue. He believes traditional approaches promote educational welfare that keep students oppressed, passively uncreative, and alienated from their personal responsibility for learning. Following Paulo Freire as well as his own philosophy of education, Miller sees the dialogical classroom as the condition for a democratic and humanistic appreciation of others. Stressing the need for continual dialogue, the mutual exchange of ideas opens into a spate of information and interpersonal validation that embraces ambiguity, respects diversity, and leads to the mutual creation of classroom reality that broadens the parameters of learning. Instead of students remaining the passive receptacles of information, Miller sees dialogue as a negotiation toward truth.

In dialogue, the interdependence of teaching and learning is repeatedly underscored. Promoting a question-friendly and question-inviting environment, Miller sees the on-the-spot oral defense of ideas as a powerful method for engendering skills at communication and rational argumentation. In his approach, he attempts to create a comfort zone for difference and disagreement while preserving the goals of mutual respect, tolerance, intellectual humility, and a complex appreciation of the quest for knowledge and wisdom.

Discovering the correct degree of interdependence, he argues, is the key to developing excellent education. Dialogue becomes the means for discovering the correct method and for creating classroom situations in which all can flourish. Miller gives some personal accounts that make for a dynamic and inquisitive classroom experience embracing holistic and integrative thinking. From his account, the dialogical classroom is the classroom of the future; lecture in its traditional form is antiquated. As a radical pedagogy, Miller makes us think about the value of interdependence.

My contribution, Chapter Five, addresses the use of empathy and provocation as an instructional methodology which serves a purpose for general education. Defined as the disclosure of care, empathy facilitates an understanding and attunement with the psychic realities of students. Provocation used under the rubric of care can also provide a catalyst for active learning, critical thinking, human growth, self-examination, and personal insight. Taken together, empathy and provocation enhance the learning process. I argue that when incorporated within teaching strategies, provocation may be utilized as a means to instill empathy in students as well as express empathy itself. The purpose of provocation is to challenge students to reevaluate the logical grounds, attitudes, beliefs, and values they passively and uncritically hold in order to develop better logical arguments, attitudes, and values that have direct personal meaning. Through empathic provocation, students feel that you care enough to relate to them as human beings in the teacher's quest to help them become and fulfill their possibilities.

Empathic-provocative techniques may be constructed and adapted to compliment the introduction of a variety of distinct topics in general education courses regardless of one's discipline or pedagogical persuasion. The scope and range of empathy and provocation are discussed along with methodological suggestions, examples, concrete exercises, and caveats. As an unorthodox alternative to traditional pedagogy, students come to understand teaching as a way of being.

In Chapter Six, Guy Allen examines the role of the teacher in fostering an authentic environment for students to grow and learn. Through the application of psychoanalytic developmental theory espoused by D.W. Winnicott, Allen shows how students often construct false selves that they project into the classroom in response to the perceived hostile demands of conventional academia. As students adopt and maintain disingenuine and inauthentic comportments in the classroom often merely to get a good grade, they stultify personal creativity and effective learning. The author shows that when students break the habit of inauthenticity, learning accelerates and potential is actualized.

Through the medium of his experience as a writing teacher, Allen shows how he constructs the optimal writing class. After detailing several teaching experiments and trials he conducted over the years, he presents us with his most unique method for teaching students how to develop good writing skills that are important for every discipline. His method consists of three distinct elements: (1) a focus on writing first-person narratives rather than expository prose; (2) individual appointments with students where he reads their narratives which he critiques and offers suggestions for improvement as an editor rather than a judge; and (3) the insistence on a tight and rigorously maintained course frame.

Allen shows a command of integrating psychoanalytic theory with his teaching methodology and seeks to produce a "facilitating environment" by being a "good-enough" or optimal teacher who fosters creativity and personal development in an interpersonal space designed to help students achieve their inner potential. The end result is that students produce far superior essays than through traditional approaches to writing which is further evinced by the fact that many of his students have gone on to becomes professional writers and editors. Allen provides us with several detailed examples of his approach including successful student narratives and case examples of his individual student appointments. Through student commitment, attunement, and mentorship, his pedagogy adds a vital dimension to the academic experience and is an important approach that all disciplines are likely to value as beneficial and adopt for their own teaching practices.

Chapter Seven is by Jeffrey Tlumak who provides an extremely meticulous procedural account of seven interconnected sets of recommendations for promoting effective class discussion. Complete with several concrete applications and examples, this seasoned teacher offers his distinct instructional methodology for generating a critical, reflective, and dynamic learning environment.

Beginning with the first day of class, he establishes eight fundamental goals from offering tips to begin generating a community of inquirers, diagnosing the background and beliefs of the class, to how to phrase responses that encourage discussion. He continues to describe further goals for the first week which include gathering information on a questionnaire that he provides in an appendix. As he takes the reader through a detailed account of his goals, organization, strategies, and specific techniques, he virtually provides a hands-on manual that will impress the neophyte and experienced teacher alike.

Tlumak shows the value of creating an object for joint focus in discussion, emphasizing specified small group work and a modified debate format, and addresses the types and uses of questions and how they affect classroom dynamics. Considering perspectives from cognitive and motivational psychology, the integrated and ongoing use of assignments, and personal narratives and case examples, he provides his best strategies for engendering active learning and fruitful discussion, while delineating the role of the teacher.

In Chapter Eight, Marc Lubin provides us with a detailed look into how the classroom experience may be transformed into a laboratory for self-understanding. Through the medium of his own personal experience teaching graduate psychology students, Lubin clarifies an approach to experiential teaching and provides a detailed review of the elements that make for a powerful learning experience based on critical self-examination, evaluation, and personal insight. In the spirit of the Delphic decree, "Know thyself!", self-observation and introspection are the tasks at hand.

Giving concrete examples, Lubin illustrates ways in which the classroom is structured toward cultivating greater skills at self-reflection and interpersonal awareness. Attention to the ways in which class time is organized and how course concepts are vividly and immediately applied to students' personal existential realities are emphasized. The full focus of his essay is to demonstrate the wide range of potential opportunities for experiential teaching geared to enhance self-understanding.

Through experimentation, empathy, and appreciation for psychodynamic processes, the pivotal focus of enhancing skills at self-observation becomes a central pedagogical role. Lubin argues that this approach reinforces reflective classroom processes, achieves a better comprehension of relevant course concepts, and aids in the development of dramatically heightened student self-awareness. In the footsteps of Dewey, Lubin shows that there is no greater teacher than experience.

In the final chapter, John Lachs and Shirley M. Lachs address the future of education in the next century. With the proliferation of technologies effecting the market economy of higher education, change strikes a resonate chord through the recalcitrant world of academia. With the information age inundating our senses at every moment, the question of the usefulness of the traditional residential university becomes central when the availability of knowledge on the Internet is merely a click away. Annual tuition increases and expanding distant learner programs may possibly displace education as we know it. When most courses are structured to provide a deluge of information mainly composed of loosely connected facts and theories in disciplinary isolation—much of which are far removed from peoples' everyday lives and pragmatic concerns—traditional education may begin to loose its appeal, particularly when average individuals become more comfortable learning through electronic means.

Despite the educational alternatives available through the electronic boon, computers will never be able to provide the human immediacy, interaction, interpersonal satisfaction, and companionship students derive from their peers and teachers they admire and befriend. The residential university prepares students for life, exposes them to diverse values, backgrounds, and social classes, broadening their worldviews and deepening their sympathies. But the future of education, the authors argue, must evolve to address the practical needs of the student including curriculum reform, but most importantly, through inter-generational immediacy, teachers should be more available to their students as human beings.

The value of student-faculty immediacy promotes, not just educational concern, but personal contact with students that goes beyond the teacher's intellectual interest in students to forming a relationship with them. This is the true aspiration of an ideal mentor, a teacher who cares about the overall development of the student. Inter-generational relationships in many ways mirror the dynamics of parents who genuinely love and care for their children and want them to grow up to be all that they can. Because the mature teacher is one who, through intellectual achievement, refinement, and self-evaluation, has arrived at some level of wisdom, inter-generational relatedness fosters guidance, direction, identification, and answers for youth who are in the process of defining themselves. While residential universities are a poor substitute for loving families, professors who care enough to form personal meaningful relationships with their students will enrich the quality of their lived experiences and make a difference in their lives. It is this predominant theme of personal caring that elevates education to a pedagogy of becoming.

Taken together, these chapters attempt to show that teaching is a process of becoming designed to foster the holistic growth of students. In the spirit of *paideia*, education should embrace the obligation to encourage and facilitate the overall development of the human being in its quest for excellence. The classroom becomes the medium for becoming, and the teacher becomes the paragon of what it means to be and live authentically. Not only is teaching about becoming, but as an invested interest in the personal becoming of students, teachers become the catalysts who generate human flourishing.

As a dynamically self-articulated process, education aspires to fulfill its potential by helping students fulfill their possibilities as virtuous and sophisticated individuals. Realizing that teaching is a way of being communicates the lesson that teaching, like life, is always a process of growth, evolution, and transcendence. When teaching embraces a pedagogy of becoming, it advances education as a whole and becomes further committed to the lived existential inquiry into the nature and expression of value.

Notes

1. Hegel, *Phenomenology of Spirit*, trans. by A.V. Miller (Oxford: Oxford University Press, 1807/1977), p. 19.

2. See Stanley Aronowitz and Henry Giroux, *Education Under Siege* (South Hadley, Mass.: Bergin & Garvey Publishers, Inc., 1985).

3. *Cf.* Gerald Graff, *Beyond the Culture Wars* (New York: W.W. Norton, 1992); Bell Hooks, *Teaching to Transgress: Education as the Practice of Freedom* (New York: Routledge, 1994); Julie Thompson Klein, *Interdisciplinarity: History, Theory, and Practice* (Detroit: Wayne State University Press, 1990); John McGowan, *Postmodernism and Its Critics* (Ithaca, N.Y.: Cornell University Press, 1991).

4. See Elliot W. Eisner, *The Educational Imagination: On the Design and Evaluation of School Programs* (New York: Macmillan, 1979). See also Allan Bloom, *The Closing of the American Mind* (New York: W.W. Norton, 1987); and Alasdair MacIntyre, *After Virtue: A Study in Moral Theory* (London: Duckworth, 1981).

5. F. Clark Power and Daniel K. Lapsley (eds.), *The Challenge of Pluralism: Education, Politics, and Values* (Notre Dame, Ind.: University of Notre Dame Press, 1992).

6. See Clive M. Beck, B.S. Crittenden, and E.V. Sullivan (eds.), *Moral Education: Interdisciplinary Approaches* (Toronto: University of Toronto Press, 1971); Dwight Boyd, "The Moral Part of Pluralism as the Plural Part of Moral Education," and Daniel K. Lapsley, "Pluralism, Virtues, and the Post-Kohlbergian Era in Moral Psychology," in Power and Lapsley, *The Challenge of Pluralism*; Markate Daly (ed.), *Communitarianism: A New Public Ethics* (Belmont, Cal.: Wadsworth, 1994); John P. Miller, *The Holistic Teacher* (Toronto: OISE Press, 1993), and *The Holistic Curriculum*, Revised and Expanded Edition (Toronto: OISE Press, 1996); Klein, *Interdisciplinarity*.

7. Clive Beck, *Better Schools: A Values Perspective* (London: The Falmer Press, 1990); Beck, Crittenden, and Sullivan, *Moral Education*; James Moffet, *The Universal Schoolhouse: Spiritual Awakening Through Education* (San Francisco: Jossey-Bass Publishers, 1994); Nel Noddings, *The Challenge to Care in Schools: An Alternative Approach to Education* (New York: Teachers College Press, 1992); Donald W. Oliver and Kathleen Waldron Gertman, *Education, Modernity, and Fractured Meaning: Toward a Process Theory of Teaching and Learning* (Albany: SUNY Press, 1989); Parker Palmer, *To Know as We Are Known: Education as Spiritual Journey*, 2nd Ed. (San Francisco: Harper Collins, 1993).

8. For a review see Robert Booth Fowler, *The Dance with Community: The Contemporary Debate in American Political Thought* (Lawrence, Kan.: University of Kansas Press, 1991); Bill Readings, *The University in Ruins* (Cambridge, Mass.: Harvard University Press, 1996); Michael Sandel, *Democracy's Discontent: America in Search of a Public Philosophy* (Cambridge, Mass.: Harvard University Press, 1996); Charles Taylor, *The Malaise of Modernity* (Toronto: Anansi, 1991).

9. John Dewey, *Democracy and Education* (New York: Macmillan, 1916/1966), p. 90.

10. Plato, *Phaedrus*, 247 (d-e); Nettleship, *The Theory of Education in the Republic of Plato* (Chicago: University of Chicago Press, 1906), p. 5.

11. See Martin Heidegger, *Being and Time*, trans by John Macquarrie and Edward Robinson (San Francisco: Harper Collins, 1927/1962), Division One: chs. 3 and 4; p. 174.

12. *Cf.* John Dewey, *Democracy and Education* (New York: Macmillan, 1916/1961), ch. 2; and R.C. Lodge, *Plato's Theory of Education* (New York: Russell & Russell, 1947/1970), p. 11.

13. *E.g.*, see Louise M. Berman, Francine H. Hultgren, Diane Lee, Mary S. Rivkin, Jessie A. Roderick, and Ted Aoki, *Toward Curriculum for Being* (Albany: SUNY Press, 1991); George David Miller and Conrad P. Pritscher, *On Education and Values* (Amsterdam/Atlanta: Rodopi, 1995).

14. *Cf.* Rene Arcilla, *For the Love of Perfection* (New York: Routledge, 1995); Stephen Brookfield, *The Skillful Teacher* (San Francisco: Jossey-Bass, 1990); Philip Jackson, *The Practice of Teaching* (New York: Teachers College Press, 1986; and Max van Manen, *The Tact of Teaching* (Albany: SUNY Press, 1991).

15. See David Hansen, *The Call to Teach* (New York: Teachers College Press, 1995) and Parker Palmer, *The Courage to Teach* (San Francisco: Jossey-Bass, 1998).

16. *Meno*, in *The Collected Dialogues of Plato*, ed. Edith Hamilton and Huntington Cairns (Princeton, N.J.: Princeton University Press, 1989), 70 (a), p. 354.

17. *Ibid*, 71 (a).

18. Aristotle, *Aristotle on Education*, trans. and ed. by John Burnet (Cambridge, England: Cambridge University Press, 1903/1973), pp. 1-2.

19. Aristotle, *Nicomachean Ethics*, trans. by M. Ostwald (Englewood Cliffs, N.J.: Prentice Hall, 1962), Book 1, Sec. 9, 1099b/30, p. 23.

20. William K. Frankena. *Three Historical Philosophies of Education* (Glenview, Ill.: Scott, Foresman and Company, 1965), p. 2.

21. I. Kant, *Education*, trans. by Annette Churton (Ann Arbor, Mich.: University of Michigan Press, 1960), p. 45.

22. *Ibid*, p. 20.

23. I. Kant, *Anthropology From a Pragmatic Point o f View*, trans. by Mary J. Gregor (The Hague: Netherlands: Martinus Nijhoff, 1974), Part II, A, 3; and *Education*, pp. 84, 98f.

24. Dewey, *Democracy and Education*, p. 329.

25. See Jim Garrison, *Dewey and Eros* (New York: Teachers College Press, 1997), p. xiii.

26. Bertrand Russell, *Mysticism and Logic* (London: George Allen and Unwin, 1917), p. 37.

One

CAN WISDOM BE TAUGHT?

David A. Jopling

> My dear Agathon . . . I only wish that wisdom were the kind
> of thing that flowed . . . from the vessel that was full to the
> one that was empty.
>
> Socrates, *Symposium*

Can wisdom be taught? Is the love of wisdom contagious? If so, then how does
the flow of wisdom from a full vessel to an empty vessel occur? Is wisdom
something that could support a pedagogy, or would this be an external
imposition that alienates the very *eros* that informs the pursuit of wisdom? Could
it be that wisdom is the antithesis of pedagogy, pedagogy's other?

Before these questions can be addressed, it is important to develop a working
idea of the nature of wisdom. Just as there are conflicting conceptions of
wisdom, so there are different kinds of wisdom, ranging from the theoretical and
practical wisdom identified by Aristotle, to technical wisdom, aesthetic wisdom,
and the folk wisdom contained in proverbs, and in religious and secular
literature.

Following this discussion, the argument I will defend is the following: (1)
Those who have wisdom have both a metaphysical understanding about the
nature of self, time, eternity, God, and mind, and a practical and action-guiding
understanding about the good life, moral excellence, and virtuous conduct; (2)
Wisdom, or some functionally close variant of it, is teachable; and (3) The
obstacles to teaching wisdom can be overcome through pressing into service both
philosophical and extra-philosophical pedagogical techniques, including *mimesis*
and rhetoric.

1. Varieties of Wisdom

What kind of wisdom do philosophers desire? Is it the kind of wisdom that
involves an esoteric metaphysical knowledge about the nature of reality, or does
it involve a much less exalted understanding that remains human-scaled,
accessible to all who work at it, and practically oriented? Some philosophers
have defended the view that genuine wisdom involves holding true metaphysical
beliefs about God, nature, and the self; and that acquiring these beliefs may

require radical metaphysical revisioning, and perhaps even liberation from a false metaphysics. This would make the transfer of wisdom dependent upon a disciplined training in metaphysical knowledge, and thus accessible only to a few. The last lines of Spinoza's *Ethics* appear to support this construal: wisdom (which he calls "blessedness") is "almost universally neglected," "rarely discovered," and located at the end of a long and difficult philosophical road.

The tension between human-scaled and exalted wisdom is not uncommon in Western philosophy. Plato, for instance, describes wisdom as "the highest of human things," and as the "most valuable of our possessions," because it involves the contemplation of eternal and immutable Ideas. Augustine also views wisdom as an intellectual virtue: it is humanity's highest good, because it involves the contemplation of an infinite realm of invisible and intelligible things. Similarly, Aquinas characterizes wisdom as knowledge of the first cause, or of the noblest causes and principles.

The Stoics and Epicureans, however, as well as a number of Renaissance humanists (such as Coluccio Salutati, Reuchlin, Guillaume Budé, Bovillus, Conrad Celtis, Sir Thomas Elyot, and Francis Bacon), sought to expand the meaning of the term wisdom from its narrow metaphysical connotation to wisdom as an *ars vivendi*, involving moral and prudential virtue, rather than purely intellectual virtue.[1] Wisdom, for them, is essential for leading good lives, and this ideal is not limited exclusively to those trained in philosophical contemplation and metaphysical theorizing about the ultimate intelligibility of the real.

The Renaissance humanist Pierre Charron (1541-1603) characterizes wisdom as involving a "universelle et pleine liberté, de l'esprit." In *De la sagesse*, one of the most important Renaissance treatises on the subject of wisdom, Charron claims that the wise person is the one who has the liberty to judge all things freely, who is bound by none of them, who is universally receptive to every point of view, and who remains acutely conscious of uncertainty and human ignorance. Charron is especially critical of the narrowly defined metaphysical wisdom that understands the human condition *sub specie aeternitatis*, in terms of the "intellectual cognition of eternal things." Human life, according to Charron, must be understood *sub specie humanitatis*, as a finite event subject to the conditions of history, community and materiality. The wisdom appropriate to this view of life is primarily an ethical virtue: the person who has it is a person of excellent moral character, who in his or her actions embodies a practical knowledge of the good, and whose judgements are sound, reliable, and attuned to matters of fundamental importance. Charron claims:

> that knowledge and wisdom are very different things and that wisdom is
> better than all the knowledge in the world, as the sky is better than the whole

earth, or gold than iron; second, that not only are they different, they are almost never found together. Usually they are mutually exclusive—the learned man is rarely wise, the wise man is generally unlearned. There are, of course, exceptions, but these are rare and great souls, rich and happy. There were such men in antiquity, but practically none can be found any more.[2]

The distinction between these two ways of understanding wisdom has also found its way into contemporary moral philosophy. Kekes, for instance, maintains that wisdom is primarily action-guiding, and does not involve metaphysical knowledge, which he claims is esoteric and largely inaccessible. "Wisdom can be possessed by anyone willing to make the arduous effort to gain it — an effort different from the one required for becoming a philosopher."[3] Nozick also defends a human-centered view of wisdom that focuses on what is of fundamental importance in human living. The wise person needs to know

the most important goals and values of life—the ultimate goal, if there is one; what means will reach these goals without too great a cost; what kinds of dangers threaten the achieving of these goals; how to recognize and avoid or minimize these dangers . . .; knowing what the true and unapparent value of various things is; when to take a long-term view . . .; [and] understanding what one's own real motives are.[4]

In contemporary psychology, the concept of wisdom is leveled down even further to merely adaptive problem-solving and creative cognition. Wisdom is construed as a cognitive achievement that is independent of both moral competence and metaphysical insight: it is a skill rather than a moral virtue. The wise person is described variously as someone who has a deep appreciation of human individuality, an ability to interact effectively with others, an understanding of change and growth, a sympathetic awareness of life-problems, an ability to make sound judgements, and a balanced awareness of emotions.

Kitchener and Brenner, for instance, argue that wisdom involves: (1) a recognition of the presence of the unavoidably difficult and inherently thorny problems that confront all adults; (2) a comprehensive grasp of knowledge that is characterized by both breadth and depth of understanding; (3) a recognition that knowledge is uncertain and that it is not possible for truth to be absolutely knowable at any given time; and (4) a willingness and an exceptional ability to formulate sound and executable judgements in the face of life's uncertainties.[5]

Arlin maintains that wisdom involves: (1) a preoccupation with questions rather than answers; (2) the search for complementarity among points of view; (3) the detection of asymmetry in the face of evidence employing symmetry and equilibrium; (4) an openness to change, and a corresponding capacity to push and even to redefine limits; (5) a sense of taste for problems that are of fundamental importance; and (6) a preference for certain conceptual directions.[6]

These are important competencies. It is doubtful if a person could be characterized as wise and as lacking these specific competencies, or at least a core set of them. But they are not enough for wisdom. First, they fail to distinguish the wise person from the person who merely happens to have adaptive, flexible, and well-developed cognitive and reflective abilities, as a result of fortunate cognitive endowment or fortunate environmental prompts. Wisdom is an achievement borne of struggle and long experience; it is not a given, nor the result of chance. Second, it is possible to have advanced cognitive development and expertise in problem-solving, and to enjoy a high level of practical intelligence in the senses established by Kitchener and Brenner, and Arlin, without being wise. For example, someone can be practically and interpersonally savvy, and reflective in a rationally calculative manner, but otherwise lacking central moral virtues such as courage, honesty, and temperance.

What serves to distinguish the person who has wisdom from the person who has well-adapted reasoning abilities and practical intelligence is the use to which practical intelligence is put, and the kinds of problems that are solved. The characteristics defended by psychologists are compatible with a range of non-moral as well as morally questionable behaviors.

While the distinction between human-scaled and exalted wisdom defended by Charron and Kekes is valuable for understanding the historical tensions in the Western views of wisdom, I will argue that they are incomplete as accounts of genuine philosophical wisdom. The claim that there is nothing specifically metaphysical about action-guiding wisdom, and by implication, that there is nothing specifically prudential about metaphysical insightfulness, undermines the unity of the concept of wisdom. Wisdom is not either an action-guiding virtue or a purely contemplative virtue; and the acquisition of wisdom is not merely a matter of the simple possession or non-possession of metaphysical knowledge. Without a philosophical, and more specifically, metaphysical component, action-guiding wisdom is blind: it amounts to little more than adaptive problem-solving and creative cognition. Without an adaptive and action-guiding component connecting it to the exigencies of real moral conduct, and situating it in the service of the ideal of moral excellence, metaphysical knowledge is empty.

Kekes also maintains that the metaphysical knowledge sought by philosophers is esoteric and accessible only to a few. This is overstated. Non-philosophers also seek to clarify their understanding of God, nature, and the soul, and the efforts they invest in this task, while unaided by philosophical tools and methods, are driven by concerns not unlike those of philosophers. In the final part of this chapter, I will argue that there are available to non-philosophers a variety of ways of mimicking the possession of philosophical knowledge—a kind of "philosophical as-if-ism"—that yields similar results to its real possession. *Mimesis*, as we will see, serves as a kind of prototypical pedagogy for the acquisition of wisdom.

To see more clearly what kind of wisdom philosophers desire, I will first consider three portraits of the wise person. From these portraits we will then be able to see how wisdom offers itself to non-philosophers for *mimetic* capture, and thus for some form of pedagogy. The portraits will be drawn from the fecund well-spring of the ancient and modern traditions of practical philosophy, with their robust models of flourishing and sageliness. In each portrait the wise person will be viewed in light of some of the following dimensions: (1) emotions, desires and pleasures; (2) interpersonal relations; (3) fundamental attitudes toward being; (4) attitudes toward necessity and chance; (5) daily routines; (6) attitudes toward body and health; and (7) spirituality.

On the basis of these portraits, a composite sketch of the wise person will emerge. As with all composite profiles, it will be imperfect and thin: at once bland and tantalizingly suggestive, it will also foreground the shared features of the portraits, and background the disjunctive ones. Despite its incompleteness, it will provide a rudimentary working model that will help orient the discussion toward the puzzle of wisdom's pedagogy.

2. Portraits of the Wise

A. The Socratic Wise Person

According to Socrates, the wise care above all else for the state of their soul. Those who have wisdom display a rational disdain toward the conventional idols worshiped unthinkingly by most ordinary people: namely, material possessions, fame, fortune, sensual pleasure, and physical beauty. These are recognized as merely transient and external goods that only distract the mind's attention away from what is of lasting importance.

Socratic wisdom is distinctive because of its corrective and prophylactic character. One of the distinguishing marks of the wise is that they understand that nothing is more mistaken and more damaging to the health of the soul than the belief that they know something when in fact they do not. Wisdom consists in the honest recognition of one's own ignorance. This, however, is neither a contemplative nor a solitary understanding. The wise apply it vigorously in everyday life, impugning, as did Socrates, the putative knowledge claims made by experts, technocrats, sophists, and rhetoricians, and the putative moral claims made by politicians, social leaders, and religious figures. As the Socratic dialogues repeatedly demonstrate, one of the conditions of successfully occupying such public positions is a supreme confidence regarding the cogency of one's beliefs, coupled with a variety of strategic mechanisms that effectively close off sustained self-reflexive criticism about those very beliefs. Satisfying these conditions is the recipe for intellectual pride.

The wise know that the most important corrective to pride is self-examination. To be properly equipped for the practical duties of life, including public office, the wise must encourage others to engage in rational reflective self-evaluation—in order that they become acquainted with the extent of their knowledge and capacities, and their defects. Only in this way will they be able to distinguish what they really know from what they only seem to know. The humility that comes with owning up to ignorance makes them better persons and more responsible knowers. Self-examination is therefore an essential component of care for the soul. Without it, there can be neither self-control nor self-direction.

One of the distinctive marks of Socratic wisdom is its critical and negative character. Those who are wise maintain a steadfast suspicion of glib sagacity, ready-made answers, and false rhetoric. They refuse to assent to second-hand opinions, preferring instead to risk thinking for themselves, and to make their own decisions about how to live. They are aware that ultimately there is no one but themselves to take responsibility for their moral way of being.

Epistemic responsibility is not a solitary endeavor. One of the public duties of the wise is the unpopular and potentially dangerous one of disturbing unreflective people from their moral complacency, by stinging their conscience, and breaking up the ossified crust of intellectual habit that prevents them from seeing the world responsibly and accurately. In this role of gadfly, the *modus operandi* must always be dialectic: that is, engaging non-philosophers in conversation about ideas about which they (non-philosophers) profess some degree of expertise—then disavowing any understanding of those ideas, requesting illumination, and pressing forward with a series of strategically placed questions, counter-examples, and demands for conceptual clarification.

Dialectic invariably reveals the ambiguities or inconsistencies of the interlocutor's initially preferred definitions. If the interlocutor is honest, these often unexpected revelations will lead to revised definitions, which then lead to renewed dialectical challenges, and so on. The process of dialectic always resists finalization.

> Dialectic must skillfully choose a tortuous path . . . in order to bring the interlocutor to discover the contradictions of his own position, or to admit an unforeseen conclusion. All the circles, detours, endless divisions, digressions,

and subtleties . . . [of Socrates' dialogues] are destined to make . . . interlocutors travel a specific path. Thanks to these detours, "with great effort, one rubs names, definitions, visions and sensations against one another"; one "spends a long time in the company of these questions"; one "lives with them" (Seventh Letter, 344b) until the "light blazes forth."[7]

The wise view themselves as midwives in the dialectical process, bringing to light ideas that are latent in others. They do not think of themselves as teachers, imparting ideas in the mind that were not there before; nor do they think of themselves as masters, because they know that they have nothing positive to say, and no substantive thesis to defend.

One of the critical components of the dialectical process is cross-examination or *elenchus*—a systematic process of examining and refuting an idea by logical argument using a graded series of questions. Using *elenchus* exploringly, the wise must be sensitive to the timing and direction of their questioning, as well as to the very form of questioning (which has the potential to adversely influence the outcome of the process). Practiced skillfully, however, *elenctic* dialogue progresses toward a moment of crisis when the interlocutors are overcome with discouragement, shame, and confusion. This is clearly expressed by Meno:

Socrates, before I even met you I used to hear that you are always in a state of perplexity and that you bring others to the same state, and now I think you are bewitching and beguiling me, simply putting me under a spell, so that I am quite perplexed. . . . You seem, in appearance and in every other way, to be like the broad torpedo fish, for it too makes anyone who comes close and touches it feel numb, and you now seem to have had that kind of effect on me, for both my mind and my tongue are numb, and I have no answer to give you. Yet I have made many speeches about virtue before large audiences on a thousand occasions . . . but now I cannot even say what it is.[8]

Elenchus has as much to do with intellectual honesty and courage as it has to do with logical acumen. Interlocutors may have impeccable logical skills, but if they do not have the honesty to say what they really think, the reasonableness to admit their ignorance, and the courage to continue the process of questioning, they would miss the point of the dialogue altogether. Humility, in other words, is an essential component of the dialectical process leading to wisdom. The unmasking of ungrounded knowledge claims is as productive as it is humbling: the person who can be made to feel humility is also the person who has the most to gain from the dialogue—while the person who out of pride refuses to acknowledge his or her own confusion remains untreatable.

To encounter the wise person, then, is to engage in a kind of moral accounting, or owning up. The wise refuse to be deceived, and refuse to allow others to deceive themselves. One of his acquaintances said of Socrates:

> Anyone who has an intellectual affinity to Socrates and enters into conversation with him is liable to be drawn into an argument; and whatever subject he may start, he will be continually carried round and round by him, until at last he finds that he has to give an account both of his present and past life; and when he is once entangled, Socrates will not let him go until he has completely and thoroughly sifted him.[9]

The Socratic model of wisdom is not without its shortcomings. First, its rationalist orientation may be more amenable to people with moral personalities and cognitive abilities that are configured around intellectual interests. People who do not have strong verbal and reasoning skills may be less likely to benefit from the Socratic method than people who are verbally adept and argumentatively inclined.

Second, the educative value of Socratic questioning is dependent upon the use to which it is put, and the consequences it yields: it is not valuable in itself. Like the *pharmakon*, Socratic questioning can be both a poison and a cure. Used irresponsibly, and without sufficient attention to individual circumstances and moral needs, it can be destructive of otherwise adaptive (and morally sound) webs of belief. For some people, this may be a welcome ground-clearing exercise that serves as a prerequisite for the acquisition of insight. For others, however, it may be tantamount to wanton destructiveness, and it may lead to psychological destabilization and moral confusion. The shaming that is constitutive of Socratic questioning, for instance, may be experienced by some subjects as a source of intimidation or authoritarian mastering rather than as an opportunity for self-exploration. It may close off potentially fruitful avenues of inquiry that could otherwise be reached by less directive methods.

Finally, placing too much emphasis on the requirement that all interlocutors provide a rational justification of their fundamental beliefs and way of life may be experienced by some interlocutors as a failure to respect their autonomy. Despite the virtues of the examined life, there is a point at which life can become over-examined: the demand for rational scrutiny, in other words, can be pressed too far. This is particularly evident in cases where an unfamiliar model of examination, with its own internal standards of clarity, plausibility, and examinability, is force-fitted onto a reality that merits reflective evaluation—but perhaps not examination—in its own terms.

B. The Stoic Sage

At the heart of the Hellenistic wisdom tradition is the view that philosophy is an exercise that is to be practiced daily for its morally edifying potential; it is not merely the intellectual mastery of an abstract set of speculative doctrines that may vanish upon emerging from philosophical study.

> [Philosophy] is a progress which causes us to be more fully, and makes us better. It is a conversion which turns our entire life upside down . . . [raising] the individual from an inauthentic condition of life, darkened by unconsciousness and harassed by worry, to an authentic state of life, in which he attains self-consciousness, an exact vision of the world, inner peace, and freedom.[10]

The Stoic sage is the pinnacle of this view of philosophy, having successfully put into practice all of the "spiritual exercises" that are necessary to realize the motto "conquer yourself, not the world."

The starting point of the long road to wisdom is the recognition of the truth of the fundamental Stoic distinction, defended most clearly by Epictetus, between those things that are totally within one's control, and those things that are not totally within one's control. Memorizing this distinction with the help of simple maxims and formulae, and applying it rigorously to their own lives, aspiring sages will learn to locate in the former class their goals, desires, attitudes, and beliefs, and in the latter class their health, wealth, reputation, pleasure, and continued existence.

A metaphysical revisioning of this order does not come easily. It requires a radical shift in perspective in order to fully appreciate the fragility of the goods in the latter category, each of which, however superficially desirable and compelling, can be taken away at a moment's notice. The powerful cravings worldly goods normally inspire, and the feelings of attachment the satisfaction of such cravings creates, have to be weighed against the disturbing truth that not even the most zealous amassing, nor the most judiciously planned conserving of such goods can guarantee one's future hold over them. Self-deception and denial often prove to be the most convenient ways to stun the pain occasioned by awakening to this hard truth.

Recognizing that the pursuit of external goods will inevitably be frustrated, aspiring sages will refocus their energies only on those inner capacities over which they have absolute control—their thoughts, beliefs and attitudes. The more they endeavor to make the best of these, in light of the ideal of moral excellence, the more they will be able to do whatever they want to do, and the closer they will come to perfect freedom.

Externally, the Stoic sage and the average person appear to pursue similar goals—health over sickness, and wealth over poverty. They are differentiated, however, by their inner attitude toward these goals. The average person sees value only in the achievement of goals, while the sage, acting always with reservation borne of non-attachment, sees that the real value lies in the attempt to achieve them. Like an archer whose goal is not to hit the target but to do his or her best to hit it, the Stoic sage knows that it is the pursuit, and not the goal attained, that matters most.

Aware of their place in the larger cosmos, sages also know that things do not happen by chance: every event, from the falling of a leaf to the eruption of a volcano, is preceded by an infinitely long chain of causes and effects that could not have been otherwise. Nature is constituted by unbending law-like patterns, and the sage, as one minuscule part of the whole, has learned to identify with Nature's unfolding, and to accept the necessity of its laws. True wisdom, wrote Seneca, "consists in not departing from nature and in molding our conduct according to her laws and model." The freedom experienced by Stoic sages is a freedom of mind, based on inner self-determination; it is not a contra-causal freedom of action.

To illustrate this, Stoic sages liken their situation to that of a dog chained to the back of a cart that is drawn forward by a team of oxen. No matter how hard the dog struggles against the chain, it cannot alter the momentum or destination of the cart. The situation is not hopeless, however, because it is still entirely up to the dog to be either dragged along unwillingly, rebelling futilely against its situation, or to trot along freely at precisely the cart's pace. Sages, similarly, are free even in chains. Their external situation and their fortune are up to fate, but their moral excellence and freedom of mind are entirely up to themselves.

Endeavoring always to instantiate this metaphysical knowledge in everyday conduct, Stoic sages will be courageous, self-controlled, rational, and never disturbed by such passive emotions as sorrow, anger, or fear, which have their origin in external attachments. They will also be magnanimous, displaying a lofty indifference to the petty worries of everyday life, and refusing to become attached to those external things that are but transitory gifts of fortune. Thus they will accept and affirm all events, however hideous, without complaint, regret, or hope that things be otherwise. They have learned to desire that "everything happen just the way it does happen."[11]

Stoic sages enjoy a kind of mental serenity. They know that it is not events themselves that are disturbing, but the views they hold of events. They know, for example, that natural phenomena such as floods are in themselves neither bad nor destructive, as these are merely human-scaled valuations that reflect parochial human interests as much as an ignorance of nature's workings. One of the conditions for the cessation of suffering is the ability to view all things with this kind of thoroughgoing objectivity of attitude.

To consolidate their metaphysical insights, and to express them in action, sages follow a daily regimen of philosophical exercises: that is, explicitly performed philosophic acts designed to develop "philosophically healthy" thinking and living habits. These include daily self-examination, frequent philosophical meditation, the eradication of slovenly personal habits, exercises of memorization, psychological techniques, rhetorical methods of amplification, the contemplation of Stoic treatises (with edifying titles such as On Restraining Anger, On Peace of Mind, On Brotherly Love, On False Shame), and the repetition of simple mantra-like Stoic maxims that help to control inner discourse.[12] Some of the maxims the Stoic sage has memorized include:[13]

(1) Demand not that events should happen to you as you wish them to happen, but wish them to happen as they do happen.

(2) Sickness is an impediment to the body, not to the soul.

(3) Of those things you love, always remind yourself of their fragile and mortal nature.

(4) If someone provokes you, remain indifferent, because it is really your attitude that provokes you.

(5) When you are hurt, you are consenting to be hurt.

(6) Know yourself, your limits, your talents, and your nature.

(7) If someone promises you a nice gift, do not be drawn in by the excitement, but delay it, slow down all of your reactions, and then abstain from it; this way you will feel much stronger, for by refusing the temptation, you have shown that no one can buy you.

The Stoic sage is as rare as the phoenix—so rare that none of the Stoic philosophers claimed sageliness for themselves.

The Stoic model of wisdom is not without its shortcomings. As with the Socratic model, its hyper-rational orientation is not suitable for everyone: some people do not have the requisite cognitive and temperamental resources to pursue the rigorous disciplining of emotion needed to become a Stoic sage. This does not invalidate the Stoic model, but it restricts its range of psychological instantiability.

One of the well-known criticisms of Stoic philosophy is that it is a sour grapes strategy for dealing with life's vicissitudes: that which the Stoic sage really wanted but could not have is conveniently reinterpreted as that which he or she did not really want in the first place. To accomplish this reinterpretation, the sage must shrink back from life in order to live within a narrowly controlled and philosophically purified world of his or her own ordering. The sage achieves this level of purification by denying emotions and desires their natural outlet, and by leveling down the world to a pale monochromatic shadow of its former richness. Life within the protective shell is secure and uneventful, but the serenity the sage enjoys is entirely inward-looking: it is for the self and by the self. The Stoic sage does not confront life fully and on its own terms, and in such a way that he or she can learn from it and grow through experience and suffering.

The retreat into the inner citadel of the self is an act of disconnection, because the sage's range of awareness of self, other, and world is sharply curtailed; so too is the range of his or her responsiveness and openness to the real. The social, emotional, and personal relations that would otherwise connect the sage to others and to the social world are progressively weakened as Stoic disciplines are progressively entrenched in thought and behavior. While Stoic disconnection can be interpreted as a source of unparalleled inner strength, it can also be seen, from the perspective of different models of human flourishing, as causing an unnecessary stunting of emotional and moral growth. This is because Stoic strategies of disconnection undermine a person's capacity to experience a large range of interpersonally specific reactive emotional states (such as sadness, shame, pride, despair, melancholy, loss, and frustration), and the corresponding capacity to experience a range of interpersonally specific reactive moral attitudes (such as disapproval, approbation, gratitude, and resentment). With diminished vulnerability and openness, the Stoic sage is distanced from aspects of his or her own humanity.

C. Spinoza's Wise Person

Spinoza's metaphysics challenges the distinction between wisdom as a purely intellectual virtue based on metaphysical knowledge, and wisdom as a purely this-worldly moral virtue. The wisdom that is the normative ideal orienting Spinoza's system of ethics requires of subjects a radical transformation of metaphysical outlook, which in turn requires a radical change of self.

Spinoza argues that the vast majority of people—the multitude or *hoi polloi*—are enslaved by the life-denying passions of greed, lust, guilt, hatred, anger, jealousy, despair, resentment, fear, and ambition. Fused onto the sad passions are the moral categories of good and evil, blame and merit, guilt and punishment, and sin and redemption. These are mystifying other-worldly values that disparage life and prey on ignorance.

Spinoza describes the mind of the enslaved person as disintegrated and fluctuating, joyful one day and depressed the next, depending on the fluctuations of external circumstance. "We are in many respects at the mercy of external causes and are tossed about by the waves of the sea when driven by contrary winds, unsure of the outcome and of our fate."[14] Cognitively, enslaved persons tend to isolate as the sole source of their joy or sorrow a single object or class of objects, such as money, fame, sensual pleasure, or power. Emotionally, they tend to crave or detest the singled-out object with a blind obsessiveness, as if its preservation or removal is alone sufficient for their well-being. Practically, they are egocentric, because they perceive the world as revolving around themselves;[15] and they fail to see beyond their immediate environment to the chain of causes and effects that have led to the satisfaction or frustration of their desires.

Behind these parallel tendencies is the error of false individuation: that is, the failure to understand the object's place within the infinitely extensive causal network of nature, and the corresponding failure to understand the complex multi-factorial form that any adequate explanation of mental and bodily states must take.

> Most men spend their lives in an alternation between one object and another as the temporary object of desire or aversion, absorbed in their own partial view of their own environment, and unable to see this environment, and their own passive reactions to it, as formed by a concatenation of causes that extends infinitely in every direction. They have therefore no consistent plan, no stable and central direction of their interests.[16]

Spinoza's moral psychotherapy does not involve extinguishing the passions, but replacing them with life-affirming emotions. The premise of the therapy is simple: knowledge of self and nature must always replace ignorance and illusion. There are four central components of the remedy.[17]

First, it must be understood that it is a fundamental law of nature that all living things seek to increase their power and vitality, and to preserve themselves in being: Spinoza's term for this was *conatus*. Once this truth is fully appreciated, there will be no occasion to be disillusioned by the self-concern generally displayed in social relations. Those who have wisdom do not scorn or hate selfish behavior, but seek to understand it as a natural psychological tendency; nor do they criticize the weaknesses and foibles of human nature, but rather seek to accept them in the same spirit that they accept the law-like processes of nature.

Second, it must be understood that emotions are not always appropriately calibrated to their objects; and that it is possible in thought to dissociate such emotions from their perceived causes. Because all emotions are constituted in part by the subject's thoughts about the object and cause of the emotion, it follows that if a particular emotion is separated from the thought of its cause, and is reframed with regard to other thoughts, the emotion will weaken. The most important change occasioned by reframing is the change from belief in single-factor causation to multi-factor causation. For example, if a person is angry at a neighbor's insulting remarks, his or her reflection upon the multiple causes that shaped the neighbor's behavior will help lessen the anger. Just as concentrating light rays on an object intensifies the heat, and dispersing the light rays reduces the heat, so considering the multiple causes of an emotion which were once fixated upon as having one single cause will disperse the concentration of emotional energy.[18]

Third, it must be understood that every event in nature stands at the tip of an infinitely extensive causal iceberg, and that no single event could have been otherwise without the entire causal network having been otherwise. Applying this to human behavior, it will be seen that people could not have acted otherwise than they did; and that many of their actions were shaped by forces beyond their control and awareness.

> Human power is very limited and infinitely surpassed by the power of external causes. . . . However, we shall patiently bear whatever happens to us . . . if we are conscious . . . that we are a part of the whole of Nature whose order we follow. If we clearly and distinctly understand this, that part of us which is defined by the understanding . . . will be fully resigned and will endeavor to persevere in that resignation. For in so far as we understand, we can desire nothing but that which must be.[19]

Once it is understood that one's own actions and character constitute but an infinitesimally small series of mental and physical events within a single infinitely extensive and interconnected chain of causes and effects, one's sufferings will seem like a tiny ripple on the surface of an infinite ocean. One will then see that anger over an insult is as pointless as anger toward a rock upon which one has stumbled and hurt oneself.

Fourth, it must be understood that through self-knowledge the negative life-denying passions can be disassociated from unrelated factors, and eventually deprived of their energy. The imagination-driven mind tends to group together ideas and images in random ways: anything, Spinoza argues, can accidentally be the cause of pleasures, pains, or desires. With enough associative reinforcement, an unyielding template of irrational prejudices and sympathies can come to imprison the self. Phobias, depressions, and hostile feelings, for instance, are often aroused by the sights or names of events or persons or objects that have nothing to do with the real cause of those feelings, but simply happened to present themselves at the right time. Learning to see through these passively-formed associations, and to replace them with a more rational and more realistic order of ideas, is a crucial step in the acquisition of wisdom.

Those who are wise live fully within the world, but they are not disturbed by its transient demands. They have learned to detach themselves from their finite egocentric point of view, and to view themselves disinterestedly as a part in the whole order of nature. As their knowledge increases, they become more and more identified in their mind with the whole system of Nature—what Spinoza would also call the mind of God—and this brings with it an everlasting joy.

> The ignorant man, besides being driven hither and thither by external causes, never possessing true contentment of spirit, lives as if he were unconscious of himself, God, and things, and as soon as he ceases to be passive, he at once ceases to be at all. On the other hand, the wise man, in so far as he is considered as such, suffers scarcely any disturbance of spirit, but being conscious, by virtue of a certain eternal necessity, of himself, of God and of things, never ceases to be, but always possesses true spiritual contentment.[20]

Spinoza's model of wisdom is not without shortcomings, the most notable of which is the paradoxical status of individuality in a deterministic and monistic substance metaphysics. The central claim in Spinoza's argument for monism is that "whatever is, is in God, and nothing can be or be conceived without God."[21] Understanding this metaphysical truth, as well as misunderstanding it, have very real practical consequences. To misunderstand it is to succumb to the illusion of false individuation: that is, the tendency to isolate individuals (including oneself) from out of the totality, and to "love or hate with blind concentration the particular thing which, through weakness of mind, has become isolated in our thought from the infinitely complex network in the common order of nature."[22]

The problem with Spinoza's monism, as many critics have argued, is that the divine substance is so all-encompassing that it threatens to engulf individuality—including the self—in the oneness of things. Heinrich Heine, for instance, claimed that instead of denying God (as Hume and Bayle had argued), Spinoza denied the human mind, presenting it as but a "luminous ray of infinite thought"[23] Hegel also argued that Spinoza's monism renounced all that is particular and determinate, and deprived finite things of their reality: there is "too much God" in Spinoza's system; the divine substance is "the One into which everything enters, in order to be absorbed therein, but out of which nothing comes."[24]

If it is the case that Spinoza's concept of God leaves little room for individual minds as they are ordinarily conceived in common sense psychology—that is, as bounded, unique, and set over and against other minds—then it is unclear how Spinoza can defend a model of wisdom as an *ars vivendi* that is sustainable in a social world the majority of whose members lack metaphysical insight about the nature of individuality, the self, and the self's relation to God. The wise person's experience of self is radically unlike that of the unenlightened person; so too is his or her understanding of the conditions of moral virtue. For the unenlightened person, moral virtue presupposes a concept of self as individuated and unique. This reflects moral, religious and metaphysical beliefs that are driven by superstition and imagination. The wise person knows these to be false. But the wise person is different from the unenlightened person not only in his or her understanding of virtue; the differences extend to the virtuous behaviors in which they engage, and the kinds of social and interpersonal relations they maintain.

The problem, then, is one of social adaptation: how can the wise person live within a form of life that involves social relations with unenlightened subjects whose actions and reactions are based on a false metaphysics and a false concept of the self? How is a common understanding possible, and how are moral differences resolved? The problem, which Spinoza addressed in his *Theologico-Political Treatise*, is even more acute given that the multitude is likely to "respond to philosophical truth with fury and intolerance, not only because it lies beyond their grasp, but because it threatens their prejudices and undermines the sacrosanct images inculcated in them by superstition."[25]

3. A Composite Sketch

The intersection of these three portraits leaves us with a picture of wisdom as a dynamic process of becoming, rather than as a static state of being. At no point could a wise person claim to have completed the journey to wisdom. Those who have wisdom are also deeply and lovingly involved in the affirmation of life. This derives from metaphysical knowledge, and presupposes some degree of philosophical disciplining. They are aware of how the very fact of being, and being in time, is a gift; and they are aware of the interplay of their being in time, and their being eternal. Their lives are thus meditations on time: they know the importance of seizing the day, and of assigning infinite value to the present moment of existence. They know that "from the point of view of death, the mere fact of existing—even if only for a moment—seems to be of infinite value, and gives . . . [them] pleasure of infinite intensity."[26]

Those who have wisdom are also in the world as fully engaged agents. Their wisdom is human-scaled and accessible. In interpersonal dealings they are reasonable in attitude and moral conduct, and formulate sound and consistent judgements in the face of objective uncertainty and conflicting viewpoints.

Compared to others of lesser vision, they are deeply oriented in moral space, in such a way that they are attuned to what is of fundamental importance in human life and what is of relatively transient importance. Despite this, they are also aware of the limits of their own understanding, and the ever-present possibility of erring in their practical judgments and moral reasoning.

Wisdom such as this does not come by chance or inheritance: it is an achievement and not a given. It is preceded by sustained reflection on the ever-increasing accumulation of life-experience, and success at dealing with the central difficulties and moral challenges that present themselves at various points in life's trajectory: loss, grief, failure, unhappiness, illness, suffering, and uncertainty. While the possession of wisdom enables a person to live well, it is not for this reason that it is one of the highest of human goods: it is intrinsically rather than instrumentally valuable. It is in the service of no other end.

The wise have achieved a degree of mastery over the irrational passions of greed, hatred, envy, anger, lust, and resentment—either by extinguishing these passions altogether, by controlling them, or by transforming them into positive emotions. The wise thus display such virtues as self-control, self-direction, and self-knowledge, but they do this without falling prey to a narrow egocentrism that takes the cultivation of the self as the sole and ultimate point of moral development.

Finally, the wise are deeply connected to reality, and do not need the crutches of illusion, deception, or wishful thinking to filter out those harsher aspects of reality that do not conform to their desires. The wise rationally accept and affirm the law-like processes of nature, and their own place within nature, without wishing that it were otherwise. They are aware of the interplay between individual and community, self and cosmos, time and eternity, and change and stability; and their lives display an adaptive equilibrium of these elements. Those who have wisdom, as Arnold said of Sophocles, see life steadily and see it as a whole.

However comprehensive this picture may be, it still fails to answer the question of whether wisdom such as this can be possessed "by anyone willing to make the arduous effort to gain it."[27] Nor does it answer the related question of whether this effort is different from the one required for becoming a philosopher.

4. Wisdom's Catch-22

Given that wisdom has these many components, how can it be taught to someone who has never before encountered or desired it? Given the arduous journey to wisdom, the absence of any immediate motivational payoff, and the sheer uncommonness of genuine wisdom, could a potential student even be capable of recognizing its value, and be open to what a teacher might say about it? If so, how is this teaching effected, and what pedagogical mechanisms are implicated? Are the conditions in which the desire for wisdom is first triggered simply a matter of luck? Is it a matter of having the right environmental prompts (for instance, wise friends or teachers) impinging at the right time on the right configuration of cognitive and personality traits?

The problem of the teachability of wisdom stems from the fact that the state of being unwise is constituted in part by ignorance of the value of wisdom. Someone who is unwise in action and thought is disposed to hold unwise—even foolish—beliefs about the value of wisdom. Whatever potentially transformative instruction that may come his or her way must pass through these filters. Not only is the starting point of the road to wisdom a state of unwisdom; the very formulation of the goal of wisdom may initially be tainted by foolish beliefs, or foolish motives such as status or power.

Pedagogically, the situation of the unwise resembles the situation of the inhabitants of Plato's cave, who cannot understand the words of the newly-enlightened philosopher who has returned to the depths to liberate them. The cave dwellers are in the midst of a way of life that systematically discourages the very possibility of being brought rationally to see the value of philosophic enlightenment. To them, the promise of enlightenment, phrased in terms starkly alien to their darkened understanding, is not a self-certifyingly obvious value that immediately stimulates desire. The words of the philosopher fall on deaf ears.

Similarly, the unwise fail to perceive the value of wisdom from within the framework of a way of life dedicated primarily to the pursuit of material well-being, sensual pleasure, power, or fame. One of the conditions of success of this framework in "delivering the goods" is that it systematically undervalues the pursuit of wisdom. Why is there such closure to philosophical engagement? Why are these life-frameworks so internally self-sufficient and resistant to change? A number of explanations offer themselves, from sociological and pragmatic explanations to psychoanalytic interpretations. The most obvious explanation is that it is morally and practically easier to remain unreflectively and uncritically committed to certain inherited (and consoling) metaphysical, moral, and religious beliefs, than it is to call them into question: philosophical inquiry is both too taxing and too threatening.

Another explanation is to be found in the epistemic conservatism that naturally underpins the web of values constituting the framework of the materialistic or sensualist way of life, and the corresponding parochialism that sharply limits the perception of alternative ways of life. The frameworks underpinning these ways of life tend toward a kind of internal self-sufficiency: their epistemic norms, criteriological practices, and norms of inference are structured to resist the destabilization that would be occasioned by externally-prompted philosophic critique and revision. Direct exposure, for example, to the rigorous philosophical and spiritual practices of Stoic and Epicurean philosophy could be traumatic:

> The practice of spiritual exercises implied a complete reversal of received ideas. The individual was to be torn away from his habits and social prejudices, his way of life totally changed, and his way of looking at the world radically metamorphosed into a cosmic-physical perspective. We ought not to underestimate the depth and amplitude of the shock that these changes could cause, changes which might seem fantastic and senseless to healthy, everyday common sense. It was impossible to maintain oneself at such heights continuously; this was a conversion that needed always to be reconquered. It was probably because of such difficulties that . . . the philosopher Sallustius used to declare that philosophy was impossible for man.[28]

To preserve the status quo, the materialistic or sensualist way of life deploys interpretive strategies and inferential norms that serve to deflect external philosophical criticism and persuasive philosophical counter-examples. The force of the external criticism is missed, because immersion within such a way of life is constituted by a prior decision sorting out what is of lasting importance from what is transient and trivial in life. Similarly, a deeply egocentric way of life is immunized against the potential destabilization that could be occasioned by exposure to philosophical discussion about selflessness. Reinforced by the self-serving actions to which egocentricity leads, little more than lip-service is paid to a teacher's instruction about the limits of the self, and its relatively insignificant place in the whole of nature.

If neither rational philosophical argument nor compelling empirical evidence are sufficient to bring the unwise to grasp the value of pursuing wisdom, and to trigger the desire for wisdom, then what will suffice? Emotional appeal, or pragmatic considerations, or non-rational persuasion? How can the unreflective person's way of life be opened up to such a different and potentially disturbing set of values and ideals? How can a common set of terms be forged to build a bridge of mutually intelligible discourse between the unwise and the wise? What kind of "fusion of horizons" is possible here?

5. "A Right Method of Living . . ."

Kekes argues that wisdom, including non-metaphysical wisdom, cannot be taught. Examples can be set, and reminders, maxims, and role models offered, but nothing a teacher says can trigger the awakening that marks the start of the journey toward wisdom.

> Fools can learn to say all the things the wise say, and to say them on the
> same occasions. But the wise are prompted to say what they do, because they
> recognize the significance of limitations and possibilities, because they are
> guided in their actions by their significance, and because they are able to
> exercise good judgement in hard cases, while the fools are mouthing cliches.
> It takes time to acquire wisdom and we must do it by ourselves. The most the
> wise can do in the way of teaching others is to remind them of the facts
> whose significance they should realize, if they want to have good lives. But
> the realization must be theirs.[29]

It is true that there are significant differences between the foolish and the
wise. But the claim that wisdom cannot be taught is overstated. If it were true,
it would mean that a genuine engagement with the unwise at any level is simply
not possible: the wise occupy one world, the foolish another, and the only
communication between them is through "reminders" of significant facts.

This leaves the problem of wisdom's Catch-22 unsolved. Nothing about the
simple dispensing of reminders to fools, or the setting of examples, assures that
the wisdom-bearing insights they convey will be recognized for what they are,
and interpreted correctly. This makes it a mystery how anyone acquires wisdom,
and a mystery that anyone acquires it at all. Kekes's suggestion that "we must
. . . [acquire wisdom] by ourselves" only postpones the problem, because what
it is for the self to acquire wisdom for itself and by itself is a claim that requires
further explanation. The claim might be coherent on the assumption that the self
is pedagogically self-sufficient (that is., capable of self-learning and self-
regulation), but this model would need to explain the large range of social and
interpersonal influences to which selves are subject, and which typically
constitute successful pedagogical contexts.

Any fool, Kekes asserts, can learn to mouth cliches. This appears to be one
of the counter-productive consequences of attempting to teach wisdom to fools.
But it is in actuality the starting-point of the search for wisdom. Pascal's advice
to unbelievers was "Kneel and you shall believe"; inner faith begins with blindly
going through the external motions. Similar advice might be given to the
foolish: "Imitate blindly the teachings of the wise to begin the journey toward
wisdom." The way to break out of wisdom's pedagogical circle is to appeal to the
universal cognitive and behavioral capacities for *mimesis* and behavioral
molding by means of which students can begin to produce the behaviors
encouraged by their teachers. From this starting point of dependence students
can gradually bootstrap their way to more autonomous forms of philosophical
thought. Mimetism is not a matter of mendacity or duplicity: it is a capacity that

underpins the creation of a new reality, through bringing about new artifacts with real physical effects, real behavioral changes, and real constitutive effects on the self.[30]

Any means at hand can be used to instruct the unwise in this mimetically-driven manner, even if these means are extra-philosophical, unorthodox, or only tangentially related (at the outset) to the specifically philosophical pursuit of wisdom. This strategy is based on Maimonides's and Spinoza's insight that each group can only be addressed according to the level of its own comprehension. As the unwise cannot be expected to fully understand the discourse of the wise, the wise can use the language of the unwise, and adopt their level of thinking, while trying to preserve the integrity of their own ideas within the new discursive level. The simplistic and imagistic systems of thought of the unwise can serve as the starting-point for a gradual reformation of those very systems into what will initially be an external imitation of wisdom. To effect this recalibration, the wise can use non-philosophical language rhetorically, imaginatively, and metaphorically in order to convey a range of simplified philosophical ideas. With the right sorts of metaphors, for instance, the non-philosophical meanings can be challenged and eventually replaced with meanings that are closer to a carefully worked-out philosophical conceptualization.

Conceptual parasitism is only the first stage in the construction of the bridge that traverses the deep divide separating the wise from the unwise. The second stage is based on the recognition of the fact that many of the spiritual and secular practices that promise personal transformation are effective only because they press into service cognitive and behavioral competencies that are common to a wide range of pedagogies, therapies, and psycho-technologies. These competencies include behavioral rehabituation, suggestion, auto-suggestion, and *mimesis*. The transformation from unwise to wise is a function, at least in part, of techniques that are not unique to the pursuit of wisdom, and to the particular metaphysical and prudential content of the instructions of the wise; they are rather a function of techniques common to a range of practices that require the external disciplining and regimentation of desire, behavior, and thought.

The education of the unwise by the wise may require the repeated use of sub-philosophical and sub-rational pedagogical mechanisms that strategically target these universal cognitive and behavioral competencies. The point is to engage not only the intellect and rationality of aspirants, and whatever incipient philosophical urging they might have, but their emotions, imagination, affectivity, habits, and aesthetic sensibility. These competencies are deployed in a pedagogical context through the use of such devices as rhetoric, persuasion, simplification, vivid imaging, metaphors, self-fulfilling maxims, role modeling, daily exercises, and psychological techniques to control inner discourse. Consider the following five steps, which constitute a partial list of the stages involved in the teaching of wisdom.

First, in order to convince initially doubtful or ignorant students of the desirability of wisdom, the wise can highlight facts and meanings which the students would not otherwise have construed as salient. Successfully cultivating these meanings and elevating them to prominence involves more than engaging the students in rational discourse: it requires using suggestion, leading questions, and repetition.

Second, the wise can deploy a range of extra-philosophical means to begin training the intellect, imagination, and sensibility of their students. This includes winning the confidence of the students through displays of their own personal qualities of enthusiasm and conviction, as well as cautiously engendering a certain sense of mystery and benign authority.

Third, to facilitate their teaching, the wise can deploy a range of rhetorical techniques to focus the attention of their students, and to make their own message more believable than what would otherwise be conveyed by purely rational means. These include the use of vivid metaphors and images, such as Descartes's evil demon hypothesis and Plato's cave analogy, as well as philosophical thought experiments.

Fourth, to consolidate their gains, the wise can provide their students with easily memorizable rituals or procedures that serve to discipline their otherwise unruly intellects and emotional states. Rudimentary philosophical exercises need to be practiced daily, even if the students at first remain unaware of the full significance of the exercises. Examples of this strategy are to be found in Stoic pedagogy, with its emphasis on the daily practice of meditation exercises, the repetition of pithy maxims and rules, and the use of memorization techniques. What begins as the mouthing of cliches eventually becomes integrated into an adaptive repertoire of behaviors that mimic those of the wise.

Finally, accompanying the use of memorizable rituals or procedures is a new rationale or conceptual framework that offers to students a coherent and comprehensive explanation of self, world, and God. This is the stage at which philosophical content enters the picture. To be effective, however, both the procedures and the rationale should bear the mark of exclusivity. Couching the teaching of the new framework in instrumentalist terms (for example, that such-and-such a procedure and rationale is only one tool amongst many equally effective tools) is often counter-productive.

A pedagogy based upon such manipulative techniques might appear to be crudely behavioristic, and might be suspected of having omitted the most important elements of wisdom. It seems to make the acquisition of wisdom dependent less on the content of teachers' instruction, and the truth-value of their insights, than on rote repetition and the unthinking mastery of exercises. The resulting behaviors seem to be merely a shell of good judgment, rather than good judgment itself; merely a parroting of the insights uttered by the wise, rather than a genuine philosophical understanding; and merely a studied appreciation of the value of wisdom, without the edifying labor and suffering that assures genuine appreciation.

This argument hits the mark if and only if the mimetic-based pedagogical framework is an end in itself. But this is not the case. The acquisition of wisdom is a long-term dynamic process. *Mimesis* is called upon only at the starting-point of the journey toward wisdom. The point of using these techniques is not merely to produce a shell of wisdom-like behavior, but to create the conditions of receptivity from which more authentic and autonomous forms of wisdom can eventually grow. Pedagogical *mimesis*, in other words, serves a higher end than itself: it is like a ladder that is climbed up to a certain level of competence, and then thrown away. As the students are exposed to philosophical ideas through extra-philosophical means, they gradually begin to develop the resources to be more autonomous thinkers. This is a boot-strapping process. The philosophical tools whose use they first crudely imitated are gradually used in a more independent manner to explore problems that are selected on more independent grounds; and the philosophical theories they first accepted on non-philosophical grounds are gradually subjected to more independent and more rigorous philosophical scrutiny that more accurately reflects their own thinking. At a certain stage, the aspirants to wisdom can even become more critical about their own relatively passive and non-autonomous starting-point, and learn to appreciate its temporary usefulness as a means of breaking out of the Catch-22 situation.

Mimetically-oriented pedagogy was successfully practiced in the ancient tradition of practical philosophy, and advocated more recently in early modern philosophy.[31] Aspirants to Stoic sageliness, for instance, were tutored in the mastery of a small number of fundamental Stoic principles, which were expressed in simple, striking, memorable phrases. Epictetus recognized the importance of memorization and repetition: "you must not separate yourself from these general principles; don't sleep, eat, drink, or converse with other men without them."[32] With sufficient habituation, the principles of Stoicism could eventually be applied with the same quick responsiveness and constancy of a muscular reflex. The training process, however, was slow, and always beset by setbacks and lapses in attention. It was necessary that the habituation to the principles begin with easy to master exercises; only later could these be worked up to more difficult tasks. The final goal of the arduous process was to make the principles so familiar that they were like a second nature, coming automatically to the aspirant's aid in difficult circumstances, when the temptation to react with irrational fear, anger or sadness was the greatest. With repeated exposure, the maxims and practices of Stoic pedagogy eventually became self-confirming: the aspirants began to give back words and behaviors which their teachers had been looking for from the start.

Another clear example of this kind of pedagogy is to be found in the Appendix to Part 4 of the *Ethics*. Here Spinoza provides an outline of "the right way of living," listing certain fixed rules of life that should be adopted even if they are not at the time rationally transparent to the person adopting them. These rules, Spinoza argued, should be practiced daily as philosophical exercises to perfect the mind, just as physical exercises should be practiced daily to perfect the body. Strict adherence to the rules will encourage in semi-rational or sub-philosophical people an outwardly rational life based on friendship, moderation, education, and tolerance.

There is a clear behaviorist ring to this. With enough reinforcement, associative re-patterning, rote learning, and rehabituation, a wisdom-mimicking way of life may be achieved even by the multitude, who will not fully understand the nature of the result, or the philosophical reasoning supporting it, yet will nonetheless reap some of its benefits. But the grounds for the practical adoption of such a method of living are not themselves open to rational inquiry or justification at the time of their adoption; they are to be taken on faith, internalized without question, and practiced with blind commitment.

The end result of this exercise is a kind of partial wisdom. Just as partial literacy that is brought about by a crude reading pedagogy is better than pseudo-literacy or illiteracy, so in the right context an incomplete mimetically-driven wisdom is better than an understanding of self and world that is based on superstition, ignorance, and fantasy. If it produces a form of understanding that closely mimics genuine wisdom, then it can be functional, adaptive, and personally and socially valuable. The advice, persuasion, and instruction of the wise, in other words, can serve as a vehicle to transform an unwise person's confused non-philosophical understanding into a practical and external imitation of genuine philosophical wisdom that is in many ways functionally equivalent, and that serves as a stepping stone along the path to genuine wisdom.[33]

> Therefore the best course we can adopt, as long as we do not have perfect knowledge of our emotions, is to conceive a right method of living, or fixed rules of life, and to commit them to memory and continually apply them to particular situations that are frequently encountered in life, so that our casual thinking is thoroughly permeated by them and they are always ready to hand.[34]

The acquisition of wisdom is a lifelong dynamic process. It is a journey that begins in a state of relative ignorance and dependence, and that moves forward tentatively through exposure to philosophical and extra-philosophical techniques which include *mimesis*, rhetoric, persuasion, and behavioral rehabituation. Eventually these techniques are surpassed, and are recognized for what they are: heuristic bootstrapping tools that manipulate the wisdom-seeker's initial dependence and ignorance in order to stimulate greater independence of thought and action. The techniques play an important role in breaking the hold of ignorance, but they are limited in their long-term effectiveness: they are not substitutes for wisdom. Without personal struggle, reflection, and action, they are merely external formalisms that have no grip on experience. Wisdom can only emerge from the coordination of the "right method of living" with right living.

Notes

1. See E.F. Rice, *The Renaissance Idea of Wisdom* (Cambridge, Mass.: Harvard University Press, 1958), p.4.

2. Pierre Charron, *De la sagesse, livres trois* [1601] (Paris: Amaury Duval edition, 1820-1824) 3, xiv; 3, 87; cited and trans. in Rice, *The Renaissance Idea of Wisdom*, p.180.

3. John Kekes, *The Examined Life* (University Park, Pa.: Penn State University Press, 1988) p.151.

4. Robert Nozick, *The Examined Life* (New York: Simon and Schuster, 1989), p. 269.

5. K.S. Kitchener and H.G. Brenner, "Wisdom and Reflective Judgement," in Robert Sternberg (ed.), *Wisdom: Its Nature, Origins, and Development* (New York: Cambridge University Press, 1990).

6. P.K. Arlin, "Wisdom: The Art of Problem Finding," in Sternberg (ed.), *Wisdom*.

7. Pierre Hadot, *Philosophy as a Way of Life*, trans. by Michael Chase (Oxford: Blackwell, 1995), p. 92.

8. Plato, *Meno*, trans. by G.M.A. Grube (Indianapolis: Hackett, 1981), pp. 68-69; 80a-b.

9. Plato, "Laches," in *The Dialogues of Plato*, trans. by Benjamin Jowett (Oxford: Clarendon Press, 1875) 2nd ed., Vol. 1, p. 89; 187e-188a.

10. Hadot, *Philosophy as a Way of Life*, p. 83.

11. *Ibid.*, p. 194.

12. *Ibid.*, pp. 84-85.

13. *Cf.* Epictetus, *The Enchiridion*, trans. by T.W. Higginson (Indianapolis: Bobbs-Merrill, 1968).

14. Benedict Spinoza, *Ethics*, trans. by Samuel Shirley (Indianapolis: Hackett, 1992), Part 3, Proposition 59, Scholium; p. 140.

15. Stuart Hampshire, *Morality and Conflict* (Cambridge, Mass.: Harvard University Press, 1983) p. 49.

16. Stuart Hampshire, "Spinoza and the Idea of Freedom," in *Freedom of Mind and Other Essays* (Oxford: Clarendon Press, 1972), p. 189.

17. Walter Bernard, "Psychotherapeutic Principles in Spinoza's Ethics," in *Speculum Spinozanum, 1677-1977*, ed. by S. Hessing (London: Routledge and Kegan Paul, 1978).

18. *Ibid.*

19. Spinoza, *Ethics*, Part 4, Appendix, 32; p. 200.

20. *Ibid.*, Part 5, Proposition 42, Scholium; p. 223.

21. *Ibid.*, Part 1, Proposition 15; p. 40.

22. Hampshire, "Spinoza and the Idea of Freedom," p. 189.

23. Heinrich Heine, *Religion and Philosophy in Germany* (1835), trans. by J. Snodgras (Boston: Beacon Press, 1959), p. 72.

24. G.W.F. Hegel, *Lectures on the History of Philosophy* (1896), trans. by E.S. Haldane and F. H. Simson (London: Routledge and Kegan Paul, 1974), Vol. 3, pp. 252-290.

25. Yirmiyahu Yovel, *Spinoza and Other Heretics*, Vol. 1 (Princeton: Princeton University Press, 1989).

26. Hadot, *Philosophy as a Way of Life*, p. 226.

27. Kekes, *The Examined Life*, p. 151.

28. Hadot, *Philosophy as a Way of Life*, p. 104.

29. Kekes, *The Examined Life*, p. 157.

30. See also K.L. Walton, *Mimesis as Make-Believe: On the Foundations of the Representational Arts* (Cambridge, Mass.: Harvard University Press, 1990).

31. See Plato, *The Republic*, Book 3.

32. Epictetus, *Discourses*, 4, 12, 7; cited in Hadot, *Philosophy as a Way of Life*, p. 84. See also Marcus Aurelius, *Meditations*, trans. by M. Staniforth (Harmondsworth: Penguin, 1964), 3, 13; p. 60.

33. See Yovel, *Spinoza and Other Heretics*, Vol.1, ch. 5.

34. Spinoza, *Ethics*, Part V, Proposition 10, Scholium; p. 208.

Two

IN SEARCH OF MORAL TEACHING

Janusz A. Polanowski

Many students find themselves taking an introductory ethics course for some reason or another. I can remember thinking that such a class would be an easy credit because "I knew ethics." Besides, what was there to learn that I didn't already know about morality? I suppose my epistemological arrogance flowed from the plain fact that anyone born into a society learns what they are expected to do and what is prohibited simply in order to live according to social norms.

However, within a few weeks of attending lectures I came to discover that the moral knowledge I thought I understood so well unfolded into a variety of philosophical systems, the diversity and complexity of which exceeded my imagination. Aristotle, Epictetus, Kant, Butler, Hobbes, Mill, Moore, Nietzsche, and others had exposed me to new ways of thinking about morality—ways of thinking vastly different from my parents' admonitions.

And yet I remember that upon my completion of introductory ethics, I felt a sense of intellectual dissatisfaction despite the fact that I found the class intellectually enlightening. Only years later when my students began to come to me with their reservations about my ethics class did I truly understand the sense of frustration that I experienced during my undergraduate days.

The problem with most undergraduate introductory ethics courses lies in the ambiguity of their purpose. This is mainly a result of the modern academic attitude that places more value on theory rather than practical knowledge. That is to say, if the sole aim of introductory ethics is to examine the philosophical history of moral discourse, then these classes undoubtedly accomplish their goals. Students attending introductory ethics courses are exposed to a multiplicity of moral systems devised by various philosophers. On the other hand, if the purpose of these courses is to produce people who are well prepared to address the moral dilemmas that life throws at them, then these courses do not accomplish their goals. Even though students are exposed to philosophical discourse about ethics, their ruminations are highly theoretical and thus removed from the immediate concrete experiences they encounter. As Robert Fullinwider aptly observes:

> The problem [with academic moral education] is that although philosophy is, indeed, the queen of science, academic philosophy is just one more disciplinary specialty given over to theory mongering. Philosophers are no

more educated in morality than their colleagues at the dairy barn; they are trained in moral theory, which bears about the same relation to moral life that fluid mechanics bears to milking a cow.[1]

Teaching ethics is much more than milking a cow. If the aim of introductory ethics courses is to produce morally enlightened human beings, then the focus on theory doesn't fit the bill. Pragmatic moral education needs to be brought back to the academy. In this essay I will argue that moral education is in need of a pedagogy that emphasizes action over theory that is critically self-reflective, practical, and grounded in active dialogical rumination which only the classroom encounter affords. Teachers of ethics need to approach moral education not as an antiseptic academic pursuit that is preoccupied with moral theories and facts, but rather as a pursuit of moral wisdom, which by definition is concerned with the practical ability to solve moral problems. Moral teaching therefore becomes a process, in which its very process is a moral pursuit.

1. Can Morality Be Taught?

One question that is often posed has to do with the justification for moral education in general. We could solicit generally accepted arguments concerning such a justification; however, any thoughtful person would not have much difficulty offering a coherent case for moral education. We could also employ a sociological argument and assert that moral education is the most indispensable part of any society, so whether or not we are able to furnish a sufficient condition for moral education is not the issue here. The fact remains that any successful interaction between individuals requires a certain set of mutually understood rules and accepted guiding principles, without which social cohesiveness would be impossible.

We are therefore not interested in furnishing a rational defense for moral education, this is simply a given. The right to teach morality is not the appropriate question to ask simply because any inquiry into the nature of morality is itself an ethical pursuit. Teaching by definition is the expression of value; hence it is a moral enterprise. Any teacher with an invested interest in the spirit of the profession cannot divest oneself from the pursuit of value, and this responsibility extends to the classroom.

The real question becomes what kind of value should one engender. Yet this question often leads us down the path of theoretical ethics potentially advocating any one of the plethora of moral paradigms. We often feel this to be highly intellectualized and thus far removed from our pragmatic concerns, merely an empty formalism. While this has value in itself, by the time students read the third page of Mill's *Utilitarianism*, they often yawn and quietly close the cover.

Thus we are neither concerned with what kinds of ethical systems one ought to teach student's to espouse; this is inevitably a highly subjective venture. The central issue we face involves the pursuit of moral wisdom; hence it is the process, not the content, that is most important.

Since we have determined that the real question is not: should students be taught to be moral?, then perhaps we should ask: can students be taught to be moral? That is, can we teach students to be moral beings or is this something they have to learn and develop independently from the classroom experience? In the past, moral education was viewed as a necessary part of people's development; virtue was a valued social quest. But the social realities of today's multicultural communities have posed a great challenge to this positive assessment of moral education. That is to say, in the past when societies were relatively culturally homogenous, moral education was characterized by the process of "indoctrination" in which students were forced—by authority of a teacher, parent, or priest—to accept ethical pronouncements as reflecting the truth about a particular moral absolute without having been afforded an opportunity to independently evaluate the validity of those judgments.

However, with increasing cultural dehomogenization of social values, traditional moral education has fallen into social disfavor precisely because of its intellectual inflexibility. Many of us have found the process of moral indoctrination to be objectionable. No longer is the passive transfer of moral values from teachers to students socially or morally acceptable. Society's recognition of the moral right to determine one's own moral comportment has made traditional moral education obsolete. Furthermore, moral indoctrination appears contrary to the modern educational ideal in which teachers relate to their students not in a master-apprentice dialectic, but as intellectual catalysts who facilitate students' intellectual growth through discourse designed to illuminate the various aspects of studied reality.

Acknowledging the structural incompatibility of traditional moral education with modern society does not mean that modern society has forsaken moral education. Quite to the contrary, we can see a proliferation of ethics instruction on various levels of our educational systems. But in order for these types of instructions to attain social support and be effective tools in moral education, they have to become rational platforms for moral discourse between students and the various social, cultural, and philosophical traditions. Students have to feel that no particular moral tradition or view is hoisted on them by their instructor, but rather together with their teacher, through a process of rational discourse, they are mutually involved in the search for the best solutions to particular moral dilemmas.

Employing dialectic between teachers and students in moral dialogue accomplishes three very important results that the traditional process of moral indoctrination fails to provide: (1) Students are allowed to engage moral dilemmas through their own struggling with an issue. Instead of being told what to do, they can freely express their opinions; (2) Having the benefit of a teacher who is adept in explicating problems associated with proposed ethical solutions, students find themselves exposed not only to rational ways of addressing moral issues but also to the intellectual complexities associated with moral thinking; (3) The process of moral dialectic may often reveal to students the existence of moral dilemmas that cannot be solved at a particular moment in history but which, nevertheless, deserve rational examination so that the students might comprehend why these dilemmas are often beyond the reach of reason. Only by allowing students to experience the process of philosophical reflection and scrutiny in moral discourse will they be able to broach moral wisdom. This is a long road and often comes from an attitude of tolerance that results from the recognition of the power of human reason as well as its fallibility in addressing the predicaments of human life.

Ethics is a dialectical quest for truth to which only the student can derive. Indoctrinal attempts to moral teaching often fall on deaf ears or are met with recalcitrance, defiance, and even rage. The process of moral reflection and its relation to concrete action and attitude change in students is ultimately a personal campaign. Human excellence is a developmental achievement often plagued by struggle and strife. And in these moments of labor there is a wisdom to insecurity that only the process affords. Students will resist this process, even within themselves. Whether the moral teacher can have any impact on their process is a matter of degree. It is simply the teacher's responsibility and moral obligation to try. By undergoing a mutual process of ethical exploration, the teacher and students evolve together. Accepting this process is part and parcel of what it means to be fully human, a process of becoming.

2. The Aims of Moral Education

Before we attempt to address a proper structure for moral education, we need to realize why we as a community believe that moral education ought to be an integral part of higher education. It is true that introductory ethics is not required by all undergraduate degree programs at many universities, and consequently most students obtain their college degrees without ever stepping foot inside an ethics class. But the fact remains that for the last twenty-five years we have witnessed the expansion of moral education from philosophy departments to law schools, business schools, and medical schools. Undoubtedly, among undergraduate philosophy courses taken by non-philosophy majors, introductory ethics courses enjoy the greatest enrollment and probably with genuine interest.

Despite society's increased recognition of the importance of moral education at the college level, we can easily argue that people receive the vast majority of their ethical teachings long before they enter institutions of higher learning. Thus, to a large degree it is an inefficient commitment of communal resources to inculcate people whose moral convictions have already been established by their families, schools, and religious and social institutions. Furthermore, in our highly technical society, a college education should provide people with facts about the world; that is, what is going on out there. This amounts to a pragmatic understanding of the world that would facilitate their ability to manipulate facts toward accomplishing particular tasks. That is, a college education should deal with what is and is not practically relevant to the real world rather than pursue such ambiguities as what ought and ought not to be the case, thereby leaving us in a realm of intellectual speculation that has no relation to facts. Recall what David Hume brought to our attention: moral reasoning almost always derives an *ought* from an *is,* thus leaving the realm of fact and entering the realm of speculation, since an *ought* cannot be derived from an *is.* Hume writes:

> In every system of morality which I hitherto met with, I have always remark'd that the author proceeds for sometime in the ordinary way of reasoning, and establishes the being of God, or makes observation concerning human affairs; when of a sudden I am surpris'd to find, that instead of usual copulations of propositions *is* and *is not*, I meet with no proposition that is not connected with an *ought,* or an *ought not.* This change is imperceptible; but is, however, of the last consequence. For if this ought or ought not, expresses some new relation or affirmation, 'tis necessary that it shou'd be obser'd and explain'd; and at the same time that a reason should be given, for what seems to be altogether inconceivable, how this new relation can be deduced from others, which are entirely different from it.[2]

The logical positivists took Hume's objection against moral knowledge and combined it with the verification principle, which holds that "a sentence is cognitively meaningful if and only if it is in principle empirically verifiable or falsifiable,"[3] and arrived at the conclusion that all "moral and aesthetic and other 'evaluative' sentences are . . . cognitively meaningless" because they are "neither confirmable nor discomfirmable on empirical grounds."[4] For these reasons, A. J. Ayer and many other recent philosophers have subscribed to the idea that ethical philosophy should deal only with a descriptive depiction of ethics without making the ethical pronouncement: "We may say decisively that [ethical judgments] do not belong to ethical philosophy [and thus] a strictly philosophical treatise on ethics should therefore make no ethical pronouncements."[5]

The essence of this view of moral philosophy is the idea that a definite boundary exists between facts and values. Facts are true propositions about the actual state of affairs whereas values are evaluative expressions of human beings about a particular state of affairs. So when we state that "human beings have moral codes," we are stating a fact, but when we express a preference for one set of morals over another we are engaging in valuation, which is subjective by nature.

For our purposes, however, it is unnecessary to argue the distinction of values from facts, for ultimately values and facts are two sides of the same coin of moral reality. For phenomenologists and Whitehead alike, facts are value laden. The manner in which we interpret factual reality is always a valuative one. We assign values to facts; facts are imbued with values and are judged according to some intelligent principle of value. Thus to exclude values from moral philosophical discourse in favor of facts not only denies the facticity of valuation in human relations but it also prohibits philosophical inquiry from addressing the acute ethical dilemmas that all human beings face in their daily lives. This consequently deprives morality of its ultimate aim, namely, making our lives and communities more socially coherent and meaningful.

If we can agree that moral education should provide students with tools that will aid them in solving moral dilemmas, then we should ask why is the moral education that students receive in their respective communities before entering college not sufficient. What is so unique about higher moral education that familial upbringing, primary and secondary school training, and religious and social institutions are unable to adequately provide?

Modernity may be equated with the truism of inevitable change. Simply examine the rapid innovations occurring in art, science, medicine, and technology and appreciate the level of development unfolding before our eyes. Our pursuit of progress is so unrelenting that we rarely find ourselves seriously questioning its benefits. What unites us all as modern human beings seems to be our unprorogued belief in progress. Even those who make it their daily business exploring the dark side of unmitigated development find themselves deeply dependent on the freedoms resulting from the developmental progress of our modern civilization. But engrossed as we are in the pursuit of progress, we feel a sense of uneasiness connected to our moral progress. Unlike the other domains of our existential activities—where progress reveals itself in our gaining greater freedoms with our incessantly developing capacities to harness nature to our own advantage—our moral development seems dubious.

This ambivalence concerning our moral development seems rooted in the paradoxical nature of moral development itself. From a historical point of view, it is unquestionable that ethical development at the community level has enjoyed unparalleled progress. No other human society has enjoyed greater moral development than ours does. As a modern liberal society, we have come to recognize the principle of the equality of all human beings in the eyes of the law, the existentially invaluable uniqueness of all human beings, inalienable human rights, and rights to medical care and education. We have come to view each other with much greater dignity. Even those societies that do not subscribe to these principles find themselves on the defensive either to justify or to deny their failures or to actively implement these moral and political principles that we deem essential parts of human moral experience—which in turn is an indication of the extent to which the world of valuation has evolved. We have only to compare ancient Greek societies with modern Western societies to see how far we have moved from the Greek version of democracy to the modern version of democracy where the ideas of slavery and second class citizenry find no moral or political merit.

And yet we are confronted with the unhappy paradox that despite all the ethical progress in our social domain, we find ourselves perplexed by the moral demise of humanity on an individual level. As William Damon and Anne Colby remind us:

> The moral quality of young people's behavior has declined steadily by practically every available indicator. Too many of today's youth are committing violent acts of assault, homicide, and suicide or more mundane violations, such as cheating, stealing, lying, and harassing others.[6]

In other words, whereas the dictatorial social institutions of our past seemed to generate relatively moral individuals, meaning individuals who were willing to acknowledge their moral relations with other human beings, our own democratic societies are giving rise to less moral citizenry—citizenry less willing to acknowledge and accept their responsibilities toward others. And so the question now pertains to the reasons for this individual moral decline as well as to solutions that might remedy individual moral deterioration.

If we look at the history of moral education in medieval Europe, we immediately see that the role of such education, as Adam Niemczynski explicates, was to "help all individuals irrespective of background learn the life ideals of the church."[7] That is, the aim of moral education was to inculcate upcoming generations with the knowledge of essential social ideals—church ideals—in order to preserve the power of certain social and political structures commanding Europe at that time. Moral education "was necessary before a person could occupy positions in society governed according to these ideals."[8] As Niemczynski further points out, "imposing life ideals has been practiced both by individuals and by groups as a universal rule, rather than as exceptional episodes, for two millennia since Jesus Christ declared that all individuals are equal in the eyes of God."[9]

As long as traditional religious and political institutions enjoyed uncontested dominance over the political and cultural realities of European societies, the moral ideals of these institutions also enjoyed the allegiance of their citizens because for centuries these ideals fostered social and political coherence. The powers that be, namely the Catholic church and the royal and magnate courts, had a vested interest in maintaining the centuries-old moral fabric of society because they wished to retain political power. They did so by placing moral instruction at the pinnacle of one's educational experience.

However, with the French Revolution, the responsibility for citizens' moral education—which had always been the church's designed to instill core values in individuals thereby preparing them to assume designated roles in society—was suddenly shifted away from the parochial educational system to state educational institutions. And with this shift in the responsibility for the moral education of citizens, came a shift in the values that were subsequently taught as well. In the new liberal state, the decline of church and state power meant that the values of the past imposed from the top down were suddenly replaced by the recognition that each person is responsible for one's own moral education.

This new and unexpected emphasis on liberty initiated by the French Revolution and fostered by modern industrial democratic societies not only unleashed creative forces in art and science but also generated a certain sense of moral panic not previously encountered by any other generation of human beings. Wilson and Natale explain: "For many people the traditional moral values, faiths, creeds, etc. have begun to lose their force."[10] Even those who are unrelenting in their convictions to their moral principles have found themselves challenged either directly or indirectly by rapidly evolving social realities. No longer are we able to live in a world of moral analgesic absoluteness as had been possible before the industrial revolution. Moral dilemmas arising from the social and scientific changes that characterize modern civilization seem to outpace the most recalcitrant moral systems. Moral dilemmas generated by genetic and medical research, artificial reproduction, computer technologies, etc. have challenged the traditional moral system, leaving individuals ill prepared for addressing these issues.

Therefore, this moral uncertainty, connected to the emergence of a modern liberal state with the tremendous growth of technological knowledge, has given rise in the sphere of education to what can be called *moral educational neutrality*. That is, as a response to past abuses of the church and the state, modern educational philosophy has shifted away from teaching values to teaching facts; for only by teaching facts, the reasoning goes, will we be able to avoid the abuses perpetrated on others by social institutions because of the value systems of the groups in power.

However, this separation of values from facts and the consequent abandonment of values education by the modern educational system has contributed to the moral decline of the individual. That is, those of us who find ourselves in the splendiferous position of being teachers quickly realize the educational difficulties involved in teaching ethics to today's students. As teachers of ethics, we are constantly faced with students whose personal histories are fraught with moral confusion generated by the notion that in modern multicultural societies there is no room for moral education that would espouse some values at the exclusion of others. Coming from disparate ethnic, political, economic, and cultural backgrounds, modern youth is truly the product of a reality where the diversity of values not only is a given fact but is also perceived as a necessary aspect of individual and communal identity. As a consequence of this modern liberal cult of individuality, moral values are no longer treated as facts but simply as individual expressions of freedom. This judgment leads to the simple minded relativization of all values, which not only acknowledges the diversity of values espoused by various societies but also denies the superiority of some values over others. Thus students come pre-programmed by a modern society under the guise of "tolerance" to embrace a skeptical view of ethics which holds that

> moral values and moral value judgments are valid only for historical epochs, cultures, or individuals; moral values are "just opinions"; moral values are but expressions of feelings; and moral values are window dressing for individual self-interest . . . [and] worse yet, many introductory ethics courses on action oriented moral theories like utilitarianism and Kantian "rights-based" theories fuel student skepticism about morality by focusing on competing principles of right and wrong and their application to moral dilemmas.[11]

As ethics teachers, we find ourselves in a rather precarious educational position. We feel ourselves compelled to instill upcoming generations of young people with values that would serve them well in their existential progress, and yet this task of moral education needs to be performed in a way that makes us appear tolerant of the cultural as well as the individual differences that characterize our students. Simply put, as teachers of ethics, we have to be able to convey to our students that moral education is not merely an academic pursuit that bears no relation to their lives; rather, moral education is like art education: if well developed and practiced, it can give birth to existential masterpieces characterized by happiness, and if badly practiced it can lead to existential distortions resulting in pain.

So the question is, how are we to approach moral education without becoming either intolerantly indoctrinating or so morally vacuous "that no particular set of values is to be advocated, no tradition is to be singled out as exemplary of the standard sought, for . . . no standard in common is either necessary or possible?"[12] In order to answer this question, first we need to understand what we mean by knowledge and education. Second we need to inquire whether there can be such a thing as moral education; and third we need to address the manner in which moral education ought to be delivered if it is going to claim genuine influence on our students.

3. The Ambiguity of Moral Knowledge

The first sentence of Aristotle's *Metaphysics* reads, "All men by nature desire to know."[13] As much as this sentiment might appear too sanguine to teachers, who often have to struggle to motivate their pupils to imbibe the knowledge they present, the fact remains that Aristotle is right about our desire to know things. We could say that without this innate proclivity to learn about the outside world, no human being would be able to function. That is, our survival as individuals, communities, nations, and as the human species depends on our inborn predilection to amass knowledge about certain aspects of our environment. All of us, one way or another, want to know something about the reality we inhabit. We all may not be interested in the same type of knowledge, but we all need some knowledge. I might not be interested in learning biochemistry or basket weaving, but other aspects of my reality must be mastered so that my life is not only sufferable but also made possible. For instance, as a non-native speaker of English, I had to learn the English language in order to function in this society.

In the Western philosophical tradition, knowledge has been understood as having both theoretical and practical aspects. Physics, medicine, languages, etc. are all types of knowledge that belong to what Gilbert Ryle refers to as "knowing how." That is to say, Ryle has pointed out that at least since the times of Socrates an exaggerated distinction has been drawn between "knowing how" and "knowing that." "Knowing how" refers to practical knowledge or skill. The ability to tie one's shoes, ride a bike, drive a car, and so on, are capacities that fall under the rubric of practical knowledge. "Knowing that," however, is what we call theoretical knowledge. So my comprehension of aerodynamic theories or knowledge of educational theories falls under the category of theoretical knowledge, even though knowing these theories would not indicate my ability to fly an airplane nor guarantee that I will be a capable teacher.

Similarly in academia we have a tendency to sunder some academic subjects into practical knowledge and theoretical knowledge. For instance, we have applied mathematics, which seeks ways in which mathematics can be utilized for practical purposes; and then there is theoretical mathematics, which is not directly concerned with the practical needs of humanity. The same epistemic division is present in physics; hence we have theoretical and applied physics. And let us not forget about the modern division of ethics into theoretical ethics, which is mainly preoccupied with discovering or establishing the principles that should guide human actions, and applied ethics, which addresses the moral dilemmas befuddling humanity.

Behind this division of knowledge into "knowing how" and "knowing that" is embedded both the descriptive observations acknowledging a distinction between propositional knowledge and practical knowledge and the social valuative processes that assign a greater or lesser value to one knowledge over the other. So in our Western cultural tradition, theoretical knowledge has been exalted as a true knowledge whereas practical knowledge has been viewed more as skills that we acquire through experience often without genuine understanding of their underlying principles.

In the *Apology*, we have a clear manifestation of this depreciative epistemic attitude toward practical knowledge. In order to disprove the oracle's assertion that no one was wiser than Socrates himself, Socrates set out to interview people from different walks of life who were generally regarded as being endowed with wisdom. Among the many people he interviewed were poets. Since Socrates logically assumed that poets would know best what their poems meant, Socrates talked to them with the hope that they would be able to teach him something about their poems that he could not learn from anyone else. To his chagrin, however, Socrates discovered that the poets themselves, even though they created these pieces of literature, did not possess any special knowledge that would explain their creative ability. We can hear Socrates' disappointment when he says,

> Well, gentlemen, I hesitate to tell you the truth, but it must be told. It is hardly an exaggeration to say that any of the bystanders could have explained those poems better than their actual authors. So I soon made up my mind about the poets too. I decided that it was not wisdom that enabled them to write their poetry, but a kind of instinct or inspiration, such as you find it in seers and prophets who deliver all their sublime messages without knowing in the least what they mean.[14]

Put in modern parlance, all the people that Socrates interviewed lacked theoretical knowledge. Yes, they could write great poems, but they were unable to furnish an account of the knowledge they utilized to generate their poems. From this ignorance of theory stemmed Socrates' dissatisfaction with their practical knowledge. By the tone of his language we can deduce that he does not even want to characterize their practical knowledge as knowledge, but rather more like "instinct or inspiration."

To a large extent our scientific and philosophical amour of theory is merely an expression of our prejudicial preferences that are reflections of our Western epistemological tradition. Following Aristotle, Ryle opines this separation between "knowing how" and "knowing that" is not as valuatively extensive as we would like to believe. And of course, our greater regard for propositional knowledge over practical knowledge also seems to be unjustifiably presumptuous. This is not to deny that drawing the distinction between theoretical knowledge and practical knowledge is intellectually vacuous and unnecessary. Anyone who has ever found oneself struggling to comprehend the reasoning behind some difficult theory can truly appreciate the sense of pleasure and satisfaction one derives when one comes to understand what motivated the originators of a given hypothesis. To many people, comprehending the theory of the big bang can be a tantalizing experience even though it can bear no instrumental value to the performance of their everyday tasks.

However, it would be myopic to underestimate the value of practical knowledge. For instance, we may have a circumscribed understanding of the physical principles underlying computer technology. Most of us in academia use computers daily to do our work, but only a few of us can in good conscience say that we know the technological principles that make computers possible. But even without that knowledge, some of us become adept in using computers to accomplish our tasks. In order to perform our tasks, we come to develop an instrumental knowledge of computers through either practice or natural talent. Often in music we are confronted with people who "know how" to play an instrument beautifully but who have no theoretical knowledge. Through my own private linguistic experience, I have come to appreciate the division between theoretical and practical knowledge. As a non-native speaker of English, I struggle with the use of the articles *a*, *an*, and *the* since my native language does not have their equivalents. And despite the fact that I know the theory behind their use, I often find myself confused by native English speakers' use of them. Even native speakers of English are often unable to explain to me why they put one article rather than another in front of a particular noun; they say only, "It sounds better this way."

Hence the benefits that can be derived from either attaining theoretical knowledge or possessing practical knowledge can be qualitatively disparate. The first one often involves an intrinsic sense of satisfaction that comes with understanding the principles guiding a particular aspect of our reality. The latter often has instrumental value resulting in the turning out of a useful product. However, the epistemological preference that we accord to one type of knowledge over the other often has to do with our subjective valuations, which are dictated by historical and cultural circumstances that shape our reality, rather than an absolute value, which tells us that this type of knowledge is always preferable to the other.

Even though we tend to exalt theoretical knowledge over practical knowledge, the fact remains that these two sorts of knowledge are inextricably intertwined with each other; they satisfy different needs. So again, I may be well versed in educational theory and "know that," but this type of knowledge will not bring me the same kind of satisfaction as does the actual process of teaching, of having the skill to capture my students' attention and interest. In our educational experiences, we probably all have had professors whom we considered to be highly intelligent and yet poor teachers. They lacked the teaching skills that would make them great teachers. One of my former professors told me that learning to teach is like learning to ride a bike—both abilities require practice, and no amount of theoretical preparation will substitute for it. Put laconically, the knowledge of teaching as a practical skill and the knowledge of teaching as a theory are intertwined, and any endeavor to separate them and selectively pursue one type of knowledge over the other will result in acquiring an incomplete understanding of teaching.

Hence, having acknowledged both the inseparability of theoretical and practical knowledge and the inseparability of value from fact, the fact remains that our modern moral educational efforts are still bound up with the pursuit of theoretical knowledge, which claims to be free of valuative expressions. That is, in the realm of moral education, we continue to exalt theoretical knowledge over practical knowledge by focusing most of our efforts on delineating the conceptual principles that constitute the moral sphere despite the fact that no other realm of human activity is more dependent on practical knowing. In fact, moral knowledge as a practical pursuit is one of those few types of knowledge that everyone is required to master to some degree if we are going to thrive in our social environment.

Despite the epistemological ambiguity surrounding the question of moral knowledge, the practical dimensions of applied ethics demands our attention because it is what we encounter everyday. So we may not be able to fully understand or agree with a categorical imperative or truly appreciate what utilitarianism is all about or how we feel about emotivism, psychological subjectivism, or egoism, but we need to be clear about our practical moral obligations toward others and especially how we are going to convey these obligations to our students.

4. Moral Education in a New Age

This brings us to the question of what is meant by moral knowledge in our postmodern multicultural society and whether our prejudicial preference for theoretical rather than applied knowledge is the root cause of our failure in moral education. The term *morality* is now so often employed in public as well as in private discourse that few of us even bother to enunciate what we mean by morality. We all assume that when we employ the term *morality*, we all are talking about the same thing. We hear parents, teachers, scientists, politicians, and philosophers constantly talking about morality and moral responsibilities without clearly stating what they mean by morality. In his poem, "Morality," Thomas Moore captures the ambiguity of the moral enterprise:

I find that the doctors and the sages
Have differ'd in all climes and ages,
And two and fifty scarce agree
On what is pure morality.[15]

When we reflect on the above remark pertaining to the definition of morality, what inevitably strikes us is its very modern tone, because for the ancient Greeks, morality was clearly understood and had to do with the pursuit of virtues such as courage, wisdom, and temperance, which were supposed to be imparted to those who were slated to be rulers. To the medieval Christians, morality also involved virtues that reflected the tenants of the Church, which was responsible for instilling them in the youth. However, for us the notion of morality has lost its clarity because of our rapidly evolving society and its institutions. In the past, religion played a dominant role in defining and disseminating moral virtues; now the sources of moral education are dispersed and highly disorganized, often leaving individuals exposed to contradictory ideas of what is morally permissible and impermissible.

The separation of church and state makes the government a rather weak social entity as far as the moral education of the population is concerned. Thus our country's government, with the exception of a very few legal prescriptions that reflect general moral values, assumes a limited role in advocating and regulating moral values so as not to foster social divisiveness. Politicians often appeal to morality in order to justify their stands concerning laws they pass, but their ability to impose one moral code on the entire society by appealing to tradition or religion is non-existent.

Likewise, religion, as a dominant force for moral education in the past, has gradually experienced a significant abridgment of its power, not only because of the aforementioned separation of church and state but also because of the increased religious and cultural divisions within our society. Whereas in the past when societies were relatively culturally and politically homogenous, modern societies are no longer afforded this sort of unity. As a consequence, upcoming generations of people find themselves exposed to the magnificent plurality of moral systems that often contradict themselves, thus leaving young people ill equipped to discriminate among which systems are the most appropriate to their existential development. Even in cases where family units are exceedingly strong and parents attempt to impress their moral values on their children, all these efforts are strongly mediated by outside social forces such as school, law, television, other people, and other traditions, thereby leaving young people to their own devices. The moral complexity of the modern world can be bewildering to adults, not to mention young people. Yet a coherent moral education is a necessary component to any social life, for as Horace Mann correctly observed, "Moral Education is a primal necessity of social existence . . . [for] the unrestrained passions of men are not only homicidal, but suicidal; and a community without a conscience would soon extinguish itself."[16]

Given that social reality is fraught with an unprecedented diversity of conflicting moral values, which are the results of social and technological changes characterizing modern society, then how can higher education be of help? Social institutions in the past were once responsible for providing a coherent moral education, but they had lost their influence because of their inability to adapt to the quick pace of social change and thus fail to accommodate everyone's needs. It seems to me that the only way we are going to retain the social moral cohesiveness so essential to the survival of any society is by rediscovering the importance of universities as those social institutions that are capable of bringing together people of various social, historical, and intellectual traditions and engaging them in the process of moral education—the purpose of which would be to provide intellectual tools that would allow people to resolve moral conflicts arising in their lives. As Kohlberg informs us:

> The purpose of morality is modest, to resolve the conflicting claims of human beings and groups in fairer and better ways. Moral decisions are choices between people's conflicting claims, and worthwhile principles are ones which resolve these conflicts in ways that are fair, just, impartial. Acting out of principles of fairness is not necessarily causing the greatest good. If there is a greatest good that men can agree on, that is fine. But when men disagree on the greatest good one either appeals to the gun or settles for a fair decision.[17]

Kohlberg's warning pertaining to the use of violence in cases where people of different value systems cannot adequately negotiate their conflicts, often comes to fruition even in such multicultural societies as ours. For instance, in the abortion debate we witness the failures associated with our inability to engage each other in a peaceful manner. This failure leads to the employment of threats, guns, and bombs by those who think that they are standing on higher moral ground.

Therefore, if we agree that among social institutions, universities are in unique positions to bring people of different backgrounds together, then it is unfortunate that these institutions seem to be slowly abdicating their responsibilities toward effective moral education by pursuing moral neutrality. Neutrality, however, is not often understood as an impartial exploration of genuine moral issues but rather is expressed in terms of highly abstract examinations of several moral systems. This approach allows instructors to stay away from controversial moral issues and leave students leading "unexamined lives."

College graduates will go on to become doctors, lawyers, engineers, scientists, technicians, etc. and never have any further formal moral instruction. Because an introductory ethics class is for many people their first and last opportunity to learn structured methods for examining their personal values, ethics instructors are obligated to produce people who have at their disposal pragmatic means of making their own judgments, rather than merely informing students of the canon of various philosophical moral theories. That is not to say that philosophical moral theories as abstract systems are not educationally valuable, but from a pedagogical point of view, these theories are better brought to light in the process of applying them to practical situations. Instructors would do better to center the class on practical applications and show how these applications are manifestations of theories.

5. A Moral Pedagogy

To make introductory ethics germane to students' lives, it is essential for an instructor to approach the class not as another academic pursuit, the sole aim of which is to transfer a definite amount of knowledge to one's students, but rather as an existential process characterized by dialogue designed to engage students' interest in moral issues that seem most relevant to their lives. By bringing out moral issues concerning real life situations, students will suddenly find themselves fully engaged in moral discourse.

Consider for example a colleague of mine who teaches medical ethics. I once sat in on one of his classes in which the topic for the day was euthanasia. To make the class more relevant, the professor brought "living wills" for the students to fill out by the end of the meeting. Students had an option either to fill them out or not. This exercise was powerfully stimulating to the students because the living wills immediately brought the issue of their personal death up for discussion. No longer were they simply reading antiseptic articles about the philosophy of mercy killing, which afforded them a degree of emotional and intellectual distance; now they had to become personally involved in the subject.

The existential distance that academic discourse often provides was suddenly diminished. By participating in the class discussion or merely listening to it, all students had to confront a moral dilemma by reasoning whether they should fill out the living will form or not. What was most outstanding was the degree of dialectical engagement that students manifested. The stakes were high because they were talking about their live. They became unusually verbal and impassioned in their justifications of their philosophical positions that were the bases of whether or not they chose to be taken off life support.

This method of instruction requires careful preparation on the part of the instructor. Unlike the traditional lecture format, in which the instructor spends most of the class time guiding the students through a particular philosophical moral system, this application requires the instructor to relinquish part of one's control over the content of the class in order to facilitate students' unencumbered engagement with the topic. To make a class beneficial for students, a teacher has to be willing to find out the initial ideas and beliefs students hold about a particular subject matter. Only by understanding first what students think and why they believe a certain way, is one able to comprehend the social and intellectual reality from which these students come.

Two additional benefits are involved with permitting people to speak their minds freely. First, by providing people an opportunity to give an explicit account of their beliefs—no matter how inchoate these beliefs may be, students become genuine interlocutors in a process of moral dialectic. They develop a sense of critical engagement when their ideas become expressed publicly and thus attain an intersubjective reality by being shared and eventually open to criticism by others. Also the students' sense of intellectual importance is enhanced when a teacher conducts a class in such a way that permits them to express their opinions. Often unrehearsed and emotionally charged remarks by students about a topic may take a discussion in directions never before explored by the teacher.

Secondly, when people are allowed to express their opinions, they often find out for themselves not only how complicated it is to convey a coherent account of their thoughts to others but also that their views are often contradictory even though they have never thought so or appeared to be before. What seems logical and consistent in one's own head often loses its lucidity when it is expressed aloud. That is why so many of us in academia give our writings to our colleagues and friends to read: we hope that they will be able to catch those unjustified presuppositions we silently hold.

Finally, in stressing pragmatic aspects of morality, we should not neglect the importance of moral experience—as opposed to mere rational discourse about morality—as a guide to deeper and richer moral understanding. That is to say, as teachers of ethics, we should not delimit moral education solely to theoretical discourse for it is often bereft of emotional components that inevitably accompany the world of moral decision making; rather we should strive to enhance students' moral imaginations by directly exposing them to moral dilemmas. Thus, we may schedule visits to hospitals, homeless shelters, drug rehabilitation centers, prisons, courts, etc. in order to facilitate students' confrontation with their own emotional responses to moral issues that incessantly arise in those particular social realities. For instance, students who are granted an opportunity to visit critical care units in hospitals and to talk directly to physicians, nurses, and patients will find themselves in a better position to comprehend moral issues arising in the health care industry than those students who would spend all their time reading and discussing professional articles without witnessing firsthand the existential aspects of medical reality; it is the same kind of experiential difference as that between merely reading a history book about the Holocaust in the comfort of one's apartment and roaming the grounds of Auschwitz, thus visiting gas rooms where millions of people where exterminated or seeing entire rooms filled with victims' hair, teeth, shoes, glasses, clothes, and toys. Put simply, the world of human moral life transcends linguistic confines, and as such it demands from us that we strive to analyze its entire complexity if we hope to make ethics classes relevant to students' lives.

A. A Word on Method

Once students are provided with an opportunity to express their ideas about a particular topic, an instructor has to be able to question students about their beliefs so that the discussion will lead toward more methodical and coherent explorations of the issue at hand. By asking the right questions in a correct, systematic manner, students are slowly being exposed to an analytical way of thinking about moral dilemmas. An ability to ask the right questions is as important to philosophical discourse as being able to provide coherent argumentation. The style, content, and range of questioning, however, will depend upon the context and philosophical sophistication of each class. A moral pedagogy should not only aim toward providing students with self-reflective critical skills at moral inquiry, but should also strive to convey that such inquiry is itself a moral and virtuous activity. Engaging students in philosophical dialectic about particular moral issues creates an opportunity for students to witness how to approach real life ethical dilemmas philosophically. Simply put, a well executed philosophical analysis of a moral issue will inevitably disabuse students from the popularly held idea that philosophical rumination has no value in the real world.

This process of dialectical questioning of students' ethical beliefs and ideas should be didactically motivated; that is, the aim of this process should be to impart the idea that philosophical moral discourse is based on a rational organization of thought, which employs such building blocks as logical rules, concepts, and principles in order to address moral dilemmas. However, to skillfully employ these building blocks, students have to recognize: (1) the importance of defining what we *mean by* particular concepts such as "good," "right," "justice," "autonomy," etc. and how these concepts relate to a particular moral issue; (2) the importance of understanding the meaning and scope of general ethical principles; (3) the import of logical rules and the consequences resulting from their employment; and (4) the importance of logical congruity in the process of analysis of ethical propositions as well as of moral rules, principles, and actions.

B. Classroom Examples

While teaching a class on prejudice, I raised the issue of women's full participation in the military. I asked my students whether they thought society's general reluctance to have women included in certain military structures was merely a reflection of societal prejudices or was fully justified by genuine concerns stemming from biological differences between the sexes. To my astonishment, the great majority of students, regardless of gender, argued that women should be confined to performing supportive duties in the military, such as clerical, medical, and mechanical occupations and all other sorts of jobs that did not involve combat duties because, they reasoned, women are generally physically weaker, more emotionally vulnerable, and less capable of prolonged strenuous activity. Furthermore, having women soldiers in combat units jeopardizes group cohesiveness and thus increases the risks for everybody involved.

Students' opposition to women's combat service was perceptively mediated by their acknowledgment of the constitutional problems involved with denying half of the population the opportunities to pursue personal liberties that the other half is freely granted. However, they argued that certain national interests, such as the security of the community, transcend such social values as equal opportunity and justice, for if the country's ability to defend itself is unnecessarily jeopardized then all other values that our society embraces are potentially threatened by external forces determined to challenge our unity.

While acknowledging the reasoning for delimiting women's participation in certain military activities, I questioned the students social assumptions behind this argument. As the discussion ensued, students became aware that even though men and women differ biologically and possibly psychologically, this fact in itself does not justify the claim that women should be excluded from combat duty simply based on gender alone. As there are men who cannot adequately perform under combat situations, likewise there are also women incapable of functioning under these demands. However, the fact remains that both genders should be afforded the same opportunities to compete for and competently attain these positions as is the case in civilian life. To establish a principle that prohibits a woman from performing tasks she is capable of fulfilling is to unjustly deny not only an empirical reality, but the very principle of liberty itself that our country so proudly upholds.

I further raised the issue of changes in military technology, which alters the nature of modern warfare. So even if we agree that in the past sheer physical strength was the major requirement for being an effective soldier, the current reality of military conflict has evolved to such a degree that strategic and intellectual acuity has replaced reliance on brute physical force. Students were able to come to appreciate the value of is reflection upon the principles guiding social and moral rules. And despite a sense of ambiguity associated with the question of women in combat, students were still able to understand that their reluctance was emotively driven rather than rationally sound.

While teaching a class on Kant's moral prescription to treat others as ends rather than means, a student brought up a case of a Californian couple who were the parents of a sixteen-year-old girl suffering from leukemia. Physicians informed the parents that without a bone marrow transplant, their child would inevitably die. After a prolonged yet unsuccessful search for a suitable donor, the parents decided—despite the fact that they had intended to have no more children—to have another child with the hope that this child's bone marrow would be a compatible match. The statistical chances of giving birth to a compatible donor were about twenty percent. So, the father had his vasectomy reversed, and one year later the couple had a baby girl whose bone marrow was perfectly compatible with the older sister's immune system. The gamble paid off. Not surprisingly, the parents were exhilarated that the older daughter's chances of survival multiplied from certain death to about eighty percent.

When I asked the students whether the parents' decision to have another child in order to increase the survivability of their daughter was morally supportable, they were inclined to follow Kant's reasoning that human beings should not be treated solely as means to achieve some objectives. My students were not alone in voicing their moral disapproval for many notable ethicists rely on this same argumentation.

However, the moral certainty that students initially held began to dissipate when I emphasized the point that we were not talking about a hypothetical situation contrived in a philosophy class, but rather we were talking about real people who were facing the death of their daughter. I asked the students to imagine themselves in the place of the parents and to answer whether they would decide to let their only child wither away on the basis of some general philo-sophical principle. Once the students imagined themselves in this situation, they were suddenly arguing that the parents' actions were not as objectionable as they had thought. As one of the students pointed out, people decide to have children for a variety of reasons. It is a well know fact that in poorer countries, people often have children so as to have additional working hands. Others have children to fulfill their psychological needs for love and validation, or to continue their family lineage, and we are not readily provoked to moral reproach. Simply put, we often decide to have kids to fulfill our own narcissistic needs; what becomes important is not so much the reason as is how we love and care for them as parents.

Often it happens that people fail to recognize the moral implications associated with certain personal inclinations and choices. I remember having a student in my class who initially was unable to recognize moral dimensions pertaining to the act of suicide. For him, suicide was no more morally significant than the daily brushing of his teeth. He reasoned that since his body was his own he was allowed to do with it whatever he wished. Only after inquiring about his definition of ethics and helping him to clarify what he understood as a moral act was he able to appreciate the ethical aspects of taking one's own life and its impact on others even though he remained convinced of his moral right to kill himself.

When possible, instructors should try to help students recognize the moral aspects residing behind personal decisions they may potentially make everyday. Daily encounters we typically think are banal may be fertile ground for moral challenges. How many of us would report a friend or a neighbor to the police even if we witnessed a crime? Perhaps this depends upon the nature of the transgression, but many of us wouldn't report a shoplifter to the manager let alone report some minor infraction such as cheating or lying. While we may condemn such activities, moving from the realm of moral reprove to action is often a big step. I strive to challenge students to think about the ethical decisions they confront in their personal lives with the aim of achieving some form of practical knowledge even if ambiguity remains. This often entails examining personal attitudes, perceptions, concrete activities, and behavioral comportments toward others, from how they relate to their family members, loved ones, friends, and strangers, to examining what kind of human beings they would like to become.

C. Toward Moral Wisdom

Instructors have to be able to guide students in discovering latent social and personal prejudices that inform their own moral values as well as communal valuation practices. Any analysis of a moral issue is incomplete if certain premises remain unacknowledged. Since moral values do not emerge *ex nihilo* but rather transpire in particular social, historical, political, and psychological contexts, then it would be philosophically neglectful not to expose their influence in the creation of moral realities to which people adhere.

Another important reason for designing introductory ethics courses as "moral practice ranges," where people not only develop analytic skills but also employ them in addressing life's genuine moral dilemmas, has to do with imparting to students the idea that no matter what type of moral system we elect to follow, the moral choices we make have real impact on other people. Whether we subscribe to emotivism or some sort of moral absolutism or follow some kind of subjectivism or even choose to question whether there is such a thing as moral knowledge at all, the end result is that our moral comportment toward others results not only in their happiness or suffering but also in ours. Thus no matter how much we might wish to consign moral reflection to the realm of spurious human activities, the fact remains that no other human activity separates us more from animals than moral rumination nor contributes more to our happiness or misery than our moral choices.

As teachers of ethics we should not overlook the importance of fostering tolerance among our students in moral discourse. Like any other human pursuit, moral philosophy is replete with intellectual ambiguities. Thoughtful people often find themselves on opposite sides of various moral issues. We need look no further than a history of moral philosophy to comprehend the diverse views associated with morality. The moral philosophical horizon extends itself from Plato to Nietzsche and postmodernism, and whether consciously or unconsciously we are all part of that horizon. That is why it is so critical that students be taught not only moral theories but also critical skills of analytical thinking about moral dilemmas so that they can have a way of talking to each other about these quandaries even if the ultimate solutions are beyond their reach. Moral progress cannot occur when we have no way of communicating with each other. We must be willing to listen to others, even if we disagree with them, for there is always a great chance that they can enrich our thinking by providing us with new ways of considering old problems.

I do not wish to leave an impression that there is no value to teaching moral theories in introductory ethics. Students should be exposed to the theoretical history of moral discourse in order to comprehend the moral reality in which they find themselves. Without being generally aware of moral history, students will not be able to recognize the hidden biases that often inhabit moral arguments, and thus they won't be in a position to approach moral discourse with a full appreciation of its scope. However, considering the fact that introductory ethics is often the only philosophy course that undergraduate students will take in their entire college careers, it becomes essential that they leave the class with a pragmatic sense of appreciation for what philosophy in general and moral philosophy in particular have to offer.

Often people make arguments maintaining that universities are not in a position to devise ethics courses that would address students' personal as well as professional moral conundrums. Besides, the argument continues, it is quite unreasonable to think that having one ethics course can result in students' changing their moral comportments—especially remembering that by the age most people enter college their personality structures are already solidified, and this is why it is much more useful to furnish students with a historical theoretical overview. Furthermore, since university education is increasingly costly and designed to furnish people with highly specialized skills and technical knowledge, there is neither time nor money to turn introductory ethics into personal development classes dedicated to solving individual moral dilemmas. This is why ethics courses are often characterized by highly theoretical expositions in order to avoid the impression that students are getting some kind of indoctrination rather than the objective knowledge putatively disseminated in the natural and social sciences.

Undoubtedly, resistance exists among the faculty and administration to modify introductory ethics courses because such a change would require instructors to give greater control over their classes to students by engaging moral dilemmas that are germane to students' interests. Instructors would also be forced to engage in potentially controversial subjects of the day that could quite possibly require their own personal participation, disclosure, and justification of privately held moral positions—a participation many professors are reluctant to divulge. From my own experience, I know that it is much easier to come to class, lecture for two hours on Kant, and then leave rather than discuss such issues as abortion, affirmative action, or any other topic which seems socially contentious. But this is reality, and instructors must use their own discretion and find their own way.

Change is psychologically uncomfortable and requires a tremendous amount of effort to endure as well as successfully implement. Having said that, I believe that it is a high time to revamp introductory ethics courses if their aim is to have a lasting impact on students. If the only aim is to expose students to a historical overview of moral theory, then we as professional philosophers have abandoned the traditional goal of philosophy, which is the pursuit of wisdom. We can no longer hide behind the veil of abstract scholarly ruminations because the increasing moral complexities of modern societies oblige us to employ our philosophical and pedagogical skills in order to help students deal with the ethical enigmas of human existence.

We need to recognize that moral education is a continuous process that occurs throughout our entire lives. What makes moral discourse sensible is the presupposition that human beings are free agents who are capable of altering their decisions at any moment regardless of their past. So whether our lives are replete with tumultuous and painful experiences or whether they are filled with a blissful harmony of orderly existence, the value and quality of living is inextricably bound to the choices we make. If choices are part and parcel of our existential reality and if they determine the value of our lives, then we as teachers have a moral obligation to prepare our students to successfully address the moral crises they face everyday.

In our search for moral teaching, we may say that moral pedagogy, like ethical development itself, is a process, a process of becoming. And like the pursuit of wisdom, this quest is itself a moral enterprise because it prepares others—those we care about—to be more thoughtful, empathic, and virtuous, hence better human beings. By being exposed to a moral pedagogy that addresses the pragmatics of concrete ethical situations, students will learn how to think critically about their own moral realities as well as develop appreciation and sensibility for the diversity of opinions that arise in our diverse time. The recognition of this diversity can in turn be a stepping stone toward developing a sense of compassion for those with whom we disagree, for as Alexander Pope says,

> Teach me to feel another's woe
> To hide a fault I see;
> That mercy I to others show
> That mercy show to me.[18]

Notes

1. Robert K. Fullinwider, *Teaching Ethics at the University* (Bloomington: The Poynter Center, 1991), p. 2.

2. David Hume, *A Treatise of Human Nature*, Book 3, Sec.1, 1739, ed. P.H. Nidditch (London: Oxford University Press, 1978), pp. 469-470.

3. Jonathan Dancy and Ernest Sosa (Eds.), *Blackwell Companion to Epistemology* (Oxford: Blackwell, 1992), p. 263.

4. *Ibid.*, p. 263.

5. A. J. Ayer, *Language, Truth, and Logic* (London: Gollancz, 1936), p. 103.

6. William Mamon and Anne Colby, "Education and Moral Commitment," *Journal of Moral Education*, 25:1 (1996), p. 31.

7. Adam Niemczynski, "Moral Education Is Not Good Enough Because Education Is Not Moral Enough," *Journal of Moral Education*, 25:1 (1996), p. 111.

8. *Ibid.*

9. *Ibid.*

10. John Wilson and Samuel M. Natale, "First Steps in Moral and Ethical Education," *Thought*, 60:237 (June 1985), p. 119.

11. Paul Hughes, "Taking Ethics Seriously: Virtue, Validity, and the Art of Moral Reasoning," *Teaching Philosophy*, 19:3 (September 1996), p. 219.

12. Robert E. Carter, *Dimensions of Moral Education* (Toronto: University of Toronto Press, 1984), p. 49.

13. Aristotle, *Metaphysics*, Book 1, in *The Pocket Aristotle*, trans. by W.D. Ross (New York: Washington Square Books, 1958), p.108.

14. Plato, *Apology*, in *The Collected Dialogues of Plato*, ed. E. Hamilton & H. Cairns (Princeton, N.J.: Princeton University Press, 1989), p. 8.

15. Thomas Moore, "Morality," *The Poetical Works of Thomas Moore* (New York: D. Appleton & Co., 1854), p. 140.

16. Horace Mann, *The Republic and the School: On the Education of Free Men*, ed. L. A. Cremin (New York: Columbia University Press, 1957), p. 98.

17. Lawrence Kohlberg, "Why a Higher Stage Is a Better Stage," in Evan Simpson, ed., *Good Lives and Moral Education* (New York: Peter Lang, 1989), p. 184.

18. Alexander Pope, "The Universal Prayer," in *Eighteenth-Century English Literature*, ed. Geoffrey Tillotson, Paul Fussell, Jr., Marshall Waingrow (San Diego: Harcourt Brace Jovanovich Publishers, 1969), p. 682.

Three

EDUCATION THROUGH COMPASSION: CULTIVATING OUR MYSTICAL VOCATION

Frank Gruba-McCallister

The purpose of this chapter is to describe how education can best be understood as the development and refinement of our inherent mystical vocation. My intention is to argue that an understanding of the central tenets of the great mystical traditions is integral to all true education. The mystical perspective provides a valuable context for how to cultivate two forms of knowing and claims to truth that must be balanced within the educational process. It also provides important insights in how to negotiate the paradoxes central to living out human existence. These insights enable teachers to nurture and promote the mystical vocation of their students and thus provide what I believe to be an optimal education. The cultivation of compassion becomes a central and critical means of wakening students to the contemplative and prophetic facets of their mystical way of being.

1. Negotiating the Paradox of Becoming

In the past few years, I have asked my students entering on their first year of graduate study in clinical psychology to engage in an exercise that I consider valuable to their personal and professional development. I have them write a personal mission statement describing their reasons for entering into the profession of psychology, their goals for the future and their vision of psychology and where they fit into it. I share with them my own mission statement as well as the mission statement of the school. I encourage them to consider how their personal mission fits with the institutional mission and how this fit or lack of fit may impact on their educational experience and their decision to become psychologists.

I see a great deal of value in this exercise. It forces students to thoughtfully examine their beliefs, values, attitudes, and expectations that will exert a powerful influence on how they approach their education and their subsequent identity as clinical psychologists. It forces them to unearth certain beliefs and values buried so deeply within them that they often go unexamined. Because these discoveries can prove to be at best incompatible and at worst antagonistic to the mission of the school and of the profession, the exercise can be a difficult and painful one. What one does with this pain is, in part, an issue I hope to address in this essay. Without this pain, there can be no true education. However, more importantly, it is the response that a student makes to this pain that will determine whether true learning and growth will occur.

The articulation of a personal mission is also important because it addresses what I believe to be the very heart of education because all education must be, in part, an education of the heart. As is true of any mission statement, it articulates an ideal, something to aspire to. It thus speaks to a transcendent dimension of human existence. It involves the recognition that there is something bigger than us that, as Viktor Frankl (1967) states, exerts a "demand quality" on us. Part of education must thus be to awaken students to this transcendent dimension and the oughts that accompany this realization. Donald Vandenberg (1971) in his book, *Being and Education*, describes the importance of this transcendent dimension as responding to the call of Being:

> To lay the ground for the possibility of the pedagogic encounter and meaningful learning, the teacher has to lead the pupil back to himself so that he can recover his being and find the world safe enough to explore without having to pretend to be other than who he is. (pp. 148-149)

There are many words that one can use to describe this transcendent dimension. Throughout this chapter, I will follow the example of C. S. Lewis (1947) in his own commentary on the importance of the transcendent dimension to education and use the term "Tao." The choice of this term is informed by my focus on the centrality of mystical philosophy and its relation to the educational endeavor. The Tao is taken from a Chinese philosophy that represents one of many mystical traditions. It captures many of the key themes that run through diverse mystical traditions. These themes, as they are examined later, provide important insights into how mysticism can be applied to education.

Defining mysticism is, in some ways, a daunting task. The meaning of mysticism is often misunderstood, in part because many of its ideas have been regarded unfavorably in our predominantly secular and materialistic culture. The term "mysticism" often evokes images of magic and the occult. However, such associations fall far short of capturing the true meaning of mysticism. The mystical tradition lies at the heart of the great religions and forms the foundation of human spirituality.

One definition that captures the heart of mysticism is provided by Evelyn Underhill (1915). She writes, "Mysticism is the art of union with Reality. The mystic is a person who has attained that union in greater or lesser degree; or who aims at and believes in such attainment" (p. 3). Mysticism is thus the search for the Real, the Ultimate, the Absolute. As such, it involves a series of practices designed to achieve a direct experience of Reality. This experience is transformative in that it provides us with true and complete knowledge of the nature of Reality and of ourselves.

One word for this reality is the Tao. It refers to a Cosmic Order beyond our conceptual grasp that is the foundation and pattern for all of existence. Like all mystical traditions, Taoism believes that there is a Reality or Ultimate that is the spaceless and timeless Ground of Being. However, this Reality is not inaccessible and remote because all of existence is a theophany, the self-expression and self-realization of this order. This self-realization expresses one of many paradoxes that are embraced within the mystical insight between the transcendent and immanent aspects of the Absolute.

The Tao, symbolized as the union between the "yin" and the "yang," is thus an apt example of the mystical tradition as it captures the notion that all seeming contradictions encountered in human existence are resolved harmoniously and transcended within the wholeness of the cosmic order. Underhill (1915) again describes this well:

> Since you are a child of Time as well as Eternity, such effort and satisfaction, active and passive love, are both needed by you, if your whole life is to be brought into union with the inconceivably rich yet simple One in who these apparent opposites are harmonised. (p. 145)

The cultivation of the mystical experience is an important dimension of mysticism. Mystics believe that all human behavior is an attempt to express the Tao, to embody it, to live it out in one's existence as fully as possible. Thus, the goal of mysticism is liberation through and direct and immediate apprehension of the Ground of Being. Since this Ground is where all being originated, such attainment is understood as a homecoming. Each of us, as spiritual beings, participates deeply and intimately in a divine and transcendent reality because our union with the Absolute is a given. Unfortunately, this knowledge is lost to us. The mystical traditions prescribe various methods for the re-attainment of this knowledge. The rediscovery of this union is also the realization of our true identity as expressions of the Tao. The cultivation of this insight employing various methods will be discussed at length later in this chapter. Ultimately, I claim that the cultivation of our mystical vocation should be an integral goal of the educational process. In particular, I will address how the mystical experience represents the resolution of still another paradox involved in the two forms of knowing that form the basis of education.

Absolute Reality is often referred to as the Good as well as the True. There is a moral dimension inescapably expressed in the Cosmic Order. Thus, the Tao also implies a doctrine of objective value expressed in moral imperatives or

natural laws that demand devotion from us. C. S. Lewis (1947) speaks to this
aspect of the Tao: "It is a doctrine of objective value, the belief that certain
attitudes are really true, and others really false, to the kind of thing the universe
is and the kind of things we are" (p. 29). As the expression of objective values,
this aspect of the Tao again refers to its transcendent nature. However, such
values would be meaningless, as Kierkegaard notes, unless they become truths
for me. Thus, the goal of the mystical insight is also to provide us with direct
knowledge of these values. Such knowledge leads to the experience of an
"ought," the demand that we bring our actions in line with such values. Thus,
the non-dual perspective of mysticism is also expressed in its understanding of
the moral dimensions of the Tao. Within the mystical experience of union, the
distinction between the subjective and the objective is transcended. This moral
dimension of mysticism will be discussed later in terms of the importance of the
cultivation of compassion in the educational process.

In light of these mystical insights, if a mission remains merely a statement
of an ideal that never becomes embodied in our concrete actions and commitments, it is ultimately meaningless. So often, we experience mission statements
as nothing more than words on a piece of paper. Therefore, another integral
element of articulating one's mission statement is requiring students to describe
concretely and specifically how they intend to express this mission in their
actions and commitments. This is very much in line with my long-time
sympathies with the existential perspective which insists upon living out our
beliefs passionately and with conviction. It is not enough to simply acknowledge
the demand that the Tao places upon us. We must respond in a caring and
committed way to that demand. This fleshing out of the mission statement gives
expression to the immanent dimension of the Tao within the educational
enterprise.

I find this dialectic of the transcendent and immanent aspects of the Tao
eloquently expressed in a quote from the journals of Søren Kierkegaard (see
Bretall, 1936) which I use in the personal mission statement I share with my
students:

> What I really lack is to be clear in my mind what I am to do, not what I am
> to know, except in so far as a certain understanding must precede every
> action. The thing is to understand myself, to see what God really wishes me
> to do; the thing is to find a truth which is true for me, to find the idea for
> which I can live and die. (pp. 4-5)

As is so often the case with Kierkegaard's thought, we encounter a powerful
paradox inherent in human existence that creates an ever-present crisis. The
truth we seek must be personal and yet also express the will of God. It requires

understanding and yet exacts a commitment that takes us beyond what mere intellectual understanding would dictate.

All true education requires the teacher to consistently precipitate this crisis in each student. As Merton (1951) asserts, the mystic quest (whose goal is the attainment of the truth Kierkegaard speaks of) is always born out of crisis. However, to awaken such a crisis without offering the means of meaningfully addressing it would thwart growth and subsequently education. This negotiation of the transcendent and immanent dimensions of the Tao is the essence of the process of becoming to which student and teacher alike must consistently commit themselves. As is true for any paradox, it is only by openly embracing what seem to be irreconcilable dimensions of human existence that our mystic vocation is realized.

Throughout the scope of this chapter, I will discuss two paradoxes that are central to a pedagogy of being. Both of these parallel the transcendent and immanent dimensions of the Tao. Helping students understand and negotiate these paradoxes is the true objective of all education. The first of these paradoxes is based upon the two ways of knowing that must be equally cultivated in order to grasp the Tao and express it in our day-to-day actions. The second is the dual roles which all true mystics must assume, what Nouwen (1972) calls the contemplative critic. These paradoxes are intimately entwined and must be the focus of all true education. Thus, teachers must demonstrate a willingness to immerse themselves in these paradoxes and convey an attitude of tolerance for the inherent ambiguity of human existence so as to enable their students to do likewise. However, the definitive attitude that will enable teacher and student alike to translate the crises precipitated by these paradoxes into growth is compassion.

I will also be discussing the importance of compassion to nurturing and facilitating the process of students' realizing their mystical vocation. Ways of balancing the two ways of knowing through teaching and integrating the roles of contemplative and critic will be offered. These methods will ultimately be regarded as means through which the attitude of compassion can be cultivated and then put to work through practical action.

2. Two Ways of Knowing

A pedagogy of being requires that we appreciate a recurring idea throughout the history of thought regarding the two ways of knowing. These two ways of knowing may also be said to reflect two distinct forms of consciousness (Wilber, 1977), each with its own set of characteristics and each appropriate to addressing different facets of human experience. The problem with the current state of education, particularly in modern, technological society (especially in the West), is that there is a one-sided emphasis on only one of these two forms of knowing. The goal of a pedagogy of being is not to correct for this one-sided emphasis by placing an exaggerated emphasis on the neglected form of knowing, but rather to effect a respect for both ways and provide students with the means to achieve a thoughtful integration of both in their approach to life.

To understand how education has become one-sided, we must first describe these two ways of knowing and associated ways of being. References to these two forms of knowing are many. However, an excellent summary of these two modes is provided by Wilber (1977). The focus of much of current education is on what can be called discursive thought. This emphasis, in large part, is due to the predominance of the materialistic, positivistic, objective, Newtonian paradigm in modern thought (Capra, 1982). Discursive thought is based upon a dualistic relation between subject and object. Both Wilber and Capra trace this dualism to Cartestian philosophy in which the realm of thought (subject) is seen as utterly distinct and separate from the objects represented by those thoughts (object). This dualism is likewise reflected in the relation between mind and body or between the realm of spirit and the realm of nature. As a result, discursive thought does not deal with the world itself, rather with our symbolic or representational understanding of the world. Thus, discursive thought is based upon abstraction with an emphasis on language and concepts as surrogates for some dimension of experience. The emphasis of discursive thought is on reason, linearity, and analysis. The posture of discursive thought is to manipulate or achieve control of the object of our knowledge.

Opposed to discursive thought is direct knowledge. In this mode of knowing, there is no separation of knower and known, but instead they are seen as intimately and necessarily interrelated. The goal of direct knowledge is to establish intimate contact with the reality that exists behind the symbols we employ to characterize that reality. The recognition that a certain dimension of reality is ineffable or beyond words is basic to direct knowledge. Such knowledge is described by the scientist/philosopher, Michael Polanyi (1966), as the tacit dimension. This tacit dimension is the greater part of knowledge. Direct knowledge seeks access to this dimension through intuition or "getting the feel" of something. Contrary to discursive thought, direct thought is circular or dialectical, systemic and non-reductionistic. Direct thought assumes a permissive, receptive, non-interfering stance toward the object of our knowledge.

As noted, this polarity has been addressed by many thinkers and in many philosophic and spiritual traditions. Martin Heidegger (see von Eckartsberg and Valle, 1981) speaks of the distinction between the calculative and meditative modes. The calculative mode is rational, intrusive, dominating, and objectifying. The meditative mode, also referred to as "thankful thinking," is respectful, open, loving, and non-interfering. It takes a reverential attitude toward what is known so as to capture the thing-in-itself.

This polarity is discussed by Martin Buber (1958) in terms of the I - It and I - Thou realms of being. In the I - It realm, the relationship to the known is tainted by our biases and preconceptions. One assumes a detached attitude toward the known and applies the laws of linear causality so as to make the relationship predictable and certain. We relate to the "It" only in terms of some facet or part of its totality and view it in terms of its utility and functionality. The I - It realm is understood in terms of time and space. The I - Thou realm is characterized by immediacy, mutuality, and reciprocity. The "Thou" is understood as unique and is accorded absolute value and respect. We seek to know the Thou in its totality and wholeness. Such a relationship can only occur in the here and now and so transcends the conventional laws of causality.

The history behind and reasons for the increasing predominance of discursive thought in how we have come to understand the world is summarized well by both Capra (1982) and Wilber (1977). An interesting example given by Winner (1996), as it relates to education, is how children are considered "gifted" in areas such as science and mathematics, but "talented" in areas such as music and the arts. The distinction implies a lower status ascribed to non-discursive ways of knowing. The emphasis of a more discursive view in professional education is likewise articulated well by Schön (1987).

However, a critique of discursive thought should not be construed as a call to somehow abolish it or underestimate its importance and value. In some ways, the attainment of discursive thought can be regarding as one of the crowning achievements of the human race, but it is an achievement that has come at a cost. It represents an evolutionary leap that has ended up being a double-edged sword.

To understand this, it is important to acknowledge some of the important and necessary functions performed by discursive thought. The first is that it provides us with the means of managing the flood of information that bombards us at any given moment. Discursive thought is based upon our capacity to selectively filter such information and, more importantly, decide what to attend to and what not to attend to. As such, discursive thought performs an important survival function. A number of thinkers have linked discursive thought to its important role in promoting our survival.

However, this selective function is merely the first stage of a process whose ultimate goal is to create a stable, ordered and predictable view of the world (Ornstein, 1972). Discursive thought is based upon labels, words, symbols, or concepts. All of these are ways of representing our experience in a simplified, condensed, and short-hand fashion. The labels and symbols are based upon categorizing a variety of objects on the basis of some similarity between them, a similarity that becomes increasingly refined and essential over time. This capability to think conceptually has made language and high levels of abstract thought possible.

It is precisely these characteristics of discursive thought, when taken to an extreme, that become problematic and even dangerous. The first disadvantage of discursive thought is that it is always incomplete and one step away from fully capturing our experience. Because of its selectivity, discursive thought places a filter on our experience and renders only a partial picture of truth. Evelyn Underhill (1915), a well-known author on mysticism, writes, "Because mystery is horrible to us, we have agreed for the most part to live in a world of labels; to make of them the current coin of experience, and ignore their merely symbolic character" (p. 7).

Goleman (1985) in his book, *Vital Lies, Simple Truths*, also describes another hazard of discursive thought. When we are confronted with information that is new or unexpected, we feel uncertain and anxious. This again refers to the filtering function of discursive thought in which information incongruent with our existing world-view is either screened out or distorted to fit our world-view. Instead it is contaminated by our own desires, expectations, and beliefs. The importance of insuring our survival is extended to our belief systems. The result is that our representation of experience is contaminated by lies that we ourselves have constructed. Eventually, these lies become so convincing and so strongly adhered to that we fall into the trap of self-deception.

This trap of deception is described in the mystical traditions as the problem of the ego and seen as the greatest obstacle to our spiritual growth. In Hinduism, this is called *maya* or the veil of illusion in which we are typically immersed. As Wilber (1977) points out, the root of the term *maya* is also the root of the word "measurement." So it is that by trying to reduce reality to something that can be observed, analyzed, and quantified, we fall into error. By seeking to fragment the essential unity and interdependence that characterize existence, we end up with a partial truth. Because we stop at the superficial, the truth evades us. Such partial truths and incomplete notions are the stuff of which self-deception is made.

This leads to the final major drawback of discursive thought. After we have categorized our experience in terms of concepts, labels, and language, we then make the mistake of believing these symbolic forms are concrete realities. Alfred North Whitehead (1966) describes this as the Fallacy of Misplaced Concreteness. We essentially miss the metaphoric nature of discursive knowledge. As the final verse of Goethe's epic work, *Faust*, affirms, "All that which is transitory is only a symbol." In line with the etymological roots of the word metaphor, to "carry beyond," all of existence points to something beyond itself. From the mystical perspective, that "something" is the Tao or the Absolute.

The problem of missing the metaphor, from a mystical standpoint, is the problem of idolatry or what Merton (1961) calls "false mysticism." As I noted earlier, an essential function of true education is to direct the student to a knowledge of the Tao, a transcendent dimension of truth that demands our devotion and a moral order that demands our obedience. The problem of idolatry is mistakening the transcendent with our narrow and limited notions about it, attempting to package truth in our own biases and preconceptions. The problem of idolatry is also confusing our own personal preferences and desires with moral imperatives that insure justice for all. It is only when education of the head is balanced by education of the heart that the dangers of narrowness, rigidity, self-deception, and idolatry can be avoided.

However, as I stated before, the ideal education does not involve the abandonment or devaluing of discursive thought. The attainment of this form of thinking constitutes a necessary and needed stage in the evolution of our consciousness. To rely on intuition or the intellect of the heart alone would also be a path fraught with dangers. The ability to detach ourselves from a situation and examine it from a distance would be compromised. The capacity to submit ideas or experiences to a rigorous examination and application of certain rules and principles would be lost. There is little question that the achievements of science and technology, which represent a very powerful expression of discursive thought, have been noteworthy in advancing the human race and enhancing human welfare. But the lack of commensurate cultivation of education of the heart has made the achievements of science and technology, like Frankenstein's monster, creations that pose a serious threat to their creators.

3. Weaving the Two Paths to Truth

There is an old story about two monks who lost their way in the woods while setting off on a pilgrimage to a holy place (Shah, 1969). One was blind. The other, while traveling through the forest, fell and became lame. For a long time, the blind monk wandered aimlessly through the forest, while the lame one was stranded. By some stroke of good fortune, the blind monk happened upon the other. The lame one said to the other, "Brother, where are you bound for?" The blind monk replied, "I was on my way to a place sacred to my order, but lost my way." To this the lame one replied, "I too am of your order and I fell and became lame. So I have been unable to continue my journey." For a moment, both monks were unsure of what to do. But then the lame one said, "Brother, let me climb upon your shoulders and become your eyes, as you will then become my legs. Together we will find our way out of this forest and complete our pilgrimage." So it was, that when the two monks worked together as one, they attained their goal.

This story is an excellent illustration of the proper relationship between discursive and direct thought and how true education must not merely cultivate both of them in students, but more importantly teach students how to integrate them in their own journey toward truth. The unitive knowledge the mystic seeks and ultimately attains represents the pinnacle of consciousness. Such an insight, as I will discuss later, results in the attainment of an attitude of compassion that becomes transformative in one's life. But such transformation does not necessarily imply that our journey is over. Regrettably, there are many who attain the mystical insight only to later lose it or let its lessons go astray.

Thus, the attainment of balance between discursive and direct thought is best regarded as an ideal toward which we must consistently aspire. As in existential literature, this embracing of both dimensions is what enables us to be fully human or authentic. However, authenticity is likewise not a goal that can be achieved once and forever. As Buber insightfully asserts (1958), there is a natural tendency to drift away from an I - Thou mode of relating into an I - It mode because human beings cannot live without an It. This is Buber's recognition of the necessity and need for discursive thought. Thus, authenticity is best understood as a process of embracing the paradox of discursive and direct knowledge, while avoiding the proclivity to deal with this polarity in a one-sided fashion (Gruba-McCallister and Levington, 1994). Authenticity, and thus true education, is based upon an openness to all facets of human existence, an acceptance of the worst as well as the best in us. And this openness again lies at the heart of compassion.

There are several authors writing from different perspectives who have discussed the importance of the integration of discursive and direct knowledge in coming to a complete understanding of truth. One is Thomas Merton (1951) who discusses at length the close and necessary relationship between faith and reason in the mystical process. Merton observes that there are two characteristics of mature spirituality. The first is discernment which is the ability to recognize the expression of the Tao in all things through the cultivation of an intuitive perception (direct knowledge). The second is detachment in which one realizes and critically examines the illusion of finding the Tao in the limited, transient material realm (discursive knowledge). Merton also discusses this as the need to balance reason with faith, since the belief that these two ways of knowing are antagonistic, again leads to a false brand of mysticism. Discursive thought is the product of the exercise of reason. Merton notes that concepts themselves should not be discarded if they help us to reach God, but likewise the desire to reach God through concepts alone is doomed to failure. The key to the proper use of conceptual knowledge of God is to understand such concepts analogically.

So a balance must be struck such that faith does not destroy reason, but fulfills it. Merton concludes, "Reason is in fact the path to faith, and faith takes over where reason can say no more" (p. 29). Thus, for Merton, reason is not antagonistic, but rather holds the key to the mystical life. He uses the metaphor of the soul as an instrument that grace eventually brings to a state of harmony with the Tao. The function of reason is to tune the strings of this instrument, but not to play it. The playing of the instrument is accomplished by the perfect union of mind and will with the Tao. A similar assertion is made by the theologian, Paul Tillich (1957) who emphasizes that reason must be a precondition for all faith.

A second perspective on the integration of these two modes of knowing is provided by Donald Schön (1987) in his discussion of professional education as the cultivation of the reflective practitioner. Schön begins by critiquing how the focus of much contemporary professional education is based upon technical rationality. This perspective places an emphasis on reason, positivism, logic, and technical expertise. The approach to problems is dictated by the application of norms and rules in order to derive a sound solution. However, Schön observes that the situations which professionals confront on a daily basis do not readily lend themselves to this sort of perspective. The problems professionals must deal with are often messy, unstructured, novel, and unfamiliar. They often present the professional with a unique set of circumstances and the need to deal with a conflict of values. Thus, set formulas and rigid strategies fail to offer much help.

To deal with such situations, professionals are required to employ artistry or a more intuitive mode of problem solving. Schön believes that professional education can gain a great deal with a careful study of such artistry and its integration into professional education. Again, this more direct form of knowing constitutes an equally valid form of intelligence central to how a problem is framed, how solutions are implemented, and the use of improvisation to deal with problems more flexibly and creatively. Such learning is accomplished by practicing in a setting where students experience an atmosphere of freedom to learn with a sense of safety that conveys a feeling of low risk. The teacher initiates students into traditions within the profession that honor and reflect this state of artistry, and functions as a coach who helps students learn by doing and removing possible impediments to the learning process.

The integration of the discursive and direct modes of knowing is captured in Schön's discussion of teaching artistry through reflection-in-action. This process begins with being engaged in an action to which we bring a spontaneous, routine response (direct knowing). At some point, this routine strategy leads to an unexpected outcome that gets our attention. This unexpected outcome then leads to reflection within the present in order to determine why the strategy is not working. Such reflection has a critical function because it forces us to question the assumptions we brought to the situation (discursive knowing). The reflection then leads to on-the-spot experimentation in which we try alternative methods of approaching the situation and assess the impact of these alternatives. Eventually, this is expressed in an attitude of reflection-in-action in which we smoothly integrate such spontaneous improvisation into the problem-solving process and eventually construct a new way of framing the solution and method of acting that becomes routine and tacit. Thus, while professional education may still need to rely on technical rationality, to a degree, by beginning with the teaching of rules (discursive knowledge), it must eventually move beyond this to the cultivation of a form of artistry (direct knowledge) and eventually to the fluid integration of the two.

One final example of how these two modes of knowing can be integrated is provided by Senge (1990), an organizational theorist, who proposes a rather radical mind-shift in how we conceptualize the optimal organization. Senge advocates for the art of practice of the learning organization. His conceptualization of corporate settings as needing to regard themselves as learning organizations fits in very well here with the emphasis on education. Senge touts the value of bilateralism which is again the integrationn of direct and discursive knowing in how corporations approach problem solving and cites the work of Schön as an example. A tension often exists within organizations and institutions between the mission it espouses and where the organization or institution realistically stands with respect to this vision. Certain perils face the organization at that moment. It may abandon the vision and settle for something far less. It may feel defeated and create a negative vision that is based upon fear. Or it may assume that mere willpower alone will be sufficient to bridge this gap.

Such ineffective responses are ultimately based upon on non-systemic understanding of the situation. The gap between vision and current realities must be regarded as a creative tension that requires first an uncompromising commitment to the truth. This is the willingness to examine our assumptions or pre-existing mental models and submit them to critical review. There must be the freedom to question the *status quo* (discursive thought). We must recognize the hazards of self-deception with a non-defensive attitude that enables us to identify obstacles to the attainment of institutional goals and vision. Indeed, Senge speaks to the value of members of an organization being committed to some form of meditation or contemplative practice and to cultivate intuitive thought through imagery and visualization (direct knowledge).

True education is not merely the recognition of these two forms of knowing and validating the value of both of them. It is more importantly the cultivation of both forms of knowing and providing students with the opportunity of learning how to creatively and effectively integrate these two ways of knowing. As I have noted, the emphasis of education has long been on the valuing and cultivation of discursive knowing. Thus, a great deal has been written on methods for doing this. Since it is the direct form of knowing that has been more neglected, some discussion on methods for cultivating it is necessary.

4. Cultivation of Direct Thought

The principal means by which direct thought has historically been cultivated has its roots in the mystical tradition. Much of the focus of this paper has been on the value of integrating a mystical perspective into the educational process in order to achieve a true pedagogy of being. Such an integration forces us to radically rethink our understanding of the nature of learning and what it means to be a teacher or a student. The origin of the word "education" is from the Latin term *educere* which means "to draw forth." This meaning is very much in accord with a mystical perspective on education. The goal is to draw forth from students what is already within them.

It is the responsibility of teachers first to devote themselves to more fully realizing and appreciating their own mystical vocation. True education begins with self-knowledge. But then the teacher must help students to likewise realize their own mystical vocation, for we are all mystics in the making. The realization of this vocation involves assisting students in recognizing their calling, a calling that is eventually articulated in their statement of a personal mission. The fulfillment of that calling requires us to help students utilize the talents, gifts, passions, and commitments that are unique to each of them.

The chief method employed by the mystics to cultivate the knowing of the heart is meditation or contemplation. A discussion of the various forms of this method is beyond the scope of this paper. Two excellent works that provide a comprehensive guide to meditation are Kornfield (1993) and Dass (1978). Meditation involves the disciplining of the chief instrument through which all learning occurs, namely, consciousness. It necessitates our learning to pay attention. This is something that we take for granted, but even a few moments reflection on what we call ordinary consciousness reveals how distracted, undisciplined, and unfocused consciousness is. Perhaps the simplest way in which to define learning to pay attention is doing one thing at a time and being fully present to whatever it is we are doing in that moment. This definition fits well with the earlier description of direct knowledge as an immediate and receptive grasp of the object of awareness.

The second key feature of meditation is to clear our knowledge of all hindrances that interfere with knowing reality fully, completely, and accurately. These include the many biases, preconceptions, expectations, and desires that frequently lead us to experience what we wish to know rather than to know something simply as it is. There have been many terms used to describe this process including non-attachment, bare attention, holy indifference, or an attitude of letting-be. This is often a rigorous, demanding, and painful process as we systematically strip ourselves of beliefs, values, and expectations that we hold dear. The ultimate goal is to make our way of knowing non-evaluative. The goal of making our knowledge as free of bias and prejudice as possible espoused by the mystic is very akin to the task set for philosophy by Edmund Husserl in his establishment of phenomenology. This close parallel is discussed by Patrik (1994). Again, the attainment of non-evaluative knowing is central to what has been described as direct knowledge.

Some recommendations on how teachers can strive to cultivate and enhance direct knowledge are offered by Aldous Huxley (1969) who was well acquainted with the various mystical traditions. In his essay, "Education on the Nonverbal Level," he notes that education must prepare students to live in a number of different worlds, some of which are contradictory and paradoxical. However, education is often one-sided and guided by a form of specialization, with a particular focus on science and technology. The result is that students are left confused and uncertain when they must function in a world that does not fit within this scientific and technological paradigm.

Huxley recommends that universal education on the nonverbal level become mandatory. He notes that simply trying to balance education in science and technology with humanities and the arts is not sufficient because much of education in the areas of humanities and the arts still relies heavily on a verbal level of instruction. Instead, he proposes that students receive a thorough train-ing in elementary awareness from kindergarten on. This training bares close similarity to the meditative techniques discussed above. The goal of this training is to provide students with techniques in improving their awareness of internal and external events. Additionally, creativity as it is experienced and channeled through spontaneous expression, is offered as a method. Examples include how to harness fantasy and imagination in a constructive manner. Techniques to enhance bodily awareness through athletics and yoga are offered. Finally, to attend to the moral dimension of life, Huxley discusses instruction in religiously sanctioned safety valves for dealing with anger and frustration.

Another approach to education that offers valuable guidelines for the cultivation of direct knowledge is offered by the Quaker tradition. Quakerism is based on the belief that there is that of God in all people. The images of the Inner Light and Inward Teacher are often used to describe an inner truth accessible to all persons. Teaching involves helping students to know this truth directly or experientially (Lacey, 1988). Such knowing again is fostered by a meditative attitude which is not passive, but attentive and alert. We create opportunities for such encounters through stillness and silence. Thus, a pedagogy of being is one that must help students to respect the value and power of silence. It is often when we remove the multiple distractions that surround us and drown out the call of being, that truth is disclosed to us.

An attitude of silent expectation and alertness is the beginning of a dialogue with the Inward Teacher. We must first listen and, having heard, then obey. Thus begins the dialogue in which one is addressed and one then responds. To merely listen is not enough. Any call from being places a burden and demand upon us that must be heeded. Some action must be taken in accord with the call. However, before acting we must submit the call to discernment to distinguish whether our actions are prompted by our own will and desire or by a higher will and desire. One such test is to see if the call results in an action that expresses a balance between the needs of the individual and the collective. If so, we can place our trust in it. It then becomes a source of insight and inspiration that is expressed in some product, work, vocation, or mission. There can be an intimidating and even terrifying aspect to such encounters because of the burden and demand they make. The Greeks referred to this as the *daimon* from which we get the term "demon." But such is the magnitude of any true mission. It is, as Kierkegaard emphasized, a truth for which we are willing to live and to die.

Yungblut (1979) also writes from a Quaker perspective on education in direct knowledge. He makes the foundation of such education the imparting of the idea of God within to all students by promoting an openness to encountering the divine in all things, from the simplest to the most mysterious. He also makes the important point that such education much come to terms with the often vexing problem of evil and suffering. Yungblut characterizes suffering as that which works against our wholeness, integrity, and sense of relatedness. Just as we must embrace both discursive and direct thought to be whole, we must find the means of coming to terms with the demonic within us. Through discernment, we distinguish good from evil and find the means of transforming evil into good. Yungblut also recognizes the importance of developing an appreciation for myth and metaphor as a means of fostering direct knowledge. The importance of silence in opening us to the Inward Teacher is likewise reiterated by him. Finally, Yungblut recognizes how all meditative practice culminates in a key insight or the unitive vision.

Therefore, such education must be devoted to helping students experience directly their sense of oneness and interdependence with all of existence. There can be no higher expression of wholeness and integration. However, this unitive insight is also the basis for the attitude most critical to a pedagogy of being, compassion.

5. Compassion: The Integration of Prophetic and Contemplative

The two ways of knowing that have formed the focus of much of this chapter are paralleled by two dimensions of the mystical vocation. Education as the fostering and nourishing of the mystical vocation of each student involves attention to both of these critical roles. When we closely examine the lives of mystics from all of the great spiritual traditions, we find that they lived out both of these dimensions of existence. The two aspects of the mystic are mutually defining and interdependent, just as the two ways of knowing. The presence of one without the other would not only be one-sided, but also could be dangerous and destructive.

Matthew Fox (1972, 1995) describes these two aspects as the mystic who is psychologically radical and the prophet who is socially radical. Nouwen (1972) describes the contemplative critic who integrates the mystical and the revolutionary ways. The attitude of compassion rooted in the mystical insight is what enables one to integrate these two roles. Thus, it is critical that the meaning of compassion within the mystical tradition is clearly spelled out.

Ultimately, it is the attainment of compassion that is the goal of the mystical tradition. As Underhill (1961) put it: "The business and method of mysticism is love" (p. 85). The unitive experience that represents the culmination of the mystic quest is likewise an experience of one's being unconditionally loved, valued, and accepted. This love is rooted in the realization that we are the loving self-expression of the Tao. It is out of love that we are created. We are sustained every moment by the loving presence of the Divine who freely and openly participates in each and every experience that comes with being human—the highs and the lows. This realization makes the unitive experience ecstatic and blissful. Our deepest longings are finally answered because we have discovered the true object of our love.

The unitive experience is also the realization of our essential at-one-ness with all of existence. The Tao is the Ultimate Reality that embraces all. Existence is a vast web of interdependent and mutual relationships. This oneness of existence in no way negates the undeniable diversity that characterizes our experience, but reminds us that beneath differences is a deep connectedness between all beings. This sense of connectedness is the basis of compassion. It makes a deep sense of intimacy and communion with another being possible. Because we are all an expression of complete and unconditional love, we owe this love to each other. In India, people greet one another by clasping their hands in a prayerful gesture and uttering a greeting in which the divine in oneself acknowledges the divine in the other. As Nouwen (1972) writes: "Compassion is born when we discover in the center of our own existence not only that God is God and man is man, but also that our neighbor is really our fellow man" (p. 41).

Unfortunately, many mistake the mystical vocation as merely based upon the attainment of this insight in the unitive experience. This is the stereotype of the recluse who retreats from the material world and engages in a rigorous practice of meditation in order to achieve oneness with the Tao. Having achieved the experience of oneness, the mystic then remains removed from the world and transported, as it were, to some higher dimension. However, this only gives expression to the mystic as a contemplative. It is through contemplation that one attains such knowledge. However, having attained such knowledge, one does not complete one's mystical vocation until that knowledge is put into practice. As noted earlier in this chapter, any encounter with the Tao is also an encounter with an absolute moral order that places a demand upon us.

Using the origins of the term "radical" as being based in "root," Fox (1972) notes how the mysticism is psychologically radical because it is based in our being fundamentally rooted in the Tao. This affirmation of our essential inter-dependence with all beings is radical because it challenges and shatters all our previous assumptions about the true nature of our identity. A consequence of discovering this interdependence and communion with all beings is compassion not merely as an intellectual insight, but as a moral imperative. The roots of "compassion" are "to suffer with." Thus, compassion means being open to the suffering of others. Such openness is unselfish and untainted by our own wishes and desires because the mystical insight enables us to transcend the narrow limits of our ego. For the psychology students I train, this means cultivating the ability to be fully present to the suffering of the client, no matter how un-comfortable and demanding. This is the authentic way to affirm the sense of communion that exists between one human being and another. The beginning of healing is the ability to embrace that suffering in life which is inherent to being human (Gruba-McCallister and Levington, 1990-1991).

However, there is also a great deal of suffering in the world that can be eradicated. Compassion as some abstract attitude that we hold for our fellow human beings is a sham. As Fox (1995) asserts, there is no love without justice. Using the term "orthopraxis," he makes clear that the true test of our commit-ment to our beliefs is how we live our lives. We must make the eradication and transformation of suffering our central concern. This fulfills the role of the mystic as prophetic or what Nouwen (1972) calls the social critic. Mysticism is thus also radical by being socially uprooting. This critical work calls upon the exercise of discursive thought, tempered by the direct knowledge we have acquired through the mystical vision. There must be a willingness to speak out fearlessly in testimony to the Truth and to challenge the *status quo*. The old order must be torn down for the work of love to be completed. Only then is love balanced by justice.

While the contemplative process carries with it terrors and fears of its own, the prophetic role is a demanding and taxing one. Fox (1972) notes that one of the marks of a true prophet is a reluctance to accept the burdens that come with being the messenger who proclaims to all, "Reform your lives!" In both processes, sacrifice is unavoidable. In the contemplative process, we must sacrifice the most dearly held beliefs, particularly about ourselves. The ego must die for the true sense of self to be born. But prophets have their sacrifices as well.

This is expressed eloquently by Simone Weil (1952) in her discussion of the relationship between obligations and rights. We live in a world sometimes obsessed with rights, but unmindful of obligations. As Weil (1952) states clearly, "The notion of obligations comes before that of rights, which is subordinate and relative to the former" (p. 3). This is because obligations are not based upon any convention, but rather are based upon an order that is eternal and unconditional—the Tao. When we cultivate a sense of silence and stillness, it is with the goal of enabling us to hear the call of Tao and the moral order it expresses. We are silent so that we can listen. We must first listen in order to obey. Compassion then becomes a duty. The call of the Tao is not a toll-free call because there is no question that it places a great toll upon us. We have the right to refuse to listen and to refuse to answer the call. So often we do because of our profound fear. But this very fear is the root of the injustice the prophet is called to oppose. Compassion, and compassion alone, is the means to move us beyond that fear. In moving us beyond it, it enables us to extend this compassion to all others.

The most powerful expression of mystic as contemplative and prophet, and compassion as the bridge that brings these two roles together, is the Buddhist concept of the bodhisattva. The bodhisattva is one who has attained enlightenment and thus is able to enter nirvana and end the cycle of death and rebirth. However, rather than do so, he or she returns to the world with the commitment of not entering nirvana until all beings have been saved. The figure of the bodhisattva is one echoed throughout all the great spiritual traditions. It is a lofty and intimidating ideal, but like all true ideals, it is worth one's commitment. And so I will conclude with an abridgement of a lengthy narrative of the vow of the bodhisattva, for I can think of no nobler aspiration for a teacher than to inspire his or her students to make these vows as a foundation of their education:

> All creatures are in pain, . . . all suffer from bad and hindering karma . . . so that they cannot see the Buddhas or hear the Law of Righteousness or know the Order. . . . I take upon myself the burden of sorrow; I resolve to do so; I do not turn back or turn away, I do not tremble. . . . For I have taken upon myself, by my own will, the whole of the pain of all things living. . . . I resolve to dwell in each state of misfortune through countless ages . . . for the salvation of beings . . . for it is better that I alone suffer than all beings sink to the worlds of misfortune. . . . I must not turn my back in my efforts to save all beings nor cease to use my merit for the destruction of all pain.

And I must be satisfied with small success. (Stryk, 1968, pp. 303-304)

Works Cited

Bretall, Robert. (Ed.) (1936) *A Kierkegaard Anthology*. New York: The Modern Library.

Buber, Martin. (1958) *I and Thou*. (2nd ed. rev.) (R. G. Smith, trans.). New York: Scribner.

Capra, Fritjof. (1982) *The Turning Point: Science, Society, and the Rising Culture*. New York: Bantam.

Dass, Ram. (1978) *Journey of Awakening: A Meditator's Handbook*. New York: Bantam.

Fox, Matthew. (1972) *On Becoming a Musical, Mystical Bear: Spirituality American Style*. New York: Harper & Row.

_____. (1995) *Wrestling with the Prophets: Essays on Creation Spirituality and Everyday Life*. San Francisco: Harper Collins.

Frankl, Viktor. (1967) *Psychotherapy and Existentialism*. New York: Simon and Schuster.

Goleman, D. (1985). *Vital Lies, Simple Truths: The Psychology of Self-Deception*. New York: Simon & Schuster.

Gruba-McCallister, Frank P., and Caryn Levington. (1990-1991) "Suffering and Transcendence in Human Experience," *Review of Existential Psychology and Psychiatry*, 22, pp. 99-115.

_____. (1994) "Authenticity as Open Existence," *Advanced Development*, 6, pp. 1-10.

Huxley, Aldous. (1969) "Education on the Nonverbal Level." In H. Chiang & A. H. Maslow (Eds.), *The Healthy Personality: Readings*. New York: Van Nostrand, pp. 150-165.

Kornfield, Jack. (1993) *A Path with Heart*. New York: Bantam.

Lacey, Paul. A. (1988) *Education and the Inward Teacher*. Walingford, Pa.: Pendle Hill.

Lewis, C. S. (1947) *The Abolition of Man*. New York: Macmillan.

Merton, Thomas. (1951) *The Ascent to Truth*. New York: Harcourt Brace Jovanovich.

_____. (1961) *New Seeds of Contemplation*. New York: New Directions Publishing Corporation.

Nouwen, Henri J. M. (1972) *The Wounded Healer: Ministry in Contemporary Society*. New York: Doubleday.

Ornstein, Robert. (1972) *The Psychology of Consciousness*. New York: Penguin Books.

Patrik, Linda. (1994) "Phenomenological Method and Meditation," *Journal of Transpersonal Psychology*, 26, pp. 37-54.

Schön, Donald. A. (1987) *Educating the Reflective Practitioner*. San Francisco: Jossey-Bass.

Senge, Peter. M. (1990) *The Fifth Discipline: The Art and Practice of the Learning Organization*. New York: Doubleday.

Shah, Idries. (1969) *Tales of the Dervishes*. New York: Dutton.

Stryk, Lucien. (Ed.) (1968) *World of the Buddha: A Reader*. New York: Doubleday.

Tillich, Paul. (1957) *The Dynamics of Faith*. New York: Harper & Row.

Underhill, Evelyn. (1915) *Practical Mysticism*. New York: Dutton.

_____. (1961) *Mysticism*. New York: Dutton.

Vandenberg, Donald. (1971) *Being and Education: An Essay in Existential Phenomenology*. Englewood Cliffs, N.J.: Prentice Hall.

von Eckartsberg, Rolf, and Ronald S. Valle. (1981) "Heideggerian Thinking and the Eastern Mind." In R. S. Valle and R. von Eckartsberg (Eds.), *The Metaphors of Consciousness*. New York: Plenum Press, pp. 287-311.

Weil, Simone. (1952) *The Need for Roots: Prelude to a Declaration of Duties Toward Mankind*. (A. Wills, Trans.). New York: Harper & Row.

Whitehead, Alfred North. (1966). *Modes of Thought*. New York: Macmillan.

Wilber, Ken. (1977) *The Spectrum of Consciousness*. Wheaton, Ill.: Theosophical Publishing House.

Winner, Ellen. (1996) *Gifted Children: Myths and Realities*. New York: Basic Books.

Yungblut, John R. (1979) *Discovering God Within*. Philadelphia: Westminster Press.

Four

ABOLISHING EDUCATIONAL WELFARE: REDRAWING THE LINES OF INTERDEPENDENCY THROUGH DIALOGUE

George David Miller

The Right is always complaining about the moochers, leeches, and freeloaders who consume resources and give little or nothing back to society. Lazy and unmotivated and unwilling to make something of themselves, the moochers, leeches, and freeloaders use their food stamps for drugs, alcohol, or the latest pair of Michael Jordan basketball shoes. Welfare and other programs have created a culture of dependency: "Kick 'em out on their asses and let them fend for themselves." Instead of independent, self-sufficient, creative go-getters, America has reared a generation of passive, irresponsible bloodsuckers. You can't throw money at the problem, says the Right. No handouts, no free lunch.

This line of thinking can be applied to other areas as well. Not only is there economic welfare, but also spiritual welfare. The way most people have chosen to solve this spiritual poverty is by throwing religion at it. Instead of seeking an authentic relationship with the Absolute or each other, many choose to inherit lifeless religious beliefs and customs. Not only fringe crazies, but the followers of mainstream religions passively accept a prescribed list of beliefs. It is no more rational to blindly accept religious beliefs of ancient peoples than to embrace wholeheartedly the reports of extraterrestrial appearances on earth in those tabloids we find in checkout lines at supermarkets. Rather than seeking faith for themselves, those on spiritual welfare inherit second-hand faith from tradition. A culture of dependency on inherited beliefs is tantamount to spiritual free-loaders. Shouldn't the same contempt be reserved for these faith freeloaders as the Right has for the welfare mother who uses her food stamps for Lotto tickets? Spiritual welfare is no less a problem than is economic welfare.

No less a problem than economic and spiritual welfare is educational welfare. In the traditional lecture format, students are the recipients of facts from teachers. Sometimes called the "banking concept" of education or educational bulimia, the traditional lecture formats cultivates students who are dependent upon teachers. Teachers control the flow of information and dictate classroom decorum. Students passively receive information and only small-scale and tepid creativity is tolerated or encouraged.

In *Pedagogy of the Oppressed*, Paulo Freire offers a blueprint for overcoming educational welfare.[1] Distinguishing between problem-posing and banking methods of education, Freire contends that while the banking concept contributes to oppression, problem-posing contributes to liberation. Whereas banking stultifies and promotes passivity, problem-posing dynamizes teaching and learning and promotes student activity and independence. Freire sees the traditional teacher-student dichotomy as the greatest obstacle. Rejecting that dichotomy, he sees the classroom as occupied by teacher-students and student-teachers. Instead of a one-way transmission of information, knowledge, and wisdom, a continuum exists between teacher-students and student-teachers. Instead of the teacher creating reality and students fitting into that reality, everybody in the classroom co-creates reality. Reality is dynamic and we play a role in dynamizing it.

The traditional banking classroom, and I might add variants of it that include "time for discussion," are the means of oppression. With a top-to-bottom leadership mold, they much more resemble fascism than even mild forms of democracy. The point of these classrooms is to maintain order and to instill propaganda. Reality is viewed as static and for good reason. For if people were to realize that reality is dynamic and that they dynamize reality, then they would realize they can change the institutions of the society.

Reality is not an immovable mountain, but clay that can be shaped and molded. In dynamizing the classroom via dialogue, contradictions emerge. People begin to see the contradictions in the economic, social, and political spheres. The monolithic banking concept, with the teacher giving his or her view, insulates itself against contradictions. The dialogical classroom, with its openness to divergent views and free-flowing structure, overflows with contradictions. Recognition of political, economic, and social contradictions Freire calls *conscientização*.[2] Without recognizing these contradictions, the oppressed cannot direct their energies toward changing the society.

One of the means to insure oppressions is to give students piece-meal facts rather than helping them cultivate a holistic view of the world. In developing a holistic view of the world, students discover interconnections and to become more politically and socially sophisticated. In contrast to holistic education, focalized education conceals reality. It prevents the emergence of political and social awareness and *conscientização*.

Freire envisions the new classroom as radical and not sectarian. In broad terms, by radical he means the recognition and creation of the dynamism of reality and embracing rather than deflecting doubt. Sectarians, on the other hand, believe that reality is static and surround themselves in "circles of certainty" or unassailable articles of faith. Sectarians from the right use an unchangeable past as a means to domesticate people in the present. Sectarians from the left view the future is preordained and thus rob people of the freedom of creating that reality.

It's not such an easy thing to break from the past and the bonds of the oppressor. This is what Freire terms "fear of freedom."[3] Oppressed people fear the responsiblity of seizing freedom and because of that willingly fall back into the arms of the oppressor. They adopt a fatalistic view of the world—"It can't be changed," they lament—and see the world as an enveloping monolithic block that cannot be carved into or molded. Stopped dead in their tracks by fear of freedom, they often sink into silence. Freire points out there is a theme in this silence, the theme of despair.

Freire's pedagogy is rooted in respect for the person. Humanization develops the potentialities of persons, whereas dehumanization prevents people from realizing their potentials. Freire labels an act violent to the extent that it deters or prevents people from realizing their potentialities. Striking an optimistic note, he sees dehumanization not as humankind's destiny, but as a distortion due to oppressive acts.[4]

Drawing from Freire's ontological views on dynamism, dialogue, and holism, I have attempted in my own philosophy of education to reexamine thinking that takes its point of departure in the description of human self-consciousness.[5] Self-consciousness by its very nature transcends itself and is dynamic. Self-consciousness is always differing. We are always ahead of ourselves.

My philosophy of education examines the nature of thinking.[6] Thinking roots and at the same time uproots. It is a continuum of believing and doubting, doubting and believing. Belief is punctured by doubt, and doubt swings into belief. Doubt and belief run into each other. The ambiguity inherent in all thinking, I believe, is not be expunged, but embraced. For such ambiguity is the stimulus to more thinking. If we can affirm thinking, then we can affirm dynamism. Reductionistic thinking tends to oversimplify in clarification; holistic thinking (viewed negatively here) offers an unlimited amount of perspectives. Between holistic and reductionistic thinking lies integrative thinking, which attempts to negotiate between the two sides. Both reductionism and holism end up in the same place: opaqueness. Holism is opaque because if offers an infinite number of perspectives. Reductionism is opaque because in reducing to the simple, one it detaches itself from other perspectives, which confers a context. One side tends toward clarity, the other toward chaos or disorder. The holding together of these tendencies is thinking. Thinking is both an order and disordering and is gelatinous. What Freire calls fear of freedom I call fear of the ambiguity inherent in thinking.

In my eyes, ambiguity is natural to thinking and a good thing to the extent that it cultivates more thinking and more reflection. If the goal is to stimulate thinking, then dialogue, I argue, is the best means for realizing that objective.

In dialogue, a multiplicity of views can emerge to challenge our own.

Freire points out that the mere memorization of facts is dehumanizing. I have argued elsewhere that values underlie facts. Even banal facts are charged with value.[7] Certain facts are valued more highly than other facts (for example, empirical truths are valued more highly than intuitive truths) only because a web of value preferences provides the basis for such judgments. Values, concealed or otherwise, determine the hierarchy of facts.

Freire contends dialogue is an act of love because it cannot exist without a deep love for the world and its people.[8] In an ideal teaching-learning continuum, I contend that each of its parties are both receptive and spontaneous.[9] This I call love or caring. I further suggest that all human acts are teaching and learning, whether we are facing others or the world.

Some educators are leery of dialogue because they believe there at times when they must emit an unadulterated stream of explanation or analysis that they call lecture. Such an unadulterated stream of information does not fit within their idea of "dialogue." But dialogue does not exclude the emission of such unadulterated streams. Students have to understand concepts in order for there to be dialogue. During the course of discussions, especially when one person knows much more than another in a certain area of inquiry, emission of unadulterated streams of information is requisite for understanding on the part of the uninformed person. Dialogue is sustained so long as there is in principle room for response on the part of less informed participants in dialogue and room for unadulterated streams of information other than those of the teacher. A one-way stream of information does not cultivate knowledge and wisdom, which involves the application and judgment of information. Dialogue is sustained to the extent that the principles of democracy and not autocracy guide the classroom. Among the tenets of democracy, as I shall suggest later, are a marketplace of ideas, the fallibility of authorities, and faith that the many can come to know and judge.

A pattern of the teacher giving a lecture and then students asking a few questions at the end of class is not dialogue. This arrangement suggests that students' perspectives are but an afterthought and not intrinsic to the classroom dynamic. In dialogic democratic schooling, students' perspectives are intrinsic to the classroom dynamic. The dialogic democratic classroom is sustained by dialogue and the self-determination of each individual.

One-way informational dispersal is not conducive to dialogue. The assumption is that the information is to be absorbed. The monolithic aspect of this dispersal prevents dialogue from flourishing, much less than emerging. When information comes from many dimensions, differences of opinion occur. These differences demonstrate the breadth and gradations of arguments and introduce ambiguity. To the extent that ambiguity emerges, thinking is possible.

We are drawn into thinking to the extent that we wish to clarify the ambiguous.

Lecture in its traditional sense is not conducive to developing knowledge and wisdom in others. For knowledge and wisdom are not mere recall of information. Knowledge and wisdom refer to the application of knowledge. Dialogue is a more effective means than lecture in providing the conditions for the search of knowledge and wisdom.

Educational welfare will continue in academic settings until students' thinking can become creative and thus autonomous. If students are thwarted from making or creating connections and prevented from full participation in the classroom, they will remain on educational welfare.

In dialogue, the interdependence of teaching and learning is repeatedly underscored. In dialogue, the interdependence of human beings is repeatedly underscored as we teach and learn from one another. Dialogue is not to be defined as chit chat or even discussion. In a Freirean sense, dialogue refers to the co-creation and re-creation of reality. From my perspective, dialogue is a negotiation toward truth. Dialogue is not talking about a subject, as if the subject were distinct from dialogue. Dialogue animates the subject by contextualizing and concretizing it. Dialogue is the soul of education, the unifying principle of information, knowledge, and wisdom.

Dialogue is question-friendly and question-inviting. It serves as the incubator of ideas because it is conducive to the friction of difference. The ambiguity arising in dialogue due to the friction of difference allows us to see the interconnectedness of viewpoints. The on-the-spottedness of dialogue cultivates a moment-to-moment responsibility for re-creating reality. Finally, the interactivity inherent in dialoguing fits the kind of thinking that is the result of interacting with modern technologies. Despite my harsh words at the beginning of this essay, please don't think for a moment that that I reject the idea of assistance. I firmly believe that in an affluent society, starvation, homelessness, and poverty are atrocities that are on par with crimes against humanity. I also firmly believe that spirituality, in its genuine sense, is creation and recreation of community.

On one extreme is rugged individualism and the self-made person. On the other extreme we find the wholly dependent leech. A third option is the best and also reflects the true nature of human reality: interdependence. Interdependence includes individual effort or will, but it recognizes that individuals exist within a social context and that individual goals cannot be realized without assistance from others. Dialogue is the best means for exemplifying, modeling, and reinforcing interdependence.

The idea for human endeavors is not to disallow assistance, but paternalistic assistance that cripples the self-development of human beings. The kind of assistance to be fostered is an interdependence that makes everybody co-responsible.

1. Creating a Comfort Zone for Discomfort or Difference

Predictions for the next century claim that the United States is going to become more diverse and that people of color will be a majority. This means, whether the dominant class likes it or not, they are going to come in contact with difference. The dialogical classroom illustrates and embraces difference; thus it prepares people for difference. The friction of difference is an everyday experience in the dialogical classroom. But the friction of difference is also creative. It can lead to the co-creation of common ground. Such common ground is earned through the sweat of dialogue instead of imposed from one or a few sources.

The dialogical classroom affords more opportunities for diversity and the broadening of issues. The more ideas out there, the more choice. The spectrum of issues is much more difficult to broaden when it comes from one or just a few sources. It may be argued that not the number of ideas but the types of ideas broaden issues. That is true. A lot of ideas from a narrow perspective does little to broaden the dialogue. But dialogue offers the opportunity for different voices and thus has the potential for broadening the spectrum of ideas.

Facts are challenged and deficiencies discovered in dialogue. Dialogue is inherently question-oriented. Teachers, others say, can ask these questions. But teachers' questions are not the only questions, and questions from different perspectives arise. The dialogical classroom creates an atmosphere and attitude of questioning. The dialogical classroom creates a climate for questioning and questioning creates a climate for examining diversity.

To create a comfort zone for difference, a new way of understanding thinking must occur. Believing thinking to be the expunger of ambiguity and contradictions, educators therefore extinguish difference. Difference is best experienced in ambiguity and contradictions. Categorization is the project of clear thinking, but these categories are segregated from one another and are not interpenetrating. Ambiguity is the truly integrated: categories trespass into other categories, ideas overlap other ideas, crooked and dimly defined borders predominate. Moments of difference are moments "other than" moments of consistency and bold demarcation. Thinking is a continuum that swerves from the consistent and boldly demarcated to the contradictory and crookedly demarcated. The first corresponds with the attitude of belief; the second with the attitude of doubt. Clear belief fades into fuzzy doubt and fuzzy doubt is sharpened into clear belief. Thinking swerves from belief to doubt and doubt to belief. If this analysis is accurate, then cultivating difference is a matter of allowing thinking to take its natural course. The natural course of thinking can be enhanced by dialogue, which allows for the emergence of different voices and also challenges to one's position.

Dialogue reminds us of something we sometimes forget: that no issue is black and white and all are fraught with ambiguity. In demonstrating difference, dialogue reinforces that thinking dwells in ambiguity and that issues are usually incredibly complex. Dialogue encourages layered rather than unlayered thinking. Such thinking tends to be holistic rather than focalized.

Dialogue illustrates the dynamism and ambiguity of thinking because it is question-inviting or question-friendly. Question-friendly environments are conducive to diversity and ambiguity because they produce diversity and ambiguity.

Part of the learning process is the evolution of ideas. Dialogue acts as an incubator of ideas, helping them to evolve more quickly than in lecture. Dialogue heats ideas, causing them to expand, change shape, and interact. The friction of difference in dialogue creates pluralistic possibilities for co-inquirers. The broader the possibilities, the more opportunity to discover ideas.

2. On-the-Spottedness and Moment to Moment Responsibility

A big part of getting students off of educational welfare is to cultivate a sense of responsibility. If students do not practice acting responsibly, then they cannot become responsible. This is similar to the argument Aristotle uses when he says in the *Nicomachean Ethics* that a person becomes courageous by acting courageously, temperate by acting temperately, just by acting justly. According to the same reasoning, a person becomes responsible by acting responsibly.

In democratic dialogical schooling, everybody has responsibility for creating and sustaining the dialogue. Each individual in the classroom shoulders the responsibility of contributing to the well-being of the class. It is not a matter of speaking when "I feel like it" or letting the instructor coax participation with veiled threats or inspirational jingoism. In democratic dialogical schooling, the concept is that the classroom flourishes to the extent that everybody flourishes. This means that everybody is on the spot.

Dialogue promotes on-the-spottedness. This means that students and instructors share in the moment to moment responsibility of co-creating dialogue and reality. Student responsibility is not limited to taking exams on 13 September, 31 October, and 8 December, but in the every-day and every-moment operation of the classroom. They must be productive in the creation of the classroom experience or else the little society called "Philosophy 101"or whatever course suffers. This moment-to-moment responsibility, in contra-distinction to intermittent responsibility (on this date and this date), is the means for developing responsibility.

We say we want to cultivate critical thinking in the classroom. Can that really be accomplished in the classroom lacking moment-to-moment responsibility? In the democratic dialogical classroom, students and instructors are routinely held responsible for the factuality and consistency of their views in the rigor of dialogue. On-the-spottedness engenders discipline and once internalized becomes self-discipline. The development of self-discipline is the gateway to independent or critical thinking.

Some students will resist being on the spot. They feel pressured to speak and only want to when they feel like it. Or, some may refuse to dialogue, claiming they learn by listening better rather than they learn by participating.

I have several things to say to these comments. In the first place, the interpersonal skills gained from dialoguing are invaluable in all spheres of human contact, including the coveted job after graduating. Would educators allow students who didn't want to write ("It isn't how I learn") not to write, or do we acknowledge that writing is an essential skill for students? Is not the ability to dialogue an essential skill? Students must be able to negotiate between viewpoints, not only to discover their own viewpoint but to reconcile conflicts that arise in their personal and professional lives.

Secondly, dialogue promotes responsibility for one's viewpoints. My experience is that the person who doesn't want to share his or her viewpoint and test it via dialogue is not a responsible learner. The responsible learner wants to test his or her views and embraces rather than flees from critique. We do a profound disservice to students by allowing them to be isolationists. In fact, we are responsible for retarding their development. Thinking about things may not be passivity, but it is by no means as dynamic as dialoguing. Dialoguing brings ideas out into the open and allows them to develop via interaction with others. The response of the student to critiques of his or her ideas makes the student aware of the shortcomings of the perspective and encourages responsibility for addressing those shortcomings. As a general rule, most of us are not good critics of our works: they are our children and we are reluctant to find flaws in our children. The person who "learns by listening" actually insulates himself or herself from critiques and flees from the responsibility of developing his or her ideas. If dialogue is the most active kind of learning and the most active kind of learning is more conducive to critical thinking than more passive kinds of learning, then dialogue is the means to the higher forms of critical thinking. A large part of critical thinking is knowing what your perspective is and what its strengths and weaknesses are. Knowing your own perspective can occur only when we know how it relates to other perspectives. Undoubtedly, this can occur in other ways (reading, watching TV, movies, etc.), but the interaction of dialogue and the specific questions of fellow dialogists that prompt response cultivates a more active and therefore a more critical view of one's perspective.

What are the means for cultivating a classroom environment in which dialogue can flourish. First, the classroom must be democratized such that we have a continuum of teaching-learning rather than a designated teacher and others designated as students. I will talk in more detail about democratization in the next section, but right now, I want to talk about some methods to make students feel comfortable to dialogue. One of the methods I use, which I realize works better in small classes rather than large, is to ask a question and go around the room and have everybody answer it. If done on a regular basis, students then become conditioned to participate.

Antagonism arises in dialogue, especially when controversial topics are discussed. One of the great mistakes I have made as an educator is to throw students into these topics without first reassuring them that my intent and the objective of the course is not to ridicule their views, but to develop them as human beings. This is why I begin all of my courses by shaking the hand of each student and telling them that I care about them and their development as a human being. Important, too, is not only allowing unpopular ideas to be presented, but to keep alive through dialogue the proponent of unpopular views who must be respected as a person, or else that person may withdraw from the process.

3. The Democratization of the Classroom

The interactivity of dialogue is the ground for the democratization of the class-room. Instead of one or a few views, there are now many views. In a climate of questioning, authority is routinely challenged and thus the student-teacher relationship is redefined. Instead of one sun and many planets circling it, we see another reality: many bodies that attract and repel one another. Dialogue fosters the democratic co-creation of reality whereas other more traditional forms of pedagogy are less conducive to such co-creation. Democracy and questioning are a much better fit than are authoritarianism and questioning. The following passage offers some suggestion about learning about democratic leadership:

> This, then, is the role of the liberal arts in higher education. Some things can be taught, other things have to be learned. Leadership must be learned. Learning about democratic leadership requires teaching and encouraging students to improve their capacities for observation, reflection, imagination, invention, and judgment. It requires an ability to gather and interpret evidence, marshal facts, and employ the most rigorous methods in the pursuit of knowledge. We should encourage the ability to ask the right questions and the ability to distinguish the significant from the trivial, and we should encourage an unyielding commitment to the truth combined with a full

appreciation of what remains to be learned.[10]

Strikingly absent from this list of things is dialogue. Learning about democratic leadership means participating in democratic leadership. How likely is this democratic leadership to arise in classroom environments without dialogue? In the authoritarian classroom, students are still on educational welfare.

If we want to get students off of educational welfare, then we must democratize the classroom. But this involves more than collaboraton; it involves the sharing of power. And when we get down to the sharing of power, we separate the those whose pursuit of democracy is authentic and those who want to give the illusion of democracy. The authentic fighters for democracy have faith the people can make decisions and, can be self-determining. The illusionists believe the masses are too stupid to make decisions. As Noam Chomsky writes:

> He [Jefferson] made a distinction between two groups-aristocrats and democrats. Aristocrats "fear and distrust the people, and wish to draw all powers from them into the hands of the higher classes." This view is held by respectable intellectuals in many different societies today, and is quite similar to the Leninist doctrine that the vanguard party of radical intellectuals should take power and lead the stupid masses to a bright future.[11]

The authentic fighters for democracy want the people to be in control, though they may not make the right decisions every time:

> Democrats, Jefferson wrote, "identify with the people, have confidence in them, cherish and consider them the most honest and safe, although not the most wise, depository of the public interest." In other words, democrats believe the people should be in control, whether or not they're going to make the right decisions.[12]

One of the biggest problems in democracy is disparate levels of knowledge that exist between people. Is it irrational for those who have less knowledge or expertise to make or help make decisions? Does it make more sense to allow those decisions to be made by those with more knowledge or expertise? Those who believe that the elite should run a country or an organization have no problem with this issue. They can argue, as Plato does in the *Apology*, that the few who possess knowledge improve things while the many ignorant corrupt things.

My question concerns the place of democracy in the classroom. I am going to define democracy in its most basic way. Democracy is generally defined as government by the people, either directly or through representatives. Equality of rights, opportunity, and treatment are three principles of democracy. From these principles others can be inferred: (1) challenge of authorities; (2) the fallibility of authorities; (3) checks and balances; (4) marketplace of ideas; (5) self-determination; (6) faith in people to make decisions; and (7) education geared to help people make decisions.

Unlike in a dictatorship, in a democracy authorities are accountable to the people. They have to justify their actions and policies, which can be challenged by the people. Allowing the people to challenge policies suggests the fallibility of authorities and also the existence of checks and balances between the rulers and ruled. When authorities are infallible, they cannot be challenged. They are golden cows. Checks and balances only occur when the policies of leaders can be challenged. Checks and balances are meant to limit the powers of authorities. This goes back to the accountability of authorities.

A marketplace of ideas provides a wide range of alternatives from which people can choose. In a democracy, a marketplace of ideas has a better chance to emerge than in authoritarian regimes. The equality of rights, opportunity, and treatment is often associated with individuals having the right to determine their own fates. One of the unstated principles of democracy is faith in the people to determine their own fates. Justifications for paternalistic authoritarianism are sometimes rooted in the lack of faith of the people making decisions on their own. This faith in the people is translated into educational programs designed to educate the people to participate in governing.

In many everyday cases, one party has more knowledge than another, such as: (1) Doctor-Patient, (2) Customer-Seller, (3) People-Government, (4) Parents-Children, (5) Car owner-Mechanic, and (6) Teacher-Student. But there are also less obvious examples; for example, the stranger in town asking for directions from a resident or even two people in the same general field, one of whom has knowledge of an area of inquiry the other lacks. For example, two people may have Ph.Ds in Philosophy, but one reads Chinese and is a Lao Tzu Scholar whereas the other may be a generalist with only a superficial understanding of Lao Tzu.

In the classroom, one person (the teacher) usually has more knowledge than the others (students). Does this mean that the classroom structure should be authoritarian? I think a clue to answering the question can be gleaned from the examples above. We make a mistake in saying that in most cases the relationship is one between the knowledgeable or the ignorant. In many cases, the relationship is between the more and the less knowledgeable. If we argue that those with knowledge ought to dictate the fates of those who have less knowledge, then we violate one of the key principles of democracy—self-determination. Following this dictum leads to absurdities. Would we allow salespeople to determine what we need because they have more expertise than we do about a certain product? Would we allow our government representatives to create policies harmful to us because they have more expertise in the area in question? Would we allow the mechanic to do repairs on our car we could not afford? Should children allow parents to be abusive to them? Would we allow the doctor to determine when we live and when we die? While we do not have as much knowledge as the experts in these cases, we still want to make the decision because it directly affects us.

In the early stages of education, the ideal of democracy is difficult to attain because of the cognitive level and inexperience of the students. But as students mature intellectually and have experience in the classroom and in the world, they can become members of a democratic classroom.

In a democracy, teachers and students co-create the syllabus. In order to be self-determining beings, students must make the key choices how the class should be run: class structure, grading, books, etc. But when students come into a course in which they have little or no knowledge, this proves to be a herculean task. This is why the course should begin with tentative guidelines suggested by the instructor. As the course progresses and students get what is going on, then the real syllabus will be co-created.

Where, then, is the expertise of the instructor in all of this? The instructor has been down these roads before and can direct students to readings and exercises that may be more fruitful. Teachers lead through the authority of reason, not the by reason of authority.

We cannot expect students to become critical thinkers if they are told what to do. They can only become critical thinkers as they challenge authority. We cannot expect students to value self-determination when their self-determination is constantly devalued. We can only be what we practice to be.

Can't this lead to anarchy and chaos in the classroom or a tyranny of the majority? In some cases, it may. This is one of many possible outcomes of democracy. But another outcome is that students will recognize the gift of freedom in the classroom and work to make learning effective and profound. Without such a hope, democracy can never occur.

Another problem concerns the degree of participation by each student. Can this dialogical democracy withstand varying degrees of participation? Experienced educators can confidently predict on no given day will there be equal student participation. Does this mean that we scrap the dialogical democratic classroom altogether? Not everybody has to participate in order to make the dialogical democratic classroom work, but the majority must. Since students are largely reared in authoritiarian and even fascist environments, even easing them into the dialogical democratic classroom will be culture shock. This is why a clear understanding of what their responsibilities are must be understood from the beginning. One of the things that I like to tell students is they must think of themselves not only as respondents but also as initiators. "If you were structuring this course," I like to say, "what would you do?" I suggest that they bring articles, film clips, and even speakers to class if they think such things can enhance the course. Again, back to a point I have made several times, educators cannot expect students to be autonomous thinkers without having them practice being responsible.

It is not enough for educators to have their little gerbils they call students do "critical thinking exercises" from books. For critical thinking creates the sense of responsibility of shaping and directing one's environment.

Educators committed to democracy strongly believe in the value of self-determination, even if it leads to error. They are also committed to the premise that people can become more educated and that the increase of knowledge and wisdom will allow the people to function as leaders of society.

4. Dialogue as Heuristic Holism

Martin Luther King, Jr. characterizes holism in this manner:

> I am cognizant of the interrelatedness of all communities and states. I cannot sit idly by in Atlanta and not be concerned about what happens in Birmingham. Injustice anywhere is a threat to justice everywhere. We are caught in an inescapable network of mutuality, tied in a single garment of destiny. Whatever affects one directly affects all indirectly.[13]

The single garment of destiny pertains to all area of our lives, as one recent article on leadership points out:

> We live in an increasingly holistic era. For example, we see the earth more and more as an integrated holistic ecosystem. In health, the trend is toward a holistic approach with added emphasis on wellness, prevention, diet, and fitness. In business, we are operating within an interconnected, mutually-dependent global market place.[14]

The dialogical classroom is a living example of interconnectedness and mutual dependence. Dialogists see how one idea depends upon others, how one discipline depends upon others, how the development of an idea depends upon interaction with others. A one-way transference of information prevents a holistic vision of the world. It is difficult to conceive of being able to see interconnections when only one view is presented. In this vision of holism, students must not think of their knowledge as a series of isolated departments or even a series of departments in which some interpenetration occurs. Nor should we think of a single discipline acting as a nucleus and other disciplines revolving around it. Instead this integrated or holistic picture involves overlapping circles that constantly contract and expand. The contraction squeezes the disciplines together; the expansion propels them away from each other. Thus, there is a continuum of contraction and expansion, which depends upon the particular stage of development of the participants.

5. Intellectual Humility and Tolerance

The friction of difference constantly imperils our viewpoints. Two of the virtues that dialogue reinforces are intellectual humility and tolerance toward alien perspectives. Dialogue is the place for testing ideas. Quickly, we see the strengths and weaknesses of our ideas. We grasp how underdeveloped our perspectives are. In dialoguing with others, we see the limitations of our intellect and of our arguments. Thus intellectual humility is one of the first lessons learned. Another lesson is tolerance for alien perspectives. Only through repeated exposure to different or alien perspectives, and to the development of our own ideas that may first appear alien to us, can help us grasp difference.

"Give people the facts and their attitudes will change" is one of the more naïve attitudes of educators, especially of the progressive era.[15] Facts are an important part of the equation, no doubt, and should never be underestimated. But changing attitudes is more than an intellectual shift: it is as emotional shift as well. The patriotic American, for example, who has made an emotional investment in his or her country, will find it difficult to shift alliances, even if facts point to the shortcomings and outright atrocities committed by his or her country. The maxim ought to read: "Cultivate thinking and their attitudes will change." As previously described, thinking swerves to and fro, from the clear and boldly demarcated to the fuzzily marked and murky. The first corresponds to the attitude of belief; the second to the attitude of doubt. Thinking reveals to us the fragility of belief, which at any moment maybe punctured by doubt. Thinking also reveals to us that the seed of belief is in doubt. Once the nature of thinking is understood and embraced, we become less hostile to the alien and more tolerant of other people's viewpoints. We recognize the dynamism of our thinking and the mutability of our perspectives. When we don't see our views as closed off from the rest of the world and impervious to criticism, then we allow other ideas and viewpoints to mingle with our own. We are intrinsically interdependent. Our views develop only through interaction with other views. The dialogical experience is intrinsically open to development. This is why dialogists can embrace the growth of ideas and are not bent on preserving them in their pristine condition.

6. Dialogue as the Glass Slipper Fitting New Technologies

Students of the 1980s, 1990s, and today are accustomed to interactive technologies. They are accustomed to video games and the Internet. They are accustomed to interaction and interdependence. Now they come to a classroom having little interaction and interdependence. Such a classroom is a mismatch for those nurtured in the electronic medium. Dialogue, inherently interactive and interdependent, is the appropriate medium in the classroom for such students.

Dialogue is the best means for cultivating community. Community is a place for common ground and such common ground, especially when people come from diverse backgrounds, must be co-created. Many people are desperately searching for community, a connectedness with others. The dialogical classroom provides a way for co-creating community.

Greater numbers of students are coming to the classroom exhausted and fatigued. This applies to both traditional and nontraditional students. Students are working more today to offset the ever rising costs of education. Nontraditional students have familial concerns and other responsibilities and are often not "bright-eyed and bushy-tailed." Dialogue is a means to regenerate the overworked student.

Finally, for a society that cultivates instant gratification and short attention spans (sound bite thinking), dialogue is a better means than lecture to keep students' attention.

7. Critique: It's a Busy Two-Way Street

It's a silly methodology, I believe, to have students do evaluations at the end of the semester. Maybe if instructors decide to read them, they will change their methods, but what good does that do the students who handed in those evaluations? Nothing. The better method would be for instructors to receive critiques from students on a regular basis during the semester and be able to adjust to these criticisms.

In dialogue, evaluation is constant. In a democratic process, critique and self-critique can flourish. In the dialogical process, critique is natural. Below is an example of such a critique that I receive from my students 6-8 weeks into each semester after asking them to evaluate my teaching performance:

EVALUATION OF INSTRUCTOR

1. Instructor addresses primary ideas in text.

   Do I hit the main themes of the texts or do I deal with too many insignificant issues?

2. Instructor relates ideas in text to classroom discussions.

    Am I able to tie in textual issues to the concerns of students?

3. Instructor clearly defines terms.

    During our discussions, do I identify and define key terms?

4. Instructor offers clear, accurate, and thorough understanding of the authors' ideas.

    Do I explain issues so that you understand them?

5. Instructor gives support for his/her position.

    Do I take time to develop my viewpoint and to give solid reasons why I believe this or that?

6. Instructor points out inconsistencies in the author's position.

    Do I point out flaws in the author's positions?

7. Instructor routinely integrates diverse perspectives.

    Do I attempt point out comparisons and contrasts between the ideas of different thinkers?

8. Instructor discusses insights gained from works.

    Do I point which ideas have had an impact on my life?

9. Instructor routinely offers self-critique of his/her ideas.

    Am I willing to say when I have gone wrong or how my ideas have developed?

10. Instructor demonstrates how readings and ideas in this course complement readings and ideas in other courses and other experiences.

Do I show the ideas in the course relate to other courses, everyday life, and the media?

11. Instructor is evenhanded, making sure to seek out, introduce, and address opposing perspectives.

Do I attack my pet theories with the same rigor when I attack the ones I don't accept?

8. Dialogue as the Fertile Soil for Knowledge and Wisdom

Dialogue transcends one directional information exchange. Dialogue is multi-directional. Dialogue is conducive to the friction of difference. Dialogue creates on-the-spottedness. Is such an environment conducive for the emergence of knowledge and wisdom?

There is a profound difference between recalling information and applying knowledge and between applying knowledge (general rules to idiosyncratic cases) and exercising wisdom (universal truths assessing the value of knowledge).

Let us take the example of open-heart surgery to suggest distinctions between information and knowledge and knowledge and wisdom.

Surgeon 1 recalls the facts: what instruments to use; certain methods for operating; what personnel is needed. Simply recalling information is not knowledge. Surgeon 1 is limited to the recall and not the application of information. This is information.

Surgeon 2 can recall the necessary information but also can adapt it for the particular situation. This is more than simple recall. This involves judgment, of deciding what recalled information will be effective in each particular case. This is knowledge. Knowledge involves judgment.

Surgeon 3 can recall the necessary information and apply it to the particular case at hand. But Surgeon 3 goes beyond judgment of applying information. Surgeon 3 examines the role of god as doctor; or when and how doctors should intervene in the "natural processes" of nature; or how a certain class of workers (doctors) is considered more valuable than other classes. Surgeon 3 applies values to knowledge. This is wisdom.

Dialogue, promoting holism and the ambiguity, fluidity of ideas, and setting the stage for on-the-spottedness and the friction of difference, is the most fertile soil for the emergence of knowledge and wisdom. This is because question-friendly environments compel application of information and knowledge.

Two questions arise: (1) Couldn't instructors encourage information-application by asking questions?; (2) Even assuming that dialogue promotes information-application, does it promote wisdom? Instructors merely asking questions does not create a question-friendly environment. We can imagine a Nazi interrogator grilling prisoners of war. A question-friendly environment means that all kinds of questions are posed from all kinds of perspectives. A question-friendly environment is a democratic environment in which checks and balances and challenging authorities is the norm. In principle, such an environment spawns a far wider range of questioning than a central source (the teacher) could ever create. A wider range of questioning affords more options for the application of information and knowledge.

I want to talk about what I call the spillover effect. The spillover effect stipulates that all questioning leads to ultimate questions and that these questions are questions of wisdom. Dialogue is more conducive to the spillover effect than are pure or hybrid lecture forms. Knowledge spills over into wisdom as more questions are asked and more ambiguities emerge. This ambiguity muck is precisely the impetus to wisdom.

The most creative acts are those that require synthesis; hence, the application of knowledge and the exercise of wisdom are more creative than the recollection of information. This is because the application of knowledge and the exercise of wisdom consist of creatively fitting general rules to specific instances. The question-friendly or question-inviting dialogical classroom gives ample opportunities for the application of knowledge and the exercise of wisdom.

9. The Value of Interdependence

Taking people off educational welfare means that they must be the most active teachers and learners possible. They must be both teachers and learners. Ultimately, this means they must be able to apply general rules to specific cases, the hallmark of any critical thinking.

A philosophy of interdependence complements dialogue. From this, an ethics of interdependence and a politics of interdependence emerge. We can pull our own weight with the help of others; others pull their own weight with our help. I don't want to throw people off welfare and into the streets to die. Nor do I want to strip people of spirituality and let them live in spiritual bankruptcy. What I would like is to create situations that empower via interdependency. The most productive society imaginable—spiritually, economically, aesthetically— will be the one that learns how to draw the right lines between individuals and masters interdependency. In the past I have addressed the issue of dialogue in a purely positive sense, in terms of love. This essay has attempted to view dialogue in terms of escaping an evil, namely, dependency. New forms of interdependent relationships emphasizing that creativity arises from individuals but is nurtured, sustained, and actualized with others must not only pervade the classroom, but economic, political, and social spheres as well.

Democratization is the key to taking students off of educational welfare. Allowing people to make mistakes with the faith that these mistakes will lead to enlightenment is a core tenet. As Adam Urbanski, President of the Rochester Teacher's Association, contends: "If you trust students with responsibility and have faith in them, they will rise to your expectations."[16] According to George Wood, principal of a high school in Ohio in which students, among other things, help to interview applicants for faculty positions and refashion the curriculum, claims: "[P]art of the mission of a high school should be showing students how to join up with the adult community. Giving them this kind of responsibility helps do that."[17] Enlightenment does not come from memorizing information, but from knowledge and wisdom. The democratic dialogical classroom recognizes facts, but also recognizes that knowledge and wisdom are the ultimate goals of education.

Dialogue is based on love and the recognition of others as self-determining beings. But this is but one aspect of interdependence. The other aspect is the responsibility of dialogists to be contributors or initiators. In the dialogic democratic classroom, all are expected to be initiators and not merely respondents. The continuum of dialogue depends upon everyone taking responsibility for the emergence of knowledge and wisdom.

Collaboration can occur in authoritarian settings. In oppressive situations, people collaborate to assassinate their oppressors. Such collaboration can occur in the face of authoritarianism. This is not to say that collaboration under those circumstances is a common phenomenon and that such an environment is conducive to the reproduction of collaborative efforts. We have what is termed "collaboration" when instructors send students off into groups. But this is a weak sense of collaboration. The strongest sense of collaboration is when everyone in the classroom works toward creating optimal learning conditions.

When students are asked about their collaborative learning experiences, they report that they are "more satisfied with their learning experience" and also evaluate them more favorably than students who are exposed to the traditional lecture method.[18] One of the common arguments used against dialogue is that dialogue is "messy" and that it is an inefficient method for presenting information. In principle, monolithic presentations are far more orderly than dialogical collaborations. This is the case when only one voice (with a chorus of meeker voices) predominates. Dialogue is by nature messier, not simply because of multiple voices, but because of the spontaneity arising when concerns other than the instructor's are addressed and guide the discussion in different directions. Yet part of the problem consists in the inexperienced attempting to run a dialogical democratic classroom. Instructors experienced in dialogue can orchestrate dialogue to hit key points and small group exercises can function to address confusing or complex points.

A commitment to dialogue in the educational system means that initial inefficiency will be rewarded by greater efficiency as participants become more effective in the system. This is because participants will in principle become more responsible in their learning as time goes on. More responsible people means less time on second-order issues (grading, attendance, behavior) and more on developing an environment in which education can flourish. The democratic dialogical classroom is the means for striking a balance between individuality and collectivity. It represents an attack on the deep-seated but often un-acknowledged strain of the top-to-bottom management style that permeates the American way of life.

Notes

1. Paulo Freire, *Pedagogy of the Oppressed*, trans. Myra Bergman Ramos (New York: Continuum, 1970/1993).

2. *Ibid.*, p. 17.

3. *Ibid.*, p. 18.

4. *Ibid.*, p. 26.

5. George David Miller, *Negotiating Toward Truth: The Extinction of Teachers and Students* (Amsterdam/Atlanta: Rodopi, 1998).

6. *Ibid.*, pp. 96-100.

7. George David Miller and Conrad P. Pritscher, *On Education and Values: In Praise of Pariahs and Nomads* (Amsterdam/Atlanta: Rodopi, 1995), pp. 12-13; *Negotiating Toward Truth*, pp. 100-102.

8. Freire, *Pedagogy of the Oppressed*, pp. 70-71.

9. Miller, *Negotiating Toward Truth*, pp. 6; 98.

10. Thomas E. Croin, "Leadership and Democracy," in *The Leader's Companion: Insights on Leadership Through the Ages*, ed. J. Thomas Wren (New York: The Free Press, 1995), p. 308.

11. Noam Chomsky, *Secrets, Lies, and Democracy* (Tucson, Ariz.: Odonian Press, 1994), p. 14.

12. *Ibid.*, p. 15

13. Martin Luther King, Jr., "Letter from Birmingham City Jail," in *A Testament of Hope: The Essential Writings and Speeches of Martin Luther King, Jr.*, ed. James M. Washington (San Francisco: Harper Collins, 1986), p. 290.

14. Lyn Joy McFarland, Larry E. Senn, and John R. Childress, "Redefining Leadership for the Next Century," in *The Leader's Companion*, p. 461.

15. See James H. Jones, *Alfred C. Kinsey: A Public/Private Life* (New York and London: W.W. Norton, 1997).

16. Kevin Kennedy, "When Students Run Schools," http://www.pin.org/library/ans5.htm

17. *Ibid.*

18. "Collaborative Learning," http://csis3.kennesaw.edu/-cyong/grpware.htm

Five

AN UNORTHODOX PEDAGOGY: FOSTERING EMPATHY THROUGH PROVOCATION

Jon Mills

Empathy and provocation are often viewed in bipolar opposition to one another: empathy—an attunement to the psychic state of the other, provocation—a solicitation of anger. While empathy is typically associated with the humanistic comportment of care, provocation is maligned as aggressive and relegated to the realm of the negative.

Empathy and provocation are underappreciated aspects of education and are together seldom practiced in the classroom. Within general education, the methodological employment of empathy and provocation are treated gingerly. Empathy requires a personal commitment to understand the inner reality of the student, which sometimes entails a painful foray into the throes of human consciousness—a commitment few teachers are prepared to undertake. While empathy is typically seen as a virtuous activity, it is rarely taught within school: there are no mandatory classes on how to listen, perceive, and understand the inner world of others—this is often left to life experiences and the development of character.

Provocation, on the other hand, is avoided like the plague. It connotes aggression and conflict, and entails an encroachment on the inner reality of the student, a confrontation that transgresses the objective guise of instruction while entering the subjective ground of individuality. Many teachers often concede that they are minimally interested in knowing about the personal attributes of their students let alone the intimate experiences that constitute their lives, for the teacher-student relationship would shift from the professional to the private. However, provocation, like empathy, also has its positive valences, particularly when utilized to engender values.

What pedagogical role does empathy and provocation have in the active classroom experience? Is there a positive significance to the negative that provocation affords, one that may serve as a catalyst for empathy? In this chapter I wish to make a case for the use of provocation in the service of empathy which further serves a purpose for general education. I will argue that when incorporated within pedagogical technique, provocation may be utilized as a means to cultivate empathy within students as well as express empathy itself. As a critical attempt to explore the nature of value, empathic provocation may provide an alternative and unorthodox approach to values education that may be seen as the expression of care. But before we delve into the nuances of a provocative pedagogy, we must first look closely at the nature of empathy in order to understand its role in an instructional methodology as well as its relation to provocation.

1. The Topography of Empathy

Empathy is a concept used to refer to myriad experiences ranging from the ethical and aesthetic to the transcendental. Generally considered an ally of humanism, empathy is often discussed in mental health fields as a therapeutic technique. While given emphasis by phenomenological psychologists as a "very special way of being with another person,"[1] empathy is described by Freud as "the process . . . which plays the largest part in our understanding of what is inherently foreign to our ego in other people."[2] Viewed as a *process* rather than merely a state one is in, empathy can be a powerful means for understanding the inner being of another.

In everyday usage, the term has acquired a number of different meanings that imply attunement with the emotional or feeling states of another often associated with acts of sympathy or kindness. Sympathy is distinguished from empathy insofar as sympathy involves the capacity to enter into and participate in the shared feelings of the other (which is often sorrow or suffering), while empathy involves an act of insightful projection into another's experience without necessarily having to feel that same experience. Clearly, empathy, sympathy, and insight can overlap, yet empathy implies a degree of subjective space within the intersubjective engagement of another distinct from his or her affective reality while still remaining positioned alongside it. In the words of Carl Rogers, "being empathic, is to perceive the internal frame of reference of another with accuracy and with the emotional components and meanings which pertain thereto as if one were the person."[3] This involves "entering the private perceptual world of the other . . . [and] being sensitive, moment by moment, to the changing felt meanings which flow in this other person."[4] From this account, empathy almost requires a subjective merger through imagination and identificatory perception of what it would be like to experience the world from the other's perspective.

Within many clinical accounts of empathy, the emphasis falls on being attuned with the affective processes of others. Helene Deutsch provides us with an initial understanding of empathy: "The affective psychic content of the patient . . . becomes transmuted into an inner experience of the analyst, and is recognized as belonging to the patient (i.e., to the external world) only in the course of intellectual work."[5] She further concludes that empathy involves the dialectical oscillation between close emotional harmony with the patient's inner life and a distant objectivity afforded by intellectual evaluation. Following Freud's claim that a "path leads from identification by way of imitation to empathy,"[6] Deutsch believes that empathy is initiated by a temporary identification with the other. Whether or not this involves a moment of merger with the other accompanied by a simultaneous sense of separateness, she does not say.[7] Yet on some level, identification (whether transient or partial) is a key ingredient in the capacity to relate to and understand the inner processes and experiences of another person.[8]

Within psychoanalytic self psychology, Kohut describes empathy as "vicarious introspection" and designates it as the primary method for comprehending the inner reality of another. "Empathy is a mode of cognition which is specifically attuned to the perception of complex psychological configurations."[9] Through the recognition of complex psychological processes, empathic observation involves an attunement to others' inner experiences, and "when they say what they think or feel, [one] imagines their inner experience even though it is not open to direct observation."[10] For Kohut, empathy is a method of observation for collecting psychological data as well as a technique that becomes employed within the clinical encounter to seek out hidden and unavailable painful, archaic, and conflicted aspects of development. The operational mode of observation may also be considered to be an important feature of empathy that extends beyond the therapy situation. Combined with a caring comportment, empathic observation can serve as a foundation for a responsive, validating, and understanding posture that one may assume toward others at large.

There are many levels of empathy that may involve attending to a complex mélange of experiences ranging from mere conceptual understanding and affirmation of the other's inner reality to affective and emotionally charged thoughts and inner conflicts that are unconsciously derived. Schafer notes that empathic appreciation of another's mental world goes beyond the simple emphasis on shared feelings to include an understanding of the individual's "organization of desires, feelings, thoughts, defenses, controls, superego pressures, capacities, self-representations, and representations of real and fantasied personal relationships."[11] While this is an objective of therapy and thereby performed by an `arcane and highly trained groups of professionals, empathy of this sort may be said to be beyond the task of teacher-student instruction. Yet empathic connections to students' conscious internal states and experiences are viable goals of teacher education that happen on a daily basis. Given the abstruse nature of empathy hitherto presented, the very issue of its utility and exactitude in education needs to be further explored.

Because empathy is billed as a special mode of perceiving the psychological states of other people, the question of its place in the classroom becomes important to address. Furthermore, because empathy is equated with derivative forms of intuition, emotive knowing, and perceptive sensing, its epistemological status becomes even more uncertain when attempting its pedagogical employment. For these reasons, empathy as a procedure usually appears in small doses among faculty instruction.

Controversy over the meaning of empathy has even divided psychology, rendering it a meaningless concept to some.[12] Given the disparate terrain of possible meanings and purposes of empathy, we are still ambivalent about, as Basch points out, whether empathy should be considered "an end result, a tool, a skill, a kind of communication, a listening stance, a type of introspection, a capacity, a power, a form of perception or observation, a disposition, an activity or a feeling."[13] Berger tells us that,

> the impossibility of specifying the accuracy of an empathic experience and the failure to acknowledge a hierarchy of experiences or to recognize that empathy becomes more complex and accurate as [human relations] continue often makes it difficult to compare and contrast empathic experiences.[14]

Therefore, it becomes unclear what empathy really is let alone what it involves.

Due to the equivocal concept of empathy, it becomes necessary to provide an operational definition within the context of instructional pedagogy. Following in the existential humanistic tradition, and recently advanced by Nel Noddings in the context of teaching,[15] empathy may be characterized as the concernful solicitude of others through the expression of care. Like Heidegger's conception of *Dasein* as the concretely existing human being whose essential structure is care,[16] empathy may be viewed as the disclosure of care. Although empathy may take an array of forms focusing on ideational content, affect, conscious and unconscious organizations, and the processes that characterize intersubjectivity within human interaction, care becomes its essential ontology—for the *desire to understand* the inner experience of the other would be absent without the intentional comportment of care.

2. Empathy Within the Classroom

From our previous account, we have seen that empathy involves identification with others concomitant with the perceptive powers of observation. But more importantly, empathy as care involves the willingness to engage the student and attempt to understand his or her inner experiences of the world. Adapting various techniques and qualities from applied clinical psychology, we may now offer a contextual meaning and suggested course of empathy that is suited for teaching and classroom instruction. Neither intended to be an exclusive nor exhaustive list governing the parameters of empathic awareness, the pedagogue may nevertheless want to focus on these five essential elements of empathy:

A. Attunement

Attunement is an essential feature of empathy. This means being attentive to the cognitive, emotional, and overall psychological state of the student. Within the classroom experience, the teacher may want to focus his or her attention on the content and rationale of the student's beliefs, perceptions, and attitudes while appreciating the possible underlying psychological motivations, intentions, and desires that influence the student's sense of individuality and social identity. This further implies that empathic observation may involve attending to unspoken, latent, or non-verbal content or communications which may be possibly influencing the student's organization of experience. Focusing on the immediate personal experience of the student becomes a central goal in understanding his or her inner reality.

B. Listening

Listening is a key component to attunement as well as an observational stance of gathering information about the student's experience. This involves an attentive awareness and observation of the student's unique perspective and organization of reality. This often entails attending to the ideational content and rationale of a student's attitudes, beliefs, argument, or descriptive narrative. Yet listening involves more than the mere attention to ideational content and can extend to deeper levels of psychic organization. In addition to focusing on content, the instructor may also observe how cognitive processes are accompanied by affective states that can sometimes saturate the immediacy of the lived experience, thus providing important information for understanding the nuances of subjectivity.

Listening for the various levels or dimensions of subjectivity may take the instructor past the immediate comprehension of the student's communication of subject matter to more deeper emotional states that may be unconsciously derived. Deeper listening also allows the instructor to track the process of the student's associations and the discussion itself, and thus take into account intersubjective, interpersonal, and transferential forces that impact on classroom dynamics. Understanding that empathic listening is rooted in an attunement to the multiple psychological processes that comprise a student's sense of self, the teacher may be better able to appreciate the complexity of student subjectivity as well as the intersubjectivity that influences class dynamics.

C. Identification

Identification usually involves an emotional tie with an individual or collective group based on shared value preferences;[17] however, identification may also be conceived as a basic expression of valuation.[18] We identify with qualities, characteristics, ideals, and values that may or may not be salient aspects of our students. Whether we agree with a student's perspective or are personally moved by his or her experience, this does not mean that personal agreement or shared sentiments are the only means of experiencing an identificatory bond with a student. Identification can be identification with a general value practice or personal ideal that one wishes to profess as a life principle.

Following our premise that empathy is a valued ideal and the expression of care, identification with this ideal is a prerequisite for empathy to become manifest. Therefore, on the most basal level, identification as empathy is simply the desire and willingness to see through the eyes of others and try to comprehend their world as they experience it. Within this context, identification is the desire to care.

Caring identification, or "identificatory caring" may involve a self-related identification with the student's experience whether this be partial, transient, or personally constructed, or this may merely entail the wish to convey empathic understanding. Identificatory caring may be augmented by the use of creative imagination that attempts to achieve a temporary alignment with the reality of the other no matter how different it is from your own. Empathic vision may also be achieved through the wonder and speculation of inhabiting another mind-set through vicarious introspection. Imagining the inner experience of the student, whether facilitated through personal self-related experiences or through creative, imaginary construction, leads to an appreciation of the power of empathy and shared identification by standing in the psychic space of another's inner world.

D. Responsiveness

Responsiveness is broadly conceived of here as a concerned attitude conveyed as the desire to understand *what* and *why* the student believes, thinks, and/or feels the way he or she does. The demonstration of interest, respect, and under-standing are important features of empathic responsiveness. While attention to the specific ideational or affective content of the student's experience and its accompanying rationale is a primary task of listening, the response one gives to the student's experience of disclosing his or her experience becomes another key ingredient in the empathic process. Responsiveness is usually verbally conveyed as an understanding and validation, affirmation, or confirmation of the other's experience, or it may be non-verbally conveyed by body language, posture, or facial expressions that communicate availability, attentiveness, and understanding. It is important to note that empathic affirmation and understanding does not necessarily mean that you do agree or that you have to agree with the student's position, but rather it denotes that you simply understand the student's position and why the student holds such a position. The communication of your understanding is itself a validating function of empathic responsiveness.

E. Giving Feedback

Up to now, we have been mainly concerned with empathy as a mode of understanding the inner experience of the student. While this involves elements of attuned responsiveness and identificatory caring through the listening process, the expression of care through student feedback can take myriad forms. At this point, I would like to suggest that empathy need not be confined to a non-conditional, non-confrontational approach to student feedback, rather confrontation may be viewed as an expression of empathy under the humanistic ideal of care.

It is a common assumption that teaching involves critically assessing the merits and limitations of students' knowledge claims and academic performance. Many teachers also feel this critique should remain focused on the cognitive and intellectual development of students while avoiding the realm of personal values, beliefs, attitudes, and emotions that may be more dubiously defined or subjectively constructed, thereby precluding objective pedagogical critique. Teacher-student feedback that is directed toward the cognitive domain of learning is not only normative, it is safe and non-intrusive. By staying on intellectual ground, the instructor maintains a standard for the critique of discussion and student performance, and thus avoids any potentially messy encounters regarding personal choice or valuation by students.

An attempt to formulate how the other perceives the world, however, may also involve challenging that person's perspective of reality. This inevitably draws teacher instruction away from the guise of intellectual critique to the domain of personal valuation. Is it enough to show empathic interest by conveying an understanding of the student's inner experience, or does empathy also require us to go beyond affirmative understanding and challenge the student's experience in the name of care? Is it not a worthy pursuit to help the overall development of students through challenging not only their way of thinking, but also their way of being? This pursuit is a two-way street and equally applies to the teacher: students can and do challenge the teacher's way of thinking and being, and both learn from this process. Challenge leads to justification and reevaluation, and reevaluation to growth. Empathy is not only the ability to share psychic space with students, it involves the intersubjective extension of care into that space, a process that leads students to reconfigure the meaning of their inner experiences.

Empathy does not always mean that you are going to agree with students' view points, beliefs, behaviors, or lifestyle choices; on the contrary, you may have to challenge these positions in the service of molding thoughtful and well articulated arguments and dispositions. This means that sometimes you may be forced to say the exact opposite of what students want to hear. You may be compelled to provoke their belief systems that they hold dear and sacrosanct. Empathy is not sugarcoating the truth, providing the most soothing or idealistic response, or offering a blind validation to a personal experience, it may require a firm challenge that provokes students sensibilities and threatens their individual belief systems in the service of constructing new ones that are better formulated.

Feedback that goes beyond mere cognitive critique and enters into the domain of valuation is a deeper expression of empathy. Perhaps Heidegger would view this as a "leaping ahead" of students' Being in an effort to make them aware of their "ownmost potentiality-for-Being."[19] This involves a personal investment in the pursuit of truth and authenticity, and the willingness and capacity to facilitate this process with students. Feedback of this sort can often lead to a confrontation of the other's reality. This is even more realized when confrontation is executed as a provocation. Nurtured through dialogue and mutual interaction, empathic feedback through confrontation and provocation can lead students to a greater integrative and holistic understanding of themselves.

Within the context of instruction, provocation is a mode of empathy as the expression of care. While I will address the ground, scope, and limits of provocation shortly, empathic provocation is designed to foster the overall development of students and their personhoods. In the spirit of *paideia* that advocates the holistic cultivation of the human being, provocation challenges students to grow and become virtuous and highly refined individuals. In the context of the classroom, it is important to note that the reason why you provoke students and relate to them in this manner is because you care about them as developing human beings. Education, as with life, is a process of becoming; by providing students with tough challenges and obstacles to their learning about themselves and the world, you are championing the student on behalf of their own personal development.

Empathy is neither a state nor an attitude, but a process. When utilized within the classroom, empathy can serve as a powerful method for understanding the meaningful aspects of the student's inner life and the over-determined processes that govern student learning. David Berger offers a comprehensive survey on the course of empathy and shows that the use of creative imagination, imagery, metaphor, descriptive narratives, affective responsiveness, and dialogue foster and promote empathic attunement.[20] While strategies for empathy are mainly discussed within mental health disciplines, these approaches may be re-appropriated as pedagogical aids and actualized within classroom instruction. They are particularly well suited for under-graduate education where active learning is a must. Yet despite these empathic strategies that may be applied to general teaching technique, the use of provocation as a modal form of empathy has been largely overlooked. In the following sections I will attempt to show the intimate relation between the empathic endeavor and the use of provocation as an instructional methodology. It is my contention that if used appropriately, provocative technique is ultimately in the service of expressing care about students' personhoods and instilling human virtue.

3. A Provocative Pedagogy[21]

Provocation is usually defined as an activity that brings about anger, resentment, and/or aggressive confrontation. Empathic provocation, on the other hand, is defined here as challenging students to examine and justify their personal values motivated by a caring inquiry.

The quest for an effective pedagogy often (but not always) differentiates the teacher from the researcher. Within the humanities and social sciences, the instructor is constantly confronted with the challenge of communicating exceedingly complex material in a novel and effective manner. This difficulty is particularly salient in teaching introductory philosophy courses where instructors endeavor to foster abstract thinking within an active classroom environment. It has been well established that active learning is bolstered by a quality of classroom instruction that emphasizes creative problem-solving, Socratic teaching methods, and critical thinking.[22] And it is no surprise that active learning often starts with a question.[23] Perhaps the thoughtful use of questions is indeed the quintessential activity of an effective teacher, for the use of questions is as old as teaching itself.

Despite the efficacy of these techniques, philosophical inquiry can sometimes lead to esoteric, pedantic, or even banal approaches to teaching that leave the neophyte intellectually lost or personally detached from the learning process. What often seems to be missing is the student's personal investment in the subject matter. Due to the sophistication and subtlety of philosophical minutiae, students may sometimes detach themselves from philosophical inquisitiveness unless they are provoked. I have found that the use of provocative questions and statements promote active learning among students.

As a discipline, philosophy itself is intrinsically provocative. Many students taking introductory courses often enter the classroom with naive, myopic, and narrowly defined views of human nature, science, and reality. I have found that provocative techniques directed toward the class force students to examine the grounds of their assumptions, which leads them to the formulation of solid, rational arguments and conclusions with logical foundations.

It is my intention to demonstrate that the role of provocation serves a purpose for general education. In the spirit of Nietzsche's infamously provocative style, the use of provocative techniques in teaching introductory college courses can be immensely beneficial. While I will attempt to provide a framework for a provocative pedagogy that is primarily directed toward teaching introductory philosophy, ethics, and values perspectives, the provocative techniques outlined here may be applied to any field, discipline, or subject matter.

4. The Purpose of Provocation

The goals of provocative teaching are grounded in a conceptual framework of empathic attunement, critical thinking, and an understanding and appreciation of the myriad psychological processes that influence mental life and classroom dynamics. The purpose of all provocation should ultimately be in the service of care. Within this context, I believe the instructor's teaching strategy may be designed to provoke or pique students to think; that is, to analyze the grounds of their beliefs, which can be directly applied to their personal lives. Knowledge without personal meaning is passionless, while personal belief without knowledge is blind.

I maintain a fundamental teaching standard—that the passive intellect is unacceptable. In order to promote insight and help students develop greater skills at critical thinking and their application, they must be provoked to think. Although neither a necessary nor a sufficient condition for effective teaching, techniques designed to rouse, excite, incite, and awaken students from their "dogmatic slumbers,"often lead to a dynamic classroom environment marked by intellectual vitality and emotional vigor. Stirring questions and statements should challenge (and respectfully critique) the method and rationale by which students arrive at conclusions. Instructors who challenge what has been passively accepted as truth help students reexamine the grounds that serve as the foundation for their beliefs and attitudes. Students come to realize that conditioning or learning alone does not merit sufficient justification for a belief. I have found that this form of intellectual interrogation leads to productive dialogue, critical discussion, and the formulation of better logical arguments, attitudes, and beliefs, which have personal meaning that students can directly apply to their lives.

5. A Note on Method

Provocative teaching must be used carefully. Ways of maintaining a sensitive balance will be discussed later; but first let us examine a few orienting points on method. While introducing philosophical issues on the basic level, provocative questions specifically addressed to the class as a whole are a fruitful way to gain interest, pique curiosity, and facilitate student involvement. As an exercise in active learning, topics that are (1) generally intriguing, (2) presented with emotional intensity, and (3) encourage class participation are often enthusiastically entertained by students. On a generic level, metaphysical and epistemological questions such as: "Does this table even exist?"; or "What is truth?", can be presented with dramatic impact that stimulates class involvement. The delivery and receptivity of such techniques, however, will depend upon how well formulated they are, as well as the stage presence and personality of the instructor. No one method naturally fits all teaching approaches, and the teacher's own style will determine how the provocation is delivered.

As a rule of thumb, questions or statements that are too profound, abstract, or vague often confuse and intimidate students, which may lead to student-instructor alienation and classroom anxiety. For example, questions like, "Why is there something rather than nothing?", or "What is the meaning of meaning?" may serve to kill a discussion rather that provoke it. Within this context, provocative methods should be brief, concrete, and contain only one or two issues at a time for class reflection. Professors may want to avoid the use of esoteric vocabulary or jargon (depending upon the background of the students) to avoid confusion and/or potential alienation. In addition, instructors who are animated and intense in their delivery may be more effective than those who give a droning lecture. From this perspective, provocative techniques are designed to "grab" students psychologically and intellectually, cultivating their curiosity and motivating cognitive and personal growth. As a motivational technique, such an emotive grip on the class leads to intellectual exploration that may transcend traditional lecturing.

I would like to recommend a few guiding principles in formulating provocative teaching techniques:

(1)   Whenever possible, orient the technique toward the entire class, not just one student.

(2)   Allow an appropriate pause time for class response. (By placing responsibility on the active learning environment, silence encourages the class to think about the task at hand and conveys expectations for

their participation).

(3)   Respond to all students' responses. Allow the class to initiate dialogue or discussion among themselves.

(4)   Validate and confirm student attempts to respond or offer an explanation (even if such attempts are incorrect or idiosyncratic).

(5)   Use the discussion to launch into a formal presentation or exploration of the material or to augment existing didactic strategies.

6. Classroom Examples

Generally, provocative techniques combined with systematic questioning may be applied arbitrarily to any topic. For instance, let us say that a student states a personal belief that many other students in the class also espouse. Upon inquiry into the grounds for the assumption of the belief, the student claims that is what he was taught by his parents during childhood. Through provocative systematic questioning, the student realizes this type of reasoning is an informal fallacy based on an appeal to authority that became conditioned and serves as the grounds for his belief. By having the student reexamine and question the logical grounds for the belief based on his previous experiences, the truth value of the premises, the validity of the source, and the integrity of the conclusion, this process promotes critical thinking in an active classroom and stimulates discussion and cogent arguments among other students.

While it is generally better to focus questions toward the entire class, in a case like this, by focusing on one student, others join in to offer competing arguments or supportive rationale that are further examined by the class as a whole. This generally leads to an inclusive process rather than an exclusive centering on one student. In addition, while one student is giving specific reasons for a position or conveying his or her experiences, others have the opportunity to relate their own thoughts or experiences to those of the student, which makes for a vibrant class discussion. This approach not only influences greater intellectual awareness and cognitive skill development, but makes the learning process itself a personal pursuit of meaning.

Specific, concrete, or narrowly focused techniques sometimes spark greater classroom enthusiasm. I have found that topics involving ethical practices, racial and ethnic diversity, and religious convictions are typically the most vulnerable to provocative techniques. For example, issues concerning the question of God always provoke debate. During one class period while lecturing on Modern Philosophy, students spontaneously volunteered to represent their argumentation concerning the existence of God in an informal debate. Six students assembled as a panel providing reasons for theism, agnosticism, and atheism, each position represented by two students. That led to an intense classroom discussion which I mediated and supervised, allowing the students to ask and answer questions without allowing any one particular position or individual to monopolize class time. At the end of class, students voted on what they thought to be the strongest arguments grounded in critical thinking rather than ones based on mere conditioned beliefs or personal wishes. This exercise was an excellent entrée to a formal lecture that was to follow.

To illustrate the point that all individuals experience anxiety that becomes manifested in behavior and personality organization throughout the lifespan, I will open the topic with the following technique: "What would you say if I told you that everyone in this room is neurotic?; that is, we are all *ill*"[24] This provocation often prompts curiosity, apprehension, and sometimes defiance, which leads to a discussion and active exploration of the construct under question. I find this technique most useful when introducing theories of the self and human nature.

While teaching an ethics course on parenting, I asked the class whether corporal punishment was immoral. Most students believed it was morally acceptable and some even made a case that it was immoral not to physically discipline children when they commit transgressions, because physical punishment teaches them morals. This situation quickly turned into an opportunity for a provocative exercise. I asked those who supported corporal punishment to come to the front of the class and face their fellow students. I then asked them to imagine themselves as children who were just beaten for disobeying their parents. I further told them to imagine their peers sitting in front of them as their parents and to think about how they are *now* feeling after being punished. After about thirty-seconds of reflection, one by one I asked each student (child) to tell the class (parents) out loud how they felt about being hit. Many students reported feeling sorrow, guilt, shame, fear, anger, and even hate. Some reported feeling abused and humiliated and stated that their parents were cruel, unloving, violating, and immoral.

This was a powerful exercise in identification and empathy, and many students came to realize the dubious ethical nature of corporal punishment. This event further led to an extended group role-playing exercise where students formed hypothetical families of four members, each comprised of two parents and two children. Each student was assigned a specific name, gender, and role along with unique background characteristics. Over the weeks, the families were given specific tasks and problems to solve that simulated "real," everyday life events that families typically encounter. Each group's solutions were analyzed and compared to the other families' solutions, which culminated in a thoughtful exploration of the moral topography of parenting.

As another example, while introducing ethics and value theory, discussing cultural diversity, or individual differences and tolerance, I will proclaim: "Every human being by nature is prejudiced."[25] After approximately four seconds of silence, the class typically responds quite intensely. This usually incites anxiety, compliant agreement (perhaps due to intimidation or fear of personal exposure), or defensiveness marked by denial. I am often challenged and provoked to defend my claims (which I try to promote in students in all contexts), which leads to a fruitful class discussion culminating in mutual understanding. Individuals come to realize that subjective bias, personal preferences, pre-conceived judgments, and reinforced stereotypes are ubiquitous to human experience. The crucial point, however, is to get them to acknowledge this universal aspect of human nature before students can individually examine their own prejudices less defensively, with the goal of acquiring (over time) new concepts and attitudes that are more critically informed and less prejudicially solidified.

It is crucial to note here that when making such general claims, the teacher should have a carefully prepared context for provocation. Making such broad assertions without a prudent and conscientious context may suggest to students that the teacher is prone to make vacuous or ill-founded pronouncements—and it is from such an undisciplined and crass approach to thinking that teachers ought to wean their students.[26]

7. The Risk of Provocation

As an inherently provocative enterprise, philosophy deals with claims that the average person views as bizarre or outlandishly false. The fact is, philosophy ponders subjects that the average person may never even consider. Within this context, it becomes the teacher's job to make philosophy attractive and accessible to students so it may be directly relevant to their lives. One is constantly confronted with the limitations of conveying exceedingly difficult subject matter and methodology indigenous to philosophical discourse in the midst of assessing and negotiating the intellectual aptitude of the students. In addition, the conscientious teacher should be equally vigilant of his or her own personal vulnerabilities that may interfere with successful classroom engagement.

Philosophy is a risk, and so is teaching. Don't be afraid to make the classroom a risk-taking environment. As Dewey reminds us, experimentation leads to success, then to knowledge and wisdom. Allow for spontaneity that breaks the rigid mold of traditional course structure, which may serve to stifle creativity and personal insight. Provocation as risk-taking tears through platitudes and trite social locutions, which further serves to foster individuality and promote authenticity in the student's search for truth.

The use of provocation lends itself to the development of imagination and creativity in the active learning environment. Teaching is an interpersonal dynamic process that is interactive and fueled by the intersubjectivity of the classroom milieu. The professor's expressed enthusiasm for the course material can lead to a group contagion marked by intellectual vigor and camaraderie that mutually nurtures and transforms itself. If students see that teachers themselves are provoked by philosophy, then philosophy may also become the object of class identification, thereby internalized, emulated, and pursued in one's own life. Is this not a major goal of teaching? Do we not seek to make a personal difference in our students' lives? Furthermore, students identify with an enthusiastic stance, which further inspires the pursuit and fulfillment of personal and educational possibilities that extend far beyond the classroom. This teaching style communicates to students that you care about their personal development—not that they are seen as an inanimate blob of matter sitting in a chair or a social-security-number in a sea of blank faces.

8. A Provocative Exercise: Defending Your Stand

As a novel, classroom-tested exercise, "Defending Your Stand" is a perfect example of pedagogic provocation. The following instructions are intended to provide formal structure to this exercise but can be modified to suit any specific course content or adapted to fit preexisting didactic approaches.

Instructions:

(1)   Have the class divide into two groups by asking them to count off out loud by numbers. (If the class is too large, additional groups may be formed).

(2)   Draw a line down the middle of a clean chalkboard. Write "Like, Agree, Positive" on the far right, and "Dislike, Disagree, Negative" on the far left of the chalkboard (see Figure 1).

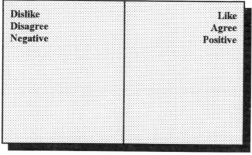

Figure 1

(3)   Then have the first group come to the front of the class and stand in front of the chalkboard.

(4)   Read the following statement:

I am going to say a number of words and phrases on various topics and I want you to go with your *gut* reaction and stand on one side of the line or the other. The closer you are to the line, the more ambivalent you feel about the topic, while the farther away, the more strongly you feel. You may go to either side and you may change your mind and move at anytime. The only thing you cannot do is stand in the middle. You must take a stand.

(5)   Now explain to the class that anyone can ask another student at anytime to defend his or her position by providing reasons or justification for their beliefs or attitudes. It is important to inform the class that the intention of the exercise is to critically examine the argumentation and logical justification for their positions and that this is not intended to attack, berate, or chasten any student. Reinforce the expectation that the ability to rationally defend a given belief system or set of attitudes promotes skills in critical thinking and oral communication, as well as personal insight into value practices that may need to be further examined. Inform the class that after a while (the instructor should determine the time frame), the other half of the class will come up to the chalkboard, and then the first group will have the same opportunity to ask the new participants to defend their stands.

The following is a list of words and phrases that may be read out loud. This list is not at all inclusive nor arranged in any hierarchical manner. You may be personally selective in the topics you wish to use. It may be supplemented, revised, or substituted for content that may be more appropriate for the specific course under question:

DEFENDING YOUR STAND WORD LIST

abortion
divorce
euthanasia (mercy killing)
homosexuality
affirmative action
prostitution
gays in the military
smoking in the work environment
mandatory uniforms in public
  schools
interracial relationships
bisexuality
giving clean needles to addicts
giving condoms to convicts
masturbation
black power
women only spaces
artificial insemination
genetic experimentation
human cloning
gay priests
capital punishment
lesbian mothers
organ donor restrictions
fetal tissue research
gay marriages
physician assisted suicide
polygamy
mandatory AIDS testing
open (sexual) relationships
pornography
nepotism
cultural right to define its ethical
  practices
castration sentence for rapists
right to privacy for convicted

felons
openly gay teachers
mandatory sterilization of the
  mentally handicapped
the right to preach hate
mandatory drug screening by
  employers
mandatory bilingual education in
  public schools
welfare programs
interracial adoption
filing bankruptcy
immigrants financially supported
  by the government
government financial support for
  political refugees
public nude beaches
scientific animal testing
sex without love
prohibition of handguns
socialized health care
illegal aliens having children then
  seeking welfare
romantic relations between
  employers and employees
prayer in public schools
school choice
legalization of marijuana
legalization of all drugs
parental choice over school
  curriculum
corporal punishment
corporal punishment in school
teaching creationism in school
atheism
multiculturalism

racial/ethnic separatism
capitalism
tax shelters
pornography on the internet
environmental exploitation in the
  name of progress
dating among teachers and
  students
profanity
censorship of any kind

The instructor should allow the students themselves to ask each other for their justifications. Explain that it is also permissible for students in front of the chalkboard to ask their fellow group members to defend their stands. As a general rule, I have found that the less interference usually works best. One may have to initiate the questioning at first, however, students gradually begin to direct the questions autonomously, particularly as the topics become more controversial.

As the instructor, one should act as a facilitator, mediator, and arbitrator if necessary. (1) As a facilitator, allow discussion to flourish and divergent positions to be expressed. Call on people if necessary, and give the individuals who are defending their stands ample opportunity to justify their positions. Finally, be mindful of time constraints and progress to the next issue if the arguments become too repetitive or if enthusiasm dissipates. (2) As a mediator, clarify and validate peoples' positions and allow for arguments to be developed. (3) Arbitration may be necessary if people become too impassioned, overly sensitive, crude or coarse, emotionally threatened, or palpably irrational. This has happened very rarely, but as a standard course of action I acknowledge the tension, sensitivities, or irreconcilable discrepancies in judgment, while attempting to maintain neutrality and empathic understanding for their feelings. Then I move on to the next topic. This strategy shows respect for the dignity of the student while maintaining classroom cohesion and structure.

One may suspect that the *either-or* structure of this exercise does not allow for diversity or a careful analysis of the constructs under question. While one cannot cover these topics with thorough precision during a class period, it is important to convey the message that these moral, socio-political issues are not to be taken superficially or treated in a shallow manner. Depending upon the instructor's level of philosophical exploration of these issues as well as the classroom dynamics in general, one may only address two or three topics per class period. This exercise may spark a protracted drawn out critique of each topic or it may go fairly quickly. This may be largely facilitated by the instructor's probing and systematic questioning aided by a spontaneous and autonomous class. The amount of time one spends on a particular topic should be up to the discretion of the instructor influenced by the general interest of the students. Whatever the case may be, this exercise provides a nice introduction to topics that can be thoroughly examined in depth throughout the length of the course.

Professors may use this exercise several times throughout the duration of the class if so desired. For example, it is a good "warm up" for introducing ethics where one can get a base level impression of students' beliefs, attitudes, and critical thinking skills. When used repeatedly, the instructor may track the level of discussion and notice the overall improvement in the logical structure and formulation of students' argumentation skills. I have found that this activity is a most effective teaching tool when it is adopted as an ongoing exercise. Students report looking forward to this ongoing activity which breaks up routine lecturing and provides a distraction from the prosaic themes of philosophy that the novice often finds tedious or mundane.

Instructors may adapt this exercise in a variety of different ways to suit particular classroom needs or assuage their own concerns over the well being of their students. Some instructors may want to provide more options for safety and control, thus allowing students to have a wider "comfort zone" in their involvement in this exercise. For example, one could make it clear from the start that participation is completely voluntary and one can withdrawal at any time without penalty. In addition, the instructor may want to allow students the option not to respond to a question if they do not want to answer by merely saying "pass." For those who are concerned that the dichotomous structure of the exercise is too rigid or confining, teachers may construct the exercise following a Likert-scale format, ranging from: (1) "Like/Agree;" (2) "Unsure;" to (3) "Dislike/Disagree," thus allowing the students more options for neutrality.

Furthermore, one may want to assign students roles in taking particular positions and then ask them to defend their stands from these assigned perspectives. This can be done on a volunteer basis or it can be given as an assignment to prepare for and enact at a later date. For example, one student may be asked to defend school prayer or gay marriages while others provide antithetical arguments. This adaptation also allows for a certain degree of individual distance from one's own personal views, thus providing safety and anonymity. Moreover, role-playing opens the floor for several positions that may be under-represented, socially undesirable, not politically correct, or less likely to be discussed if there were not the veil of impersonation.

Finally, if teachers are very sensitive that the psychological safety of the students may be jeopardized due to the controversial or potentially painful material that may be associated with one's own personal experiences or suffering, the teacher may want to be very selective in the topics discussed, omitting the most blatantly controversial subject matter. If this cannot be reasonably satisfied, then the instructor may use this exercise as a prototype for creating writing assignments that will allow a certain margin of distance from the potential interpersonal anxiety generated from being confronted by the class. This option also permits students time enough to develop their ideas and argumentation about the material that the "on the spot" method clearly does not afford.

Given the sensitivity of some of the topics, some students will not be honest in their responses. Due to the awkwardness, social vulnerability, and the proclivity to be "politically correct" due to fears of being judged or non-accepted by others, misrepresentation is to be expected. After the exercise, I generally acknowledge this observation as well as thank the class for their courage and willingness to participate and defend their positions. I also reiterate the purpose of the exercise and further attempt to summarize the various positions and reasons offered in support of their attitudes and arguments which I explain will be examined more thoroughly as the course progresses. As a general rule, thoroughly critiquing these issues at a later date gives students greater personal safety and distance to reflect on their own views while allowing them time to acquire critical thinking skills that they did not possess before the class. This also maintains the neutrality of the exercise and the instructor's role as a facilitator rather than someone who is likely to take a personal position or a philosophical stance that directly opposes other students.

At times students will want *you* to take and defend *your* stand. When this happens, instructors should remind themselves of the purpose of the exercise. While it is a natural desire to present your own personal viewpoint or provide the most cogent philosophical argument (in your opinion) for or against a particular stance, I feel that neutrality allows students to feel safe about you and open with their views rather than guarded, dishonest, or ingratiating. While one may impart his or her personal views at a later time, neutrality during the exercise opens and encourages the discussion and presentation of divergent view points rather than fostering a truncated and inauthentic atmosphere where resistance is high and honesty stymied.

A criticism to neutrality deserves our attention. How can teachers model provocation and place themselves outside of the process? Neutrality, if possible, doesn't allow students to connect with you as a human being, only as an encyclopedia. But within this context, the instructor has a responsibility to define his or her role in the process. If clearly defined, a frame is established with an eye on safety and optimal learning. We must remember that provocation is designed as an empathic tool and if students feel that the instructor's real interest is garnering personal pleasure by poking holes in their positions or values then they will not only see you as an "asshole" but they will not feel that you truly care about them during this moment of vulnerability, which may negatively color their impression of you and their overall learning experience in general.

There may be times, however, where the neutrality rule must be amended or even abandoned. In some situations, you may be forced to take a stand. For example, I had a student who was a vociferous racist and exclaimed to the class that be was openly prejudiced toward Blacks. This incited anxiety, disgust, and even rage by some class members. When asked to defend his position, he relied on over-generalizations of his personal experiences largely conditioned by his upbringing in the South and could offer no rational explanation other than this was how he felt and how he was taught to think. With my mediation, the class pointed out the gaps in his reasoning, which allowed him to openly admit that his beliefs were irrational, yet nevertheless a true conviction. In this instance, I was forced to take a stand and point out the illogic of his hate while still attempting to demonstrate to the student that I understood why he felt this way. While I did not validate the legitimacy of his beliefs, I did validate his *need* to believe a certain way, yet one that nevertheless needed to be reexamined and changed. Interesting enough, I met with this student after class to discuss his views and to see how he felt about the class confrontation. As a result, the student ended up writing a paper examining his racism. While attitudes like these are unyieldingly resistant to haphazard abandonment, the student was at least motivated enough to examine his thoughts and feelings on such a sensitive subject rather than merely chalk it up to apathy or displace his own anger onto me and the class.

Over the years, I have found this exercise to be a unique and productive device in provoking thoughtful inquiry and self-exploration about philosophical issues, personal values, and worldviews. Students often comment about how much they enjoy this exercise and how it facilitates extracurricular discussion and debate that is important for their personal growth. Provocative exercises may provide a personal utility for self-discovery that departs from the traditional procedures of pedantic pedagogy.

9. Caveats

Let me reemphasize that provocative teaching must be used carefully. Teachers need to be aware of their own personal biases, preferences, and agendas that may be foisted upon students and seen as an attack. It is one thing to expose students to particular philosophical positions that challenge their attitudes and lifestyles, yet it is another for their teacher, their guide, to encroach upon their psycho-

logical security and emotional safety. We have our own philosophic identifications that will inevitably be introduced in class. The trick is, however, to
present one's own views while bracketing one's biases and prejudices that other
philosophic disciplines are likely to point out.

To what degree is one's own philosophy truly distinguished from oneself?
The undeniable fact is that, as instructors, we cannot avoid projecting our own
identifications onto others, and such projections should be responsibly balanced.
Indeed, this can truly be difficult. Furthermore, it is very difficult to provide
concrete procedures on how far to go in provoking students. Because we are all
subjective human beings with our own sense of individuality, there is no golden
mean or step-by-step method to follow. This must be left to personal judgment
and discretion.

When we examine controversial issues in class, we should be sensitive and
respectful of individual and cultural differences that may influence certain
beliefs and practices, while still maintaining intellectual integrity. It should be
a tacit assumption for students that acts of provocation are designed to bring
rational and emotional constructs under the rubric of knowledge. No provocation should be executed merely for "shock value." Because some students
may feel intimidated by philosophical questions, the professor should try to be
sensitive to the students' cognitive acumen as well as their emotional
development. Sometimes, students who are overly emotional, cognitively rigid,
or psychologically vulnerable to a particular topic simply need to be reminded
that the discussion at hand is only an object of intellectual investigation and
certainly not a personal attack on their attitudes or lifestyles. Students need to
know that philosophical inquiry is about the critique of ideas and not personality.

It is vital not to create (either directly or indirectly) a hostile environment for
learning. No student should be forced to respond or participate. This could be
easily viewed as malicious, shameful, or exploitive. Consider personal security
and "ways out" of potentially detrimental situations. Be sensitive toward
individuals who you think may have suffered trauma. If this is suspected or
disclosed in the course of an exercise, do not pressure anyone; simply respect the
other's "safety zones," validate their experience, and move onto the next position
or topic—keeping in mind that a personal inquiry about their feelings may be
necessary to pursue after class. Insensitivity or perfunctory responses to personal
disclosures can be experienced as abusive and thus re-create a repetition of an
earlier traumatic event. One should never subject a student to such potentially
precarious psychological conditions even if it is under the guise of reason. As
a guideline, strive for neutrality through empathy; and if need be, step back from
the personal realm to the philosophical. While it is true that some students will
feel uncomfortable, that should not be a reason for avoiding provocative
techniques. By approaching sensitive issues that are directly anchored to

personal identity or ways of life, you communicate to students that you care about their well being, and that is why you challenge them.

You learn the most about yourself through *discomfort*. By leaning into discomfort, students discover the reward of achieving personal insight. It is important to note that both the material itself and its presentation can cause discomfort within the classroom. If done tactfully, however, with a caring and empathic attitude, provocation can lead to knowledge and personal growth, which is another movement on the ladder toward wisdom. While most of the time the goal of instruction is inclusion (so that the class and the teacher feel on the same side in their exploration of the subject matter), it may still be necessary to introduce an opposing stance in order to pique a more thorough examination of the material that could be easily "dropped." In fact, it is the responsibility of the teacher to provide students with all perspectives to an issue (when possible) as well as an exegesis, and some of these perspectives will unavoidably be distressing.

It is easy to mistake the meaning and use of provocation as tantamount to an aggressive attack on students' beliefs. Even though it is true that provocation is confrontational, it does not mean that it is aggressive. The boundary may at times be cumbersome to maintain, for provocation is inherently risky. When we confront the class or a particular student, our intention should be to illuminate and cultivate insight, not to tear down, disparage, or dismiss students' views, for this can be easily interpreted by students as a dismissal of them. Within the proper context, confrontation is merely approaching the problem or issue head-on, providing feedback, and pointing out the lacunae in argumentation and rationale, while at the same time confirming students' "attempts" by validating their need to think a certain way; thereby affirming their sense of self. This leads to a positive role model identification marked by respect and a concernful solicitude for them as persons.

Nothing is worse than invalidating and debasing a student. We as teachers are in a privileged position of power and authority, which should be positively channeled rather than used, even unconsciously, as a baneful weapon. Provoking students to become and fulfill their possibilities, I argue, is the core responsibility of an effective teacher—not to see students as objects to be used and disposed of because they do not fit one's desired profile, or merely seen as a mass conglomeration with no real interest in their selfhoods.

One may question the amount of discomfort one can legitimately cause students in the name of good pedagogy. One may further ponder the ethical implications of causing students discomfort in the name of self-knowledge. Nothing in life is devoid of conflict or uneasiness, particularly personal development. Learning is a struggle and knowledge is much more than the assimilation of facts. Discomfort itself is knowledge. Any teacher of philosophy who strays away from making people feel uncomfortable is intellectually disingenuous, for philosophy itself is about valuation; and values often conflict with one another. The exceptional pedagogue not only helps students understand the world, but helps them understand themselves, including the values they espouse. Professors who feel that the goal of teaching is merely to impart information and not foster valuation are divorced from their responsibility to contribute to the overall personal growth of their students. By showing students that there is more to philosophy than mere scholarly erudition, provocation allows philosophy to infiltrate the personal realm of being. A good teacher is someone who disseminates information effectively. But a great teacher is someone who *moves* you as a human being. What could be more ethical than this?

10. Conclusion

Empathic-provocative techniques may be constructed and adapted to compliment the introduction of a variety of distinct topics in general education courses regardless of one's discipline or pedagogical persuasion. No method will reach everyone. We must find a method that suits our personalities and didactic styles. Instead of traditional lecturing, the combined use of provocation and empathy that forces the class to respond to a particular issue may have more impact and personal meaning than formal approaches. This is especially salient with younger undergraduates who are generally intellectually curious, demonstrate some interest in the course but may have enrolled merely to satisfy general requirements, or who are entrenched in the psychological priorities of individual and social development. Furthermore, the use of probing and systematic questioning gears students toward an introspective analysis of their personal beliefs, not only grounded in reason, but also linked to emotional and intrapsychic motives that influence their causal attributions.

I have found that these techniques motivate students to explore, question, and actively seek out truth—not just to accept information passively as unquestioned dogma. In addition, one will notice progress in their critical thinking skills over the length of the course. Rather than professing an impetuous position based upon unreflective conditioning, students offer more solid argumentation with developed rationale for their beliefs and attitudes. I believe this process of teaching itself can be more important than the knowledge disseminated through traditional pedagogy.

More important, students often find personal meaning and values behind their beliefs that they directly apply to their lives. This may even be more intrinsically rewarding than the assimilation of the subject matter itself. Often, what students remember most about you is not your words, but the way you relate to them. The goal of teaching is not merely to bestow information or nurture skills in critical thinking, but to set an example of what it means to be, for teaching is a way of being.

Notes

1. Carl Rogers, *A Way of Being* (Boston: Houghton Mifflin Company, 1980), p. 137.

2. Sigmund Freud, *Group Psychology and the Analysis of the Ego* (Standard Edition of the Complete Psychological Works of Sigmund Freud, Vol.18, London: Hogarth Press, 1921), p. 108.

3. *Cf.* Rogers, *A Way of Being*, p. 140.

4. *Ibid.*, p. 142.

5. Helene Deutsch, "Occult Processes Occurring during Psychoanalysis." In *Psychoanalysis and the Occult*, ed. G. Devereaux (New York: International Universities Press, 1926/1970), p. 136.

6. Freud, *Group Psychology*, p. 110.

7. *Cf.* David M. Berger, *Clinical Empathy* (Northvale, N.J.: Jason Aronson, Inc., 1987), p. 22.

8. *Cf.* R. Fliess, "The Metapsychology of the Analyst," *Psychoanalytic Quarterly*, 11, (1942), pp. 211-227; M. Furer, "Some Developmental Aspects of the Superego," *International Journal of Psycho-Analysis*, 48 (1967), pp. 277-280.

9. Heinz Kohut, *The Analysis of the Self* (Madison, Conn.: International Universities Press, 1971), p. 300.

10. Kohut, "Forms and Transformations of Narcissism." Originally published in the *Journal of the American Psychoanalytic Association*, 14 (1966), pp. 243-272; reprinted in *Self Psychology and the Humanities*, ed. C.S. Strozier (New York: W.W. Norton, 1985), p. 115.

11. Roy Schafer, "Generative Empathy in the Treatment Situation," *Psychoanalytic Quarterly*, 28 (1959), pp. 342-373, p. 345.

12. See Theodor Reik, *Listening with the Third Ear* (New York: Grove Press, 1948), p. 357.

13. Michael F. Basch, "Empathic Understanding: A Review of the Concept and Some Theoretical Considerations," *Journal of the American Psychoanalytic Association*, 31 (1983), p. 102.

14. Berger, *Clinical Empathy*, p. 22.

15. See Nel Noddings, *The Challenge to Care in Schools: An Alternative Approach to Education* (New York: Teachers College Press, 1992).

16. Martin Heidegger, *Being and Time*, trans. by J. Macquarrie and E. Robinson (San Francisco: Harper Collins, 1927).

17. See Freud, *Group Psychology*, p. 105; *New Introductory Lectures on Psycho-Analysis* (1933), Standard Edition, Vol. 22, p. 63

18. Jon Mills and Janusz Polanowksi, *The Ontology of Prejudice* (Rodopi: Amsterdam-Atlanta, 1997).

19. Heidegger, *Being and Time*, p. 344.

20. Berger, *Clinical Empathy*.

21. *Cf.* Jon Mills, "Better Teaching through Provocation," *College Teaching*, 46:1 (1998), pp. 21-25.

22. See M. E. Gorman, A. Law, and T. Lindegren, "Making Students Take a Stand: Active Learning in Introductory Psychology," *Teaching of Psychology*, 8:3 (1981), pp. 164-166; R.E. Mayer, "Cognitive Views of Creativity: Creative Teaching for Creative Learning," *Contemporary Educational Psychology*, 14:13 (1989), pp. 203-211; and J.C. Overholser, "Socrates in the Classroom," *Social Studies*, 83:2 (1992), pp. 77-82.

23. *Cf.* R. J. Bonnstetter, "Active Learning Often Starts with a Question," *Journal of College Science Teaching*, 18:2 (1988), pp. 95-97.

24. See Freud, *Introductory Lectures on Psychoanalysis* (1916-1917), Standard Edition, Vols. 15 and 16, p. 358.

25. *Cf.* Mills and Polanowski, *The Ontology of Prejudice*, p. 1.

26. From personal correspondence with Eugene Kelly, Social Sciences Department, New York Institute of Technology.

Six

THE "GOOD-ENOUGH" TEACHER AND THE AUTHENTIC STUDENT

Guy Allen

I teach writing at the University of Toronto. That I became a teacher of writing surprised me. The discoveries I made in my writing classes surprised me more. I felt frustrated when students didn't learn. I experimented with different ways of teaching writing and, partly through good luck, discovered procedures that produced a high level of learning. These experiments pointed to the decisive role played by nonrational determinants in the way people learn.

The university sees itself as a place of logic and reason. So my perceptions, new to me, about the role of nonrational factors contradicted the reason-based Enlightenment outlook that even in the post-modern era commands most assumptions about learning in universities. People who examine learning and development carefully—some educational theorists, philosophers, and psycho-analytic thinkers—will see nothing new in my findings, but people who understand the nonrational features that condition human learning do little of the educating or policy making in our universities. The Enlightenment paradigm —that people learn through the application of logic and reason—prevails.

This paradigm dominates in the teaching of writing as much or more than it does in other fields, and yet for people learning how to write, as opposed to people learning physics or philosophy, this paradigm appears to be particularly inappropriate, as the experience I report in this essay shows. In the teaching of writing, this paradigm surfaces as the preoccupation with formal properties such as rules of usage or spelling and the conventions of formal academic style. I, like others who have preceded me (for example, see Britton, 1970; Wyatt-Brown, 1993), have found that these preoccupations retard learning and neglect the conditions that actually do produce development. In universities the fixation with the formal properties of writing, despite challenges, guides most teaching practice and thinking about writing skills.

I looked for theory to explain the results of my experiments whose outcomes seemed to mock the rationalist paradigm. When I consulted the writing of psychoanalytic thinkers, and especially the British psychoanalyst Donald Winnicott, I found a description of the psychic processes of human development that matched what I had been seeing for myself. Winnicott describes early human development in nonrational terms. The ability to function rationally, Winnicott tells us, stems from nonrational development. As Jane Flax (1990) puts it, Winnicott sees the "capacity to reason" not as the "engine of development" (p. 117). Instead, Winnicott sees the capacity to reason as an outcome of development. In other words, nonrational factors determine whether or not the subject—for our purposes, the learner—achieves, or does not achieve, potential.

In this chapter, I detail my observation of nonrational determinants in students' learning in my writing courses. A critical related issue, I have found, is authenticity. Students often project inauthentic constructed selves in the classroom. Students construct artificial selves to survive in an environment they perceive as hostile to their authentic selves. They construct the self they see the academic environment is demanding. The academic setting often seems like an unsafe place for the authentic self so that the presentation of a constructed self becomes a kind of academic habit. Progress in the university writing class depended, it turned out, on breaking this habit. I shall argue that when students perceive a safe, supportive place for their authentic selves their learning accelerates. Winnicott's account of human development helps explain why, though for me, observation came first, theory later.

I describe the writing class experience, but these observations, like Winnicott's theory of development, describe the conditions for learning of any kind. Peter Rudnytsky (1993a) points out: "Winnicott's ideas remain comparatively unknown among those in universities" (p. xi). Anne Wyatt-Brown (1993) points out that when *College English* devoted two issues to psychoanalysis and pedagogy, "Winnicott's name never appeared" (p. 292). In this project, I will show what those of us in universities concerned with learning lose by neglecting this thinker who so articulately described the conditions of human development and the nonrational forces that govern these conditions.

1. "The Writing Problem" and Conventional Procedures

In 1979, the Dean of Humanities asked me to teach *Effective Writing*, a one-semester course meant to teach students to write an acceptable expository essay. *Effective Writing* had been put on the curriculum a few years before to address "the writing problem." Students who met demanding admissions requirements to get into university could not, once there, produce coherent essays or even correct sentences. Faculty members despaired—and still do—about "the writing problem."

I had little idea how to teach this course, so I took on the practices of my predecessors, the standard practices for quasi-remedial university courses in expository writing. I drilled grammar, lectured on structure and style, and assigned readings in *The Norton Reader*, the standard collection of model essays by E.B. White, J. Didion, Martin Luther King, Jr., Plato, and others. I assigned essays based on the readings. The assignments went like this: "Sartre's 'On Christianity' argues that people use religion to dodge responsibility for the choices they make. In a well-reasoned, logical essay, show why you agree or disagree with Sartre's position."

A week later, in came the students' essays. I read them and despaired. Clauses tangled, modifiers dangled, clichés governed, subjects and verbs disagreed, and premises masqueraded as conclusions. Worse, few of these essays had any meaning. These essays faked the making of meaning.

The students wanted only to please. Yet the more I tried to show them how to please, how to produce writing that would engage me, or anyone, the drearier the enterprise became. The more I drilled them in prose basics, the more frustrating the results became. If I did not mind mechanical reproductions of the examples I gave in class, then they progressed, but, if I sought real engagement with writing process then my teaching failed.

I felt ashamed. This was a sham. Dread swelled as I walked through hallways to classrooms where I would once again act like the "one who ought to know," as Lacan has put it. "Here I go," I muttered to myself, "to teach *(IN)Effective Writing.*"

One day in a course meeting at the end of term, I listened as colleagues who taught other sections said they doubted their students' writing had improved as a result of the course. They talked about "students these days...." Some said, "They just don't care." I never wanted to sound like these complainers. I saw things differently. I cared. My students cared. But their caring and my caring had between them a profound gap. We reinforced each other's estrangement. My teaching expressed my alienation. The students' writing expressed their alienation.

A. Ignorance and Luck

I was ignorant, and I knew I was ignorant. Even though the ignorance embarrassed and depressed me, that ignorance was surely the possible knowledge for my situation. My sense of myself as "the-one-who-ought-to-know"-but-who-does-not-know made me alert and receptive.

Students made the first move in the break that eventually, seven years later, led to discovery. The first, Kathleen Johnson, an early 1980s new-waver with green and orange hair, transformed a *Norton Reader* assignment based on an essay by John Kenneth Galbraith into a hilarious personal narrative about a job she worked at in a mice-infested bakery. When the bakery failed a health inspection, the piggish owner blamed Kathleen and another worker. Johnson's narrative engaged. The phoney, characterless, pseudo-objective, academic voice I had come to hate was gone. In its place was a distinctive, honest, personalized voice that made a meaning that the author cared about. I read Johnson's essay in class. The essay engaged the students, who laughed and applauded. One said, "I'm surprised she had the nerve to write that." Another said, "That's very honest; I don't know if I could write something like that for a university professor." I did not recognize Johnson's essay as a decisive moment; but I did appreciate relief from the tedium. I did not even see anything significant when three other students in the next class meeting tried, as Johnson had, to engage meaning in the way real writers do.

I made a copy of Johnson's essay and read it, for amusement, to my next section of *(IN)Effective Writing*. The reading spawned another spirited narrative, this one a tale of adolescent shoplifting. I asked the writer, Glen Ricketts, to read his piece to the class. Intense discussion followed. The class debated Rickett's moralizing conclusion: about half the students argued that the moral detracted from the honest narrative voice, and the other half argued that the writer needed the moralizing to make the piece respectable.

Ricketts brought another draft of the story, without the moral, to the next class, and the debate resumed. The talk around this piece heartened me. Students spoke like writers and editors. They engaged real writing issues, and the issues mattered to them. Issues of meaning, what the meaning would be and how best to make it, centered the talk. Rickett's piece inspired others to write narratives in voices that expressed their culture and experiences and about subjects they cared about and felt qualified to write about. The *(IN)Effective Writing* corpse twitched. The potential life in these twitches felt out of place and perhaps illicit, in the university setting. Something was happening. I little understood. I felt excited and threatened by it.

What was different about the work of these two students and those who followed their lead? Three factors distinguished this writing: (1) The students wrote in an honestly subjective, first-person narrative voice; (2) The students drew their content from their own direct experience; and (3) The students used informal language and style appropriate to their subjects. All of these features seemed like violations of formal academic propriety, and yet these students made an impact because they were doing what real writers do. They wrote from direct experience and observation in a distinctive and appropriate voice.

This writing brought life to a dead enterprise. I welcomed the life and in one small part of the courses I gave assignments designed to encourage these first-person narratives. To show the students what I meant when I gave these assignments, I read and distributed examples of good personal narratives I had collected from previous classes. This part of the course felt fun to teach, and I looked forward to reading the work that came out of it. The students liked it too and made comments like this one: "Can't we do more of this and just forget those other essays?" But the personal narratives felt like breaks from real academic work, like recess, and I insisted that the students spend most of the course writing formal expository essays based on their reading of masterpiece models.

Over time, it seemed to me, despite my academic preconceptions, that the work in the course on expository essays saw partial selves going through mechanical motions. The work on personal narratives engaged whole human beings. The students took this writing seriously and worked hard at editing and revising it. The lessons I wanted them to learn about writing—economy, clarity, precision, directness, detail—came alive when they worked on personal narratives and fell stillborn when they worked in conventional academic formats. What was I seeing here? I felt as though I was seeing something significant, but I had no idea what it was. I wanted to find out more.

I decided to experiment. *(IN)Effective Writing* was administrated through an academic no-man's land called "Interdisciplinary Studies," an assortment of courses that had no legitimate academic home, and drew students but did not attract the scrutiny and rule-setting that courses in traditional academic departments, English for example, did. As long as enrollments remained steady and there were no complaints, administrators paid *(IN)Effective Writing* little attention. Because this course lay outside the academic main channel, I had freedom to try out and test procedures that might challenge common academic wisdom. Even when orthodoxy is wrong, like the idea that the sun rotates around the earth, it looks like common sense. Without the freedom from close scrutiny and regulation that accompanies most instructional activity in our universities, I could not have made the discoveries I report here.

2. Experiments

Much teaching practice is based on handed-down "knowledge." Little of it is tested in the way we insist that research knowledge be tested. The course, however, provides an ideal experimental format: the predictable structure allows the experimenter a repeatable situation, one where variables may be isolated and observed. For many trials, one independent variable became the kind of assignments I gave my students. For others, I tested grading procedures, the course format, or the course readings. The dependent variable was the measurable impact of the course on their writing ability. I measured this impact by assessing the quality of their writing at the beginning and end of the course, by tracking their writing results in other university courses before and after the course, by conducting surveys of students' impressions of the impact of the course and by having students submit finished writing to publications and granting agencies that assess writing outside of the academic setting.

This is not the place to detail my experiments that took place over a decade through about thirty sections of university courses in basic prose. I will mention three.

I designed one set of trials to determine what type of writing assignment produced the best learning. How could learning be assessed? I decided to assess learning using a conservative, conventional measure: students' performance on the expository prose they use in the essays, lab reports, book reviews, essay exams and critiques they write in their university courses. Because the work around personal narrative seemed so much more alive than the work on expository prose, I posed this question: Does intensive work on personal narratives improve students' performance in writing expository prose? The data I collected produced a surprisingly clear answer: the personal narrative work, despite its differences from conventional academic writing, did improve performance on expository writing.

Furthermore, the personal narrative work appeared to improve academic writing performance more assuredly than did instruction in academic writing. Guided by this result, I shifted the balance of assignments and course time from 30 percent personal narrative/70 percent expository prose to 70 percent personal narrative/30 percent expository prose. The students' writing and their results on writing assignments in other university courses improved so much as a result of this changed balance that I eventually posed a more radical question: Does the inclusion of instruction on academic writing improve academic writing skills? In other words, was the 30 percent of course time spent on academic writing the best use of time, or would it be better to devote the whole of the course to the journalistic narratives the students wrote from their own experience? I taught sections with 30 percent of the course time given to academic writing and sections with no attention to academic writing. The results of repeated trials showed that instruction in academic expository prose did not improve students' performance on academic assignments as much as did further work on personal narratives. Put another way, the results showed that the time spent in the course on expository prose was wasted.

Without these careful tests, I would have scarcely believed the conclusion: that the best way to improve students' performance in academic writing was to offer intense training and experience in personal narratives, seemingly a very different kind of writing. While I did not know how to account for this result, the evidence was convincing. I felt in one sense better informed but in another more profoundly ignorant. The world was not revealing itself in the ways my academic common sense would have predicted.

A second set of trials tested the effect of changing my relationship with the students. In the original configuration, this relationship emphasized authority, detachment, and judgement. I took the students' assignments back to my office where I read, graded, and wrote comments. Like many instructors, I spent lots of lonely, alienated time reading and assessing papers. I hated this part of the job so I decided to try another arrangement that I read about in an instructor's manual that accompanied a writing text by Roger Garrison. In the manual *One-on-One: Making Writing Instruction Effective*, Garrison (1981) outlines another kind of professor/student relationship in a writing class setting. Instead of collecting his students' assignments and taking them away to grade, Garrison held five-minute appointments with students and read their work as the student watched. Instead of grading the assignment, he recommended edits. Instead of judge, he became editor. An editor operates as the writer's ally. The editor, who assumes the first draft of a piece of writing will respond to positive attention, works with the writer to make the writing as good as possible. I liked the sound of Garrison's one-on-one editing practice because it more closely resembled the way writers who are not university students work. Garrison warns that this system requires discipline and focus on the part of the instructor, or else the student meetings take too long and become unmanageable.

I modified Garrison's procedures and applied them to my course. Students came for fifteen-minutes appointments and sat in a chair facing me as I read and edited their work. Given the short time, I had to restrict myself to important points or specific passages. At first, I felt terrified. "What if I don't know what to say?" "What will I do when I cannot say anything positive about their writing?" I pushed past my fears and tried this system. My trials proved without a doubt the superiority of Garrison's procedure. With experience I got better at these instantaneous editing sessions. While I could not comment on every aspect of the students' work, they remembered the things I said. Because the trials of the Garrison one-on-one procedure gave such decisive results, I made it a permanent part of my writing teaching. At least in the initial response to their writing, I changed my relationship from authority/judge to expert/editor. I later extended the one-on-one procedures to place all assignments on the draft system. Students can write as many drafts of original work as they like. I grade nothing until our work as writer and editor is complete at the end of the course. Since the writing is so much better, the standard for the course is much higher than it was before I used this one-on-one method.

The third set of experiments I will summarize involved the course frame. The frame includes the rules about deadlines and attendance, the times the class starts and ends, the structure of the class session, and the explicit standards for evaluation. The frame defines the boundaries that separate the course from the world around it. The frame establishes what will be acceptable and what will be unacceptable within the temporary social container established for the operation of the course. Every course has a frame, but the frames may vary greatly. Some courses operate with rigid, tightly defined frames; others use flexible, vaguely defined frames. Sometimes the boundaries that surround the course change as the course proceeds. Sometimes students push announced boundaries and the instructor yields. Sometimes in response to events in the course the instructor may announce new boundaries or tighten existing ones. Since a writing course operates without the predefined content of subject matter courses, the question of definition of boundaries seems especially important.

I set up trials to see if frame changes made a difference in student learning. In some sections I used a loose frame. That meant flexible deadlines, optional attendance, casual structuring of class sessions, student choice for assignments, and class sessions that varied in format. In other sections I used a tight frame: strictly observed deadlines, mandatory attendance, highly structured class sessions, firm assignments without options, and a format that repeated in each class session. The syllabus for the loosely framed course took one-half page to set out rules and procedures; the syllabus for the tightly framed course took two full pages to define these guidelines. On first look, students favored the syllabus for the loosely framed course; the syllabus for the tightly framed course intimidated many students, and some dropped the course after they read it. But my trials produced a clear result: the tightly framed course produced better learning. When I presented a paper about the value of the tight course frame at a conference, one faculty member in the audience blurted, "Your students must hate you!" The tight frame does not produce hatred. Rather it has produced glowing reviews where students praise the course for what it has helped them to accomplish.

I have summarized three experiments and their results. These trials, along with others I do not describe here, have led to the design of the basic writing course as I have taught it since about 1990. I still experiment and I still make adjustments in response to the results, but the course as I teach it now has these basic features: (1) assignments that encourage students to write first-person narratives based on their experiences and observations; (2) an instructor/student relationship defined by the instructor's operating as editor (supportive other) rather than simply as judge; and (3) a clearly defined and rigorously maintained course frame.

The level of student achievement in the revised course has astonished me, the students, and other faculty members. Instructors in other courses comment on the extraordinary rise in writing performance they see in students who have taken the course and even in students currently enrolled in the course but who have not yet completed it. I first thought of these unexpected results as flukes belonging to a particular group of students. But these results have continued and have become expected. Students in this basic writing course often write publishable prose. I encourage and help students to publish assignments they write for the course. In 1989, I collected 111 pieces of student work from the course in an anthology and used the anthology as the course text (Allen, 1989).

This collection of peer models accelerated positive outcomes. A number of students who have taken the course have gone on to become writers and editors of creative, journalistic, and organizational publications. The course at the University of Toronto, under-subscribed in its early years, has now become difficult to get into; student demand for the course has led to more sections and eventually the creation of a sequel—an advanced course set on similar pedagogy. Over the years, these positive results have brought the course a good reputation in the university community. Six years ago, in a coming out of the academic closet, I was able to propose and have accepted a title change: *Effective Writing* became *Expressive Writing*.

One other feature of this experience deserves comment. This pedagogy appeared to enhance learning of students working at very different levels. Writing courses have often presented discouraging obstacles to students with poor academic backgrounds, students who speak English as a second or third language, or students who have trouble mastering the formalities of the academy dialect. These students benefit most from expressive writing pedagogy and often make stunning breakthroughs. Many are able to bring into the academic setting rich life experiences and vital language that they have, until this course, done their best to hide or forget.

The interesting point is that these students, once they have brought themselves and their language into the academic setting via this course, often appear to lose their phobia about academy dialect; the formal essay, which once defeated them, becomes a form they can manage. High achievers, less surprisingly, also prosper with this pedagogy and claim it adds a vital dimension —psychic growth and integration—to their academic experience. I have applied this pedagogy in community literacy projects and in workshops of university professors. Most people, whatever their level, claim to benefit from it. Many report breaking through personal or academic barriers as a result of the writing they do.

3. Meaning

What do these results mean? I set out to understand the principles that underlie the apparent power of this pedagogy. In particular, I wanted to know why many people who had been working at writing in one form or another for most of their lives made a sudden lurch beyond personal and academic barriers in this course (see Allen, 2000). I looked for theory that would explain the events that seemed to me both mysterious and yet, after years of observation, routine and predictable. Because the shift in students' performance was often dramatic and sudden, unlike an incremental learning process, I felt that something about this pedagogy enabled a release of latent capacity, a freeing of trapped potential.

And because people frequently reported changes that extended beyond the academic material presented in the course—increased self-knowledge, enhanced confidence—it seemed this process sometimes catalyzed personal development. I looked to psychoanalytic theories to account for the apparent capacity of this pedagogy to encourage, or permit, positive change, not just in writing, but in the person as a whole. Here I found powerful arguments about the value of expression and the damage of repression. Freud made the case for the "talking cure" and its capability of liberating the talker. With the help of a trained interpreter, the talker might find meaning in seemingly meaningless, disorganized pieces of discourse and emancipation through the interpreter's interpretation. Freud validates expression, but his theory does not account for the development I witness in student writers. The process I describe operates without the interpreter (analyst). Student writers, like most writers, may free associate as part of their writing process, but it is they alone who give shape and meaning to their words and to their experience in the course.

Another psychoanalytic thinker, Jacques Lacan (1953-1954), points to the centrality of language in psychic life: "Empty Speech," language that hides meaning, prevents development while "Full Speech" reveals meaning and makes change possible (p. 61). Language, for Lacan, defines limits. Yet the student writers I observe, once they find a writing voice that they hear as their own, experience language as possibility. Freud and Lacan, each in different ways, suggest why intensive work with reflective narratives might stimulate development. However, it is Donald Winnicott who describes the conditions that make development possible and likely. Whereas Freud emphasizes conflict and Lacan alienation, Winnicott stresses connection. This is what I see in the successful writing course: I see students making connections. They make these connections—between inner world and outer world, between self and other, between past and present—without interpretive direction from me. They move to these connections if they are allowed, if they feel it is safe to explore connections. And their writing improves drastically as they approach these connections.

How do we account for this? The title of a collection of essays by Winnicott (1984) points the way: *The Maturational Processes and the Facilitating Environment.* The "facilitating environment," I discovered, makes the difference in the writing course. According to this view, the teacher does not provide students with a set of meanings. Instead, the teacher creates an environment where students can make meaning or discover for themselves. My work shows people do this naturally—but only under certain conditions. A skilled practitioner can learn to create these conditions.

4. Winnicott's Theory: How Environment Enables Development

Unlike Freud, who focuses on innate drives, Winnicott concentrates on environmental factors that constrict or expedite development. These are a person's relations with others. People are naturally "object seeking," and the child's first and earliest relations are the most important. A pediatrician and a psychoanalyst, Winnicott observed mothers, babies and early development closely. The *good-enough mother*, Winnicott's term for an adequate primary caregiver, devotes herself to fulfilling the newborn's needs. At this stage, the infant "is able to have a brief experience of omnipotence" (Winnicott, 1962, p. 57) and sees the good-enough caregiver as an extension of self. When the infant grows "from absolute dependence to relative dependence, and towards independence," (p. 62) the infant sees the good-enough caregiver as an object outside of self.

Winnicott calls the psychic space between caregiver and infant *potential space*. This potential space, a creative place for both caregiver and child, is a place where play, the "work" of childhood, happens. Here we find paradox, both separation and connection. In the potential space child and caregiver are separate, but through creative play, the psyche of the child connects to the psyche of the caregiver. It is important to recognize that this space is only "potential" and depends on the "good enough" caregiver making and maintaining that space. If the caregiver interferes with and dominates the space, then the space and its potential are compromised. If the caregiver is negligent, there will be no defined, protected space where "the work of play" can happen. The development that happens in this space endures as the child learns to connect inner world and outer world. The child internalizes this potential space and recreates the space between itself and other objects.

According to Winnicott, an important event in this potential space is the infant's identification of a *transitional object*. This is some object, like a toy or a blanket, that becomes the infant's first "not-me" possession. As separation between the "good-enough"caregiver and the child begins, the child uses the transitional object to create the illusion of the comforting caregiver. The child utilizes the transitional object to evoke a mental representation of the caregiver. The transitional object provides an illusory sense of a soothing, responding, sustaining object experience. The illusion is crucial and positive. It not only provides a sense of security but allows autonomy since the object, unlike the caregiver, is under the infant's control. The "transitional object" symbolizes the union between baby and caregiver. It is the "first use of a symbol." Here in this "potential space" with this first symbolization, we find, according to Winnicott, the origin of culture. Culture consists of various "transitional phenomena" that mediate the space between inner self and outer world. Culture, because it operates in the "potential space" between "inner psychic reality" and "outer reality"offers an area of play. Play "expands into creative living and into the whole cultural life of man" (Winnicott, 1967, p. 102).

Finally, Winnicott relies on the concepts of a "True Self" and a "False Self" to describe psychic structures that all persons carry within them (1960). The True Self is the primal unmediated "experience of aliveness," "creative and spontaneous being" (1960, pp.148, 150).   In the "spontaneous gesture" Winnicott sees "the True Self in action" (148). Creativity here suggests the True Self interacting with or changing an environment. The False Self forms as a defense *against* the environment. Where the True Self acts on the environment, the False Self reacts by complying with environmental demands. The False Self acts as protector. As Winnicott puts it, the "False Self has one positive and very important function: to hide the True Self..."(pp. 146-147). A mild and healthy form of False Self is seen in the social compliance of good manners and consideration for others when, for example, we avoid saying everything we think.

There are degrees of False Self. Habitual compliance can swamp the True Self and produce an individual who does nothing but react. "Where," Winnicott writes, "there is a high degree of split between the True Self and the False Self ..., there is found a poor capacity for using symbols and a poverty of cultural living" (p. 150).   The False Self as a defensive organization protects the authentic core of personal autonomy from the abyss of psychic annihilation. Yet this defensive structure can lead to such a degree of falsehood that authenticity is strangled and a false existence perpetuated as a maladaptive attempt to protect the self from a hostile object environment.

Because Winnicott shows persuasively how environment facilitates or precludes development, his theories speak to teachers. Teachers create environments of one kind or another in their classrooms, presumably spaces meant to encourage students to develop their potentials. The university students in my writing classes are not babies, and I am not their parent. However, the teacher/student relationship does mirror the parent-child dyad in some ways. Teachers have authority to reward and punish. Teachers can, like parents, neglect, overwhelm, support, protect, or threaten their charges. When I confront my students with their freedom to write about what matters to them, most present experiences, good and bad, with parents and teachers in their first few narratives. "These people," they seem to say, "are keys to understanding who I am now." The teacher, like the parental caregiver, need only be "good enough," not perfect. And "good enough" means, if Winnicott is right, making the classroom a "facilitating environment."

5. The Student as False Self

Nowhere can we find a better example of the False Self than in the prose submitted by university students in essays submitted for humanities and social science courses. The lab reports done in science courses offer other examples, though the detached, "objective" style of the sciences may disguise the issue of self. Even in so-called creative writing courses, the False Self prevails: here many young writers fail to develop a voice of their own as they hide behind imitations of Hemingway, Nin, Joyce, and produce some of the most pretentious, hollow prose imaginable.

Faculty members despair about "the writing problem" in our universities —the apparent inability of many students to produce clear, readable, communicative prose written in grammatically correct sentences. Most often they blame teaching in the high schools. High school teachers blame the elementary schools. Elementary teachers blame parents. Amidst the blaming and displacement of responsibility for this crisis, these voices of despair present "the writing problem" as an issue of competence: students have not been taught the fundamental skills they need to write acceptable prose. Lax standards, lazy students, a poverty of grammar instruction, too much television watching, and not enough reading are commonly cited components of what is seen as the decline in writing skills. People routinely assert these connections with confidence—and without evidence. Their comments suggest a lost paradise, a time when high standards and competent performance prevailed. The complainers see themselves as fighting a lonely, weary, and probably hopeless battle against the decline of civilization. The same people propose a general crackdown as a remedy: a stiffening of standards and a system of penalties for those who cannot meet their standards.

My classroom-based research shows that "the writing problem" is not a problem of students' competence. Instead, it is a problem of trapped potential, potential that often fails to materialize when students write. With "good-enough" instruction, I have shown, students can go through what looks like a revolution in writing performance in six weeks or less. Learning by skill building, accumulating information and practice is too slow a process to account for the degree and speed of the change. Many students, who when I meet them produce trails of sentence fragments, run-ons, and other structural breakdowns in their incoherent writing, make perfect sentences in their coherent speech. Obviously, they have internalized grammar and structuring principles in order to speak they way they do. These students have the ability and the knowledge— the potential—to produce good writing. "Good enough" instruction releases this trapped potential.

What is there about the act of writing that traps this potential? Many people rarely write at all except when compelled in school or business or other institutional settings. This is true for most students. I can spot right away students who write frequent letters or who keep diaries; this minority, of course, has an easier and more positive relationship with writing than do those with only forced experience.

The majority, those with only forced writing experience, fear writing and the negative judgements they associate with it. Writing brings them under the scrutiny of a judge, usually a teacher, who usually finds defects. In surveys I have done, better than 90 percent of students in my courses associate writing in an academic setting with harsh negative judgements (and these are students who have chosen to take a writing course as opposed to the many who avoid courses with any writing in them). Many students report that when they write they run afoul of a mysterious labyrinth of rules that they feel their teachers understand but that they do not. And when someone judges their writing, students feel the judgement touches them as persons in a way that a judgement about their knowledge of chemistry does not.

Students construct False Selves as a defense against the intimidating, alien environment they see themselves in when they write. The university environment, with its relentless focus on evaluation and judgment, maximizes this defensive behavior. The poor writing our students produce speaks in the voice of the False Self.

The False Self, Winnicott (1960) tells us, hides and protects the True Self by "compliance with environmental demands" (Winnicott, p. 147). Students perceive the university as a place of elevated knowledge, difficult ideas, and complicated, specialized language. The compliant response of the False Self leads many students, especially students who feel marginal in the university —students from working class families, and students who speak English as their second language—to imitate the elevation and complexity they associate with academy dialect. Since this dialect seems opaque to them, they reproduce its opacity. Sometimes they do this unconsciously. Other times, they intentionally imitate this opacity. They shift into complicated syntax and inflated vocabulary they have no experience using—and naturally this alien style looks awkward and suffuses with errors. No wonder, the readers, faculty members, complain. Reading this compliant prose, like eating sawdust, offers nutritionless bulk, a cloying emptiness. Faculty members know the flavor well. And if it alienates its readers, it certainly expresses the alienation of its writers. The False Self articulates the alienation of the True Self. Yet, as Winnicott (1960) writes, "Only the True Self can be creative and only the True Self can feel real" (p. 148).

6. The Student as True Self: Or, Making a Place
for the Self in University

The honest, personalized voice I saw in Kathleen Johnson's piece about the bakery that failed the health inspection represented the voice of the True Self. That voice registered as authentic because the author expressed in language which belonged to her experience and a personal reality. The voice of her essay is not a compliant, defensive voice; rather it is an expressive voice. Instead of trying to blend herself into the environment, she acted on the environment by bringing the spontaneous expression of a True Self into it. She created her own environment. We might say that she achieved a rapport, or a symmetry between herself and the university. This differs from the one-sided relationship of the False Self. The False Self is swamped by its environment.

Winnicott's theory of play explains why writing personal narratives facilitates learning and development. Personal narratives are objects of play because they exist in a space between the student's world and the outer world of the classroom and the university, are objects of play. Winnicott (1971) would call them "transitional phenomena"—things which mediate the potential space between inner and outer, things which operate in "the third area" (p. 53) between self and other. When students reach into themselves for their content, they play. They make a connection between what is them and what is outside them. In this sense, the personal narrative is play while the political science or the English essay, where the students address subject matter that lies outside of their experience, are usually not.

Too often universities with their rigid allegiance to academy dialect falsely suggest to students that writing is a mainly a matter of formal form. The dynamic relationship between content and form, surely the essence of writing, gets lost here. The indiscriminate application of academy dialect is like putting on a tuxedo every time we step out of the house. The tuxedo that looks sharp at the wedding doesn't work for gardening, and it looks absurd in the grocery store. Many of the worst examples of "the writing problem" I have seen involve prose where the writer applies a ludicrously pompous and formal style to a situation that calls for straightforward functional communication.

The play of personal narrative takes the student away from the rigid demands of the expository essay where composition follows an externally prescribed structure and style. The student moves into storytelling, where structure and style arise from the story the student tells. Style becomes a matter of appropriateness, not correctness. The writer must decide what level of formality is appropriate to the story being told. In this system, students do what writers do. They make tricky and difficult decisions about diction, theme, tone, structure, length—decisions that writers outside of the academy must make. Like real writers, the students must play with the elements that make up a piece of writing until they find what is right for the story they want to tell. That rightness is dictated by the connection the writer must make, the connection between the inner world of the self and the other world, the reader, that the writer wants to reach. These truisms, commonplace for writers, come as new information to most of the students I teach. Here is the opening of a personal narrative titled, "Going to Chinese School" by Jennifer Lee, a second-year university student when she wrote this essay.

> I never got to see a complete line-up of Saturday morning cartoons. On Saturday mornings, while Adrienne and Marie watched *Casper*, *Alvin and the Chipmunks*, and *Spiderman*, I went to Chinese school. Chinese brush painting classes kept me busy over the summer. Chinese speech contests and writing Mandarin com-positions kept me from going to birthday parties all year. I was born in Canada and taught Canadian values and traditions. My parents always found ways of reminding me of my Chinese roots.
>
> "You don't want to grow up not knowing how to read and write in your own language," said Mom. She made me copy paragraphs out of ancient Chinese study books before I could ride bikes with Adrienne and Marie. Every time a Chinese holiday came up, Mom and Dad made my brother and me call my grandmother. We always had the same conversation.
>
> "Wai-po how!" I yelled into the phone.
>
> "You eat supper yet?" she asked.
>
> "Yes."
>
> "You study in school?"
>
> "Yes."
>
> "Lots of homework?"
>
> "Yes."
>
> "Good. Nice girl."
>
> Every year the same thing. Sometimes I just wanted to tape my voice and play it back over the phone.
>
> "No respect for your grandparents," Mom would have said.
>
> When our grandparents' anniversary came up, Mom bought a card for my brother and me and made us write a long message in Mandarin to our grandparents. I asked Mom if she would write the message on the card and we could just sign our names at the bottom. She looked shocked, slapped the card over my head and said, "Tao yang!" (nuisance). She made me write an extra long Mandarin message.
>
> My parents first took me to Chinese school when I was six years old. Because my mother was a teacher, she knew all the other teachers and often spoke to them to find out what I learned and what I needed improvement in.

I always needed improvement. (Lee, 1996, p.18)

Lee goes on to present hilarious details about Chinese school, where she encounters other sons and daughters of Chinese immigrants whose parents want
them to know their roots and who, like her, feel the split between the place they
live in now and the culture of their parents.

Lee's narrative is stylistically right. Through her choice of words and her
simple, direct sentences, she sets the right tone and level of formality for a piece
about a young girl who mourns the loss of Saturday morning cartoons to the
demands of Chinese school. The tone is light, but the theme is serious. Lee
presents a piece of her inner world—the sometimes awkward blending of her
Chinese heritage and her life in North America—in a way that readers who have
not had this experience may understand it. This, like most successful personal
narratives, works as what Winnicott would call a "transitional object." This
object, the story, is under Jennifer Lee's control. It furthers the sense of
autonomy that Winnicott (1963) sees as the outcome of *"the object that is
created, not found"* (p. 181). Paradoxically, the playing which creates this
object also "leads into group relationships" (Winnicott, 1971, p. 41). Other
students reacted to Lee's narrative with comments like, "I never thought about
what it's like for a person from another culture before," or as one Serbian
woman notes: "My parents want the same; they want me to grow up and succeed
in Canada, but they want me to keep the old country values as well."

Another narrative, "Lakeview Indian Day School," by Mary Lou C.
DeBassige (1989), an Anishnabe woman of about forty who grew up on West
Bay Reservation on Manitoulin Island in Georgian Bay, opens this way:

> Real fast, I turn around in my desk to look at my cousin. He says
> something in our Odawa and Ojibwe language. This is a mistake.
>
> The teacher, Miss McNulty, walks with a limp. She uses a cane. We
> all jump when she hits a desk with that cane. I'm sure the cane would cry
> if it had feelings. She doesn't need her cane this time. She stands in front
> of me waving a new yardstick.
>
> Another yardstick. How many has she broken so far on someone or on
> the blackboard? Crack! Across my knuckles. It happens fast. I half cry out.
> I try to hold it in. A big lump rises from inside, pauses at my throat, stops
> at my nose. My eyes hurt. Tears roll down my face. My nose drips.
>
> "Mary Louise, you must never speak that whatever language again!
> Never! Never! It is not a proper language. You must forget it totally! Speak
> English only. Hear me?" She shakes me by the shoulders.
>
> "Yes, ma'am."
>
> She glares at me. "Repeat after me. I will not speak Indian ever again."

I chokingly speak every word after her because I am scared she will hit me with her yardstick. But my habit is to speak anishinabe and English together. I don't understand why speaking Anishnabe is wrong. Miss McNulty makes my mother language sound evil and ugly.

Catechism begins another day at this Indian Day School. Miss McNulty asks, "Who made you, Jane?"

Jane looks around and says, "God made me."

"Dick, where is God?"

Dick answers fast. "God is everywhere." I look at Dick in wonder. He is smart.

"Mary Louise, say The Hail Mary in front of the class."

I get up in front of the classroom and try to keep my eyes straight ahead. I'm ready to die. Miss McNulty will kill me if I forget a word or a line of this English prayer. She tells me to fold my hands.

I start.

> *Hail Mary, full of Grace*
> *the Lord is with Thee.*
> *Blessed art thou amongst women,*
> *Blessed is the fruit of . . .*

I wish I could say this prayer in Anishnabe. N'mishomiss, my grandfather and the chief of the West Bay Reservation for many years, taught me to pray in Anishnabe. N'mishomiss is a devoted Roman Catholic.

This morning, I feel scared as I try to remember. I've said this prayer at The Legion of Mary, the religious group on the reservation. There, we pray together. I am not forced to say every word or sentence. I feel safe and happy there. This morning, my mind empties and I forget. Nobody is allowed to help me. I have to say this prayer by myself. For sure, this is doomsday. (pp. 41-43)

DeBassige's piece ends happily. Her grandfather, the chief of West Bay Reservation, gets Miss McNulty replaced by "a new, kinder teacher."

The scene DeBassige describes at Lakeview Indian Day School is the perfect inversion of Winnicott's "facilitating environment." She cannot learn, or even say the Hail Mary, because the school is not a safe place, as the reservation is because there "we pray together." And this school does not allow the vital connection between the self and the world it inhabits. Miss McNulty tells her with words and gesture that her True Self, which includes her language, is unacceptable. Precisely what personal narrative does for university students —giving them a way to bring themselves into the academy—Miss McNulty's classroom excludes.

DeBassige's piece, like Lee's, uses simple language and style. DeBassige sets a more serious tone to convey the grim experience she had of the cultural genocide First Nations peoples in the Americas have endured. The style is appropriate, and it makes a successful connection between the experiences that have formed the inner life of the writer and the outer world of the university and of the readers of her story. This story operates not only in the transitional space between writer and reader but also in the transitional space between cultures. Through the story the writer achieves autonomy—the story belongs to the writer who creates it—and the writer achieves connection to readers. Other students in the class said to DeBassige that they had heard about the abuse of First Nations peoples in schools but that they had no idea what this really meant until they heard her read this story.

Like most of the student writers I work with, their first pieces identify straightaway a critical, central issue that defines their experience in the world, an issue that both connects them and sets them apart from others. People use playing, Winnicott tells us, to "work" at resolving the tension between what is them and what is outside them. DeBassige, who had written nothing other than school assignments before she wrote this piece has gone on to become a well-published writer and recognized voice for her community. A characteristic feature of DeBassige's writing has become her mixing of Anishnabe and English, something we see the faint beginnings of in the passage quoted her. Lee, still an undergraduate English major at the University of Toronto, has published several of her narratives and is working on her first book, a collection of stories about being at once Chinese and not-Chinese. "Going to Chinese School" was her first piece of "real writing," as she calls it.

Personal narratives reach beyond the walls of the academy; the world will publish and read journalistic prose. Many of my students, even in the basic prose course, publish work written for assignments in magazines, newspapers, and literary journals. The validation and recognition achieved through publishing in the community beyond the university amplifies the sense of connection and personal empowerment. Few traditional academic essays can reach an audience outside the academy. Cultural experience, Winnicott asserts, grows directly out of transitional phenomena and playing. The play of the personal narrative leads students into the life of the cultures they live in. They become makers as well as students of culture. The vitality of the connection becomes the vitality of the course.

Students use narratives to make links between their inner and outer worlds, links between the university and the culture the university studies, and links between the academic and the personal. Many students use the potential space provided by the narrative to make connections between things that without these links seem to conflict and split their attention. Students use this space to grow personally and academically, and the growth comes partly by bridging the artificial gap between the personal and the academic. The skills they gain through rigorous work in the personal narrative transfer to more traditional academic writing because the self experiences the division between the personal and the academic as artificial and imposed. The transfer of skills is not a transfer but a linkage that integrates the self and yields confidence. An unfortunate side effect of the split between the personal and the academic is that students fail to see that their own lives can be a source of knowledge. Their work with personal narrative brings them to recognize their lives as places where meaning may be found.

Students who have learned under this pedagogy sometimes carry this perception into other courses. A daughter of Chinese immigrants to Canada made an interview with her mother the basis for an essay she submitted in an upper-level Chinese history course. The professor who read the essay gave it an A+ and commented on its extraordinary freshness and originality. The student who wrote this essay told me it never would have occurred to her do research outside of the library, and certainly not in her own family, without the experience of writing about her family in the course she took with me. She has since published a collection of pieces based on her observation of and interviews with her mother (Chong, Kofie, *et al.*, 1993); these pieces were originally writing course assignments. One further interesting note on this writer involves her relationship with her mother. Before she wrote her writing-class pieces, she told me, she wanted only to put distance between herself and her mother. She used the potential space in the writing course to address this split.

Play, Winnicott (1971) tells us, "is an experience, always a creative experience, and it is an experience in the space-time continuum, a basic form of living." Play involves risk: "playing is always liable to become frightening." Play is precarious because it sits "on the theoretical line between the subjective and that which is objectively perceived" (p. 50). The activity my students undertake happens at this line. They explore themselves, they take charge of meaning, and they face down and fill the blank page—all precarious events that unsettle people. They speak about risk and fear. Yet they push forward: these courses have very low drop rates, and in the end students evaluate the course highly as a learning experience. Something secures them against the precariousness of their play.

Perhaps one securing element is storytelling. Storytelling offers illusory security. Alamatea Usuelli (1992) writes: "The attraction of *story-telling*, from children's tales to myths, from popular literature to the novel, consists largely in the creation of a meaningful universe, a closed world, in which each element has its place (p.183)." When they write their narratives, students become makers of stories.

Usuelli goes on: "Story-telling creates the illusion that the subject and object, the inner and the outer world correspond, and that the subject's experience has meaning and is preserved from chaos" (p. 184). For Winnicott (1971), "Transitional objects and transitional phenomena belong to the realm of illusion which is the basis of the initiation of experience." This illusion is experienced in later life "in the intense experiencing that belongs to the arts and to religion and to imaginative living, and to creative scientific work" (p. 14). The illusion of security and continuity allows play, itself precarious and risky, to occur. Development happens in the presence of this useful illusion. For a while, in the secured space of the classroom, the securing illusion of the narrative gives experience apparent order and logic. The world, it seems, makes sense. This illusion offers the security people need to risk real learning.

Others have written about the power of pushing students to make their own subject matter and to make their own meanings. James Britton (Winnicott's brother-in-law), the influential educational theorist, who thought "like a clinician" and wrote about "how British children learned or failed to learn to write" (Wyatt-Brown, 1993, p. 297) asserted his belief in the creativity of people and argued that teachers should permit their students to write about what interests them. Britton rebelled against the prevailing English department attitude that literature is "'something *that other people had done'*" (Tirrell, *et al.*, 1993, p. 297). Britton argued that children master writing skills, not through drilling and programmed writing, but through using their freedom to make their own meanings.

I do not know if Britton realized that his observations about children apply with little change to the students of various ages in university. As Winnicott (1971) put it, "the task of reality-acceptance is never completed" and "no human being is free from the strain of relating inner and outer reality...." The "relief from this strain is provided in an intermediate area of experience..." (p. 13). The personal narrative provides this intermediate space for what Christopher Bollas calls "transformational object seeking"—finding "the word to speak the self," the word that facilitates our urge to change ourselves (Bollas, 1993, p. 43).

7. Collaboration: "Making Use of" the Teacher

Britton's (1970) theories express his faith in children's creativity and in their capacity to express themselves to "an interested audience" (Wyatt-Brown, 1993, p. 297). Britton resisted the notion that the teacher comes to the classroom as "culture-bearer." Instead, he advocated the teacher as collaborator with the student.

Winnicott took a similar approach with his patients. He minimized the value of the analyst's interpretations: "it is the patient and only the patient has the answers" (1969, p. 87). Patients get better, Winnicott says (1971c), not because the analyst gives them answers but because of "the patient's ability to use the analyst" (Winnicott, p. 87). "Interpretation," Winnicott writes (1971c), "when the patient has no capacity to play is simply not useful, or causes confusion" (p. 51).

I discovered that it is more important to facilitate "play" than to deliver expert opinions when I began working one-on-one with writing students as collaborative editor rather than judging authority. A crucial ingredient of this relationship is my interest in what they have to say. I look forward to reading their work. They sit a few feet away and watch me read it. They cannot mistake my excitement when their writing connects. When their writing does not connect, I comment on how difficult it is to make this connection, and I offer advice.

A typical first session with a writer/student goes like this. The student comes to my office at an appointed time and sits in a chair that faces my chair. My desk sits against the wall—not in the center of the room as a barrier between the student and me. I turn my chair at right angles to the desk and face the student. I take the student's work from my desktop and place it my lap so the student sees what I am doing. The student cannot see the words I write because from their position the paper is upside down. But the student sees the activity. It is important, I think, that I read the student's work for the first time as the student watches. This creates some vulnerability for me: I have not rehearsed or planned my reaction to the student's work. Typically the student starts the session with a nervous, defensive comment.

Student: So, tell me what's wrong with it. Tell me my mistakes.

Teacher: I work as your editor, and it's an editor's job to identify a writer's strengths and to help the writer emphasize those strengths. Editors also point out weaknesses that pull away from the strengths. But we have to know the strengths before we know what the weaknesses are. So the most important part of my job is to locate your strengths, at least as they appear to me.

Student: Show me my grammar errors. My teachers always said I make grammar errors.

Teacher: What kinds of errors?

Student: I don't know exactly. Commas. Spelling. Sometimes my sentences are wrong.

Teacher:	When we identify the strength of your writing and when you build on your strengths, I think you'll find these technical matters fairly easy to take care of. We don't have much time, and I am going to read now. I'll talk to you about this when I finish reading.

I make editor's notations as I read. The student watches. I react to the content spontaneously as I read. If something moves me, I might say "This is powerful." If something is funny, I laugh. I might mutter, "That's interesting" about some detail. When I finish, the dialogue resumes.

Student:	So what's wrong with it? You've made lots of marks.
Teacher:	Editors always make marks. We make marks to help the writer, to suggest changes. I really like the passage in the middle about how you got around the dress code in your high school by fooling the hall monitors. You provide good, precise details there, and as your reader I can really see the scene. It's alive. It's funny. It's enjoyable. Your sentences in that part are sharp and clear too. I've marked this passage that I like so you can see where it is. Now you should revise this piece. Change the beginning so that it has just as much detail in it as this strong passage in the middle. You know where this story happens. You can picture the place. But you don't put any of that picture down here. Show me the high school. Give it a name. Show me the teachers. Show me the students. You have that picture in your mind. Get it down on the page. New writers almost always forget to do that. I have another suggestion. Get rid of the moral at the end of your essay. You don't have to moralize. I didn't really believe you when you told me you had learned your lesson. Do you really think that changing the hem on your skirt to fool the hall monitor was wrong? Do you really regret doing this?
Student:	Not really. I sort of think it's funny.
Teacher:	That's what I think too. Be honest with your reader. You don't have to tell us that you are a good obedient person. Show us who you really are. That will make the best writing. I look forward to seeing your revision of this piece. Expand on what works here, and get rid of or change the things that

don't work. Take this with you, and use it as notes for your revision. Look at the writing in the course text [a collection of published peer models] and see if you can get ideas from other writers. If you don't understand anything in my edit notes, ask me in class. It is hard to produce a piece of writing that really says something and that expresses you clearly. This is a good beginning. The real work of writing is revision. I have to get to another student now. Thanks for showing me your work.

Student: Thank you. That wasn't too bad. I was so nervous I almost didn't come. I almost dropped the course. Do you really think I can do this course?

Teacher: Yes, you can do it. You can write well. You'll be amazed at what happens over the next few weeks. Build on your strengths. Goodbye. I'll see you in class.

This procedure emphasizes a boundaried human relationship. Two people sit in a room. One reads a narrative the other has written. The reader reacts to the narrative by articulating its strengths and by suggesting ways to make it stronger. The writer, the student, learns, in Winnicott's terms, to make "*to make use of*" this collaborator. How? First, the writer/student uses the "holding" provided by the collaborator/editor. Holding is Winnicott's term for the protective, empathetic, space-creating function of the caretaker. Holding means making a secure place. Writing, especially when the writer struggles to make original meaning based on self-experience, is a lonely, threatening activity. Holding does not make the writing experience less lonely or less threatening. Holding does offer the beginning writer "the experience of being alone while someone else is present" (Winnicott, 1958, p. 30). This experience of being alone in the presence of another leads ideally to autonomy—that is, the writer develops the capacity to take on the aloneness of writing experience in the presence of the empathetic other who understands the difficulty of the experience the new writer is going through. The effect is supportive. Students speak to me about the value of holding. They tell me, for example, that as they sit alone writing they visualize the moment when they will sit with me in my office and I will read what they write.

Winnicott describes a further stage in object-relating. Sooner or later the subject tries to destroy the object by attacking it. In the case of mother and child, the child (subject) attacks the mother (object) by defying her or by expressing anger and disappointment. In the case of therapist and patient, the patient may criticize or manipulate the therapist as a reaction to the therapist's perceived inadequacy. In the case of teacher and writing student, the student will try to "destroy the object" by criticizing the teacher, by breaking the boundaries the teacher has set, or by suggesting that the teacher's view of writing and learning process is not valid. In some cases, the student may try to "destroy the object" by asserting an inappropriate shift in the editor/writer relationship, such as informal friendship or a love affair. Winnicott goes on to say that the object's (teacher's) response to attempts to destroy it will determine whether or not developmental work can continue. The object must "survive" the attack without retaliating. If the object does retaliate then development is truncated. The retaliation wrecks the interplay between subject and object, between student and teacher. The student will either discontinue the relationship, or more likely will continue it in name only by hiding behind a compliant, False Self.

If the object (teacher) survives the attack without retaliating, then the subject (the student) will have placed the teacher outside of the student's "omnipotent control, that is, out in the world" (Winnicott, 1969, p. 91). The student places the teacher "outside the area of objects set up by the [the student's] projective mental mechanisms" (p. 94). That is, the teacher becomes a real person, rather than the student's mental projection of infallible expertise and authority. "In this way," writes Winnicott (1969), "a world of shared reality is created which the subject can use. . ." (p. 94). The student, in this way of looking at this interaction, takes responsibility for learning and development. The student decides how to use the teacher. The student decides what is valuable and what is not. This taking of responsibility on the part of the student, in my view, represents the desired outcome of the student/teacher relationship.

Here are examples of student attempts to "destroy the object." Sometimes the student's rejection of the teacher's commentary, particularly in trying to discredit praise, may also represent a form of self-defilement. These interactions take place after we have met two or three times and the students have lost their initial fear of the one-on-one editing sessions.

Teacher: This is a fine piece of writing. You have done a stunning job of showing just how random and risky creative process is. The details are precise and vivid. You really got me involved in this piece. This is an exceptional piece of writing. I see a distinctive voice here, and I see powerful expression. Congratulations.

Student: [Laughs.] That can't be. This is stupid. I wrote this assignment in ten minutes sitting on the floor in the hallway outside the classroom. I didn't think I'd get it done on time. Ten minutes. I spent hours on other assignments, but this one was a throwaway.

Teacher: In my view, this is brilliant writing. How you wrote it may provide a clue to your own mental processes. Maybe you write best when you write fast and spontaneously. I don't care how you wrote it. I just react to what I see here.

. . . . .

Student: Isn't writing all subjective? Isn't this just your opinion? How can you say what good writing is?

Teacher: Yes, you're right. These are my opinions. You need to decide whether or not they have value for you.

. . . . .

Teacher: I had an appointment with you in my book for 10:00 this morning. Did I have that wrong?

Student: No. We had an appointment, but I had to study my Physics.

Teacher: I missed seeing you and hope we can meet again soon. If you can't make it, call me so I can give that time to someone else. I don't like unused appointment times because I have a long line of people who want times.

. . . . .

Student: I'm think I'm going to quit the course. You made me very angry the last time I saw you. The things you told me to change were the things that had my soul in them. I felt like you wrecked my project. I was inspired before. Now I hate it.

Teacher: I'm sorry. What did I say?

Student: Not anything really. Maybe I was just mad because I wanted you to think it was perfect, and you didn't say that.

Teacher: My goal is to work with you to help you produce the best writing that you can. But this is not science. I make guesses based on my experience, but I might be wrong. I make suggestions, but you do what you think is right. Maybe you'll teach me something.

Student: I don't know what's right. That's your job to know what's right.

Teacher: No. It's your job to decide what's right. I have experience, but I cannot say what's right for what you want to express. Writing is a difficult and uncertain enterprise. Trial and error are part of writing. You try things to see if they work. That takes courage, and I respect your courage for taking on this difficult project. I respect how hard this is. You have to decide how to write it. If my advice helps, take it. If not, disregard it.

Student: I did manage to pull together one piece along the lines you suggested. I have it here. Would you mind having a look at it?

Teacher: Let's see it. I'll tell you what I think. Even though this has been tough, you have still produced work. I admire your perseverance. That usually leads over time to good results. Let's see what you've done.

I see many things happening in these dialogues which contain kernels of the complex interpersonal dynamics between student and teacher. At one level, I see these as fairly typical attacks against the object/teacher as I have experienced them in teaching writing. When I handle them as the teacher in these examples does, the attack usually turns out to presage a positive breakthrough by the writer. In Winnicott's terms this represents the object's survival of the subject's attempt to destroy it followed by the subject's enhanced ability to "use the object." In the writing-class case, using the object means students' ability to use their relationship with me to develop their writing and themselves.

Like many teachers, my own insecurities tempt me to use my position and experience to retaliate. On occasions when I have retaliated, I have seen the development that makes this work so fulfilling abruptly stop. Certainly, play, as Winnicott defines it, will not happen in an environment where a power figure retaliates. The most damaging action occurs when in a bad moment I retaliate against an attacker in a classroom. There, I have found, that even when other students feel irritated by the challenge presented by the attacker, they identify with the attacker as the victim of my authority the instant I use my position to retaliate. All the students become timid and fearful and present false, compliant selves in the face of the retaliating authority figure. The False Self does not produce authentic writing so this is death for a writing course. Such slips damage the teaching environment so that it no longer facilitates development. When I realize I have retaliated, I acknowledge the mistake, make a direct apology and hope for time to repair the damage.

When I speak about collaborative one-on-one work with writing students, some colleagues react skeptically. One reaction is: "I would never have the time to do that." They see this procedure as inefficient. I spend no more total time on the writing courses than I would if I took the students' work back to my office, read it, wrote comments on it and handed it back to them in class. The student sitting in the office with another scheduled to arrive in fifteen minutes provides strong incentive to focus attention and keep moving. Colleagues who have adopted this procedure agree that it takes no more total time. It *is* more intense, and I and those who try one-on-one say, it is much more effective than taking the writing away to read. My tests show this procedure improves the quality of the learning in the course and the writing of the students. Winnicott's theory shows us why. On balance, one-on-one is highly efficient.

Other colleagues say, "I couldn't sit and read work for the first time while a student watched; I would be worried I wouldn't know what to say. And what do you do if it's terrible?" Teachers, like students, feel exposed by one-on-one teaching. I think one-on-one provides balance. We ask our students to expose their work to us and our judgements. Putting ourselves on the spot in the one-on-one editing session gives us some of the uncertainty and risk the students feel all the time. I think the image of the teacher/editor working while the student watches is powerful. Sometimes I don't know what to say after I have read a piece. I have to say, "I don't feel sure; I'll think about this for a few days, and then I'll have more to say." When the writing is terrible, I know that if I can locate some strength, any strength—one sentence will do—I know from past experience that this terrible writing can change quickly and that the student who sits before me and watches me sweat through a draft may surprise both of us before we are finished. My teaching has taught me not to pre-judge anything. I have seen too many little miracles. My job is to provide a setting, the "facilitating environment," where these miracles will likely happen.

Another feature of one-on-one involves identity. Many graduating students come to me for recommendations, and I often hear this refrain: "After four years here, you are the only professor who knows my name." If self-reflective writing encourages individuation, the teacher's knowledge of the student apart from the sea of faces in the classroom must enhance that process.

8. The Frame: Making a Container for Development

The most surprising result in my experiments with pedagogy came from my observations of the impact of different course frames. My experiments have shown that the tighter the frame—that is, the more rigidly defined the boundaries and procedures of the course are—the better the learning environment. This result surprised me because I came of age in the late 1960s, and many people, including myself, felt general antagonism against academic and social limits. I am also aware that many writing courses, especially "creative" writing courses, see writing as privileged activity that must make allowance for unreliable inspiration and flighty muses; these courses, often loosely organized, see creativity as compromised by structure. My view is the opposite.

My writing courses, while they encourage freedom and responsibility in the content of the students' writing, impose austere regulations in the formal procedures of the course. Classes meet for two hours once a week. Students must submit a substantial original piece of writing in every class after the first class, a "bootcamp" writing exercise based on the previous week's lecture, and revisions of work that we have edited. I check the bootcamp exercises by calling names randomly at the beginning of the class and asking people to read their exercises. The course has no late policy because I do not accept late work: "In this course," I say in the first class, "we operate on a no-excuses system: put your creativity into your work, not into your reasons for not doing your work; no excuse is valid." Attendance is, of course, mandatory. And I don't read the students' work until they come at an appointed time to my office and sit with me while I read it. If they don't come, I don't read their work.

The structure of the class sessions is formal and repetitive. Each session includes a fifteen-minute review of the previous week's bootcamp exercise, a forty-minute lecture, a new bootcamp exercise, a ten-minute break, and a forty-minute group editing session. I structure the editing session carefully. When I announce the editing sessions, students dread them because they fear exposure in front of their peers and because they associate university seminars with rambling, seemingly pointless discussions dominated by a few students. I call students' names at random in these session, I organize comment so that positive identification of strengths comes first, and I intervene when the discussion becomes vague or threatening. In other words, I see to it the editing session become part of the facilitating environment. Students learn to listen, to make constructive comment, and to take individual responsibility for group enterprise. By the end of the course students speak highly of the disciplined group work. The editing session becomes a form of group play within a protective frame that makes risk possible.

The structure of class sessions, the assignment schedule, the workload, and the one-on-one interview schedule remain a constant pattern from the beginning to the end of the term. In most of the University's courses, the workload clusters in large assignments and tests at midterm and at the end of term a concentration that maximizes stress. The constant weekly pattern in the writing course, while rigorous and demanding, provides stability and reliability. This pattern appears to minimize stress. So while in terms of quantity of work and the difficulty of the task (ten original pieces of work in ten weeks) the course seems demanding, the tight frame with its regular patterning provides a securing container that allows students to build strength in the face of pressure. Students report distress mainly at the beginning of the writing course—before the pattern is established.

The frame also operates as a securing container for the uncharted exploration of self and voice that goes on in the students' writing. I have identified this work with Winnicott's concept of play in the potential space. The search for self is conditioned, according to Winnicott (1971), by the "reliability or unreliability of the setting in which the individual is operating" (p. 55). For there to be a potential space where this play can occur, Winnicott explains, there must be "trust and reliability." Where these elements are absent, there can be "no relaxed self-realization" (p. 108). Where there is trust and reliability "there develops a use of symbols that stand at one and the same time for external world phenomena and for the phenomena of the individual person who is being looked at" (p. 109).

Personal narratives, because they connect between the writer (the inner world) and readers (the outer world), operate in the potential space that links the individual with the culture the individual inhabits. Without a trustworthy, reliable environment, the potential space that makes possible linkages between outside and inside, between past and present, cannot be accessed. "The potential space," Winnicott writes (1967), "happens only in relation to a feeling of confidence..., that is, confidence related to the dependability of ... environmental elements..." (p. 100). What, we may ask, is a space without any kind of securing boundary? It is, Winnicott would say, a space without potential. Only when we delineate a space from the anarchic void of unboundaried space do we sense our own potential within it. Pioneer farmers fenced their fields before they planted them.

The frame must itself be reliable if it is to provide the reliability and elicit the trust that underwrites the potential space. For the teacher, this means striving to produce a regular pattern of course activity, one that students can rely on. The frame imposes dual obligations: the students must meet the require-ments and live within the limitations laid down by the teacher; the teacher must complete the contract by also respecting the obligations and limits imposed by the frame. It is easy for teachers, who hold power, to breach their part of the contract. I remember from my own undergraduate career a professor of Anglo-Saxon coming into an afternoon class: he told us he hadn't been able to prepare that day because he had taken a well-known visiting scholar to lunch and had had too much to drink. In Anglo-Saxon class, this probably meant less than it would have in the writing class I describe. In the writing class, such a breach would have an immediate, and lasting, impact on the quality of the writing the students produce. The securing frame would have a crack in it, a crack that would draw attention from the vital activity inside the frame.

Recently a colleague who has worked hard and successfully in adopting my writing course pedagogy in a course of her own phoned me about a problem. She told me she had canceled one session of her weekly writing class so she could attend a conference. Because of this break, she told me, the class lost its momentum, the quality of the writing plunged and she felt she had to start over again. Even when students welcome a break in routine, as my colleague told me her students did in this case, the break will likely compromise the environment that leads to the best work. Frame breaks in the form of illness, professional obligations, and unforeseen circumstances occur, and we must deal with the consequences as best we can. The inevitable consequences of frame breaks show us how important the frame is.

Students always challenge the frame. The frame challenge has a hidden purpose: to make sure the securing limit provided by the frame is really there. The attacks, or attempts to "destroy the object" that I described in the previous section are often tests of the frame. While the teacher should not retaliate, the teacher should preserve the frame. Here is an example.

Student: I have a lot to do next week. I have two tests and an essay due in other courses. Is it okay if I don't hand in an assignment next week? I'll hand in two assignments the week after.

Teacher: No. You must hand in an assignment every week. There are always a lot of things to do besides these assignments. My work with writing students shows that they develop most when they work regularly. So I want you to hand in an assignment next week. You may not have as much time to spend on it as you would like. You may have to write it faster, but you may learn something from that. And you can revise it later. Hand in your assignment next week.

Through careful experiments, I have learned that the compassionate response is one that maintains the course frame. By maintaining the integrity of the frame the teacher is most likely to create and maintain a space where the student can work productively and balance the competing demands the world makes on a person's resources. When the teacher allows that space to be compromised, the teacher treats that space as though it has little value. The fact is that space may offer one of the most valuable opportunities the student may ever have. Some students arrive at university without much sense for boundaries or protected space. These are likely students who, because of unfavorable circumstances in their pre-university lives, may not have experienced boundaried potential space before in their lives. Their impulse is to test it, in part because they may fear it and in part because they may want to make sure it is really there. They may be the ones who, when this space is treated with respect and protected, will profit from it most.

When I conceptualize the frame in the writing course I teach, I see more in it than rules and procedures. Some aspects of the course operate in an illusory way. I have already noted Winnicott's emphasis on the role of illusion in creating the potential space: the caregiver presents an illusion of safety and coherence that the caregiver cannot really give. The parent promises the child that the parent will protect the child from external threats. Parents know life may present circumstances that render this promise empty. However, the illusion is useful because it fosters the child's ability to develop. There is an equivalent in the writing course. I give forty-minute lectures about writing in every class. These lectures are the firmest, most predictable part of the course experience. Yet, I know even as I lecture, that writing, like life, is a slippery business and that what I say about it in my lectures could be successfully contradicted by a knowledgeable sceptic. That does not mean I lie in my lectures. I do my best to lay out principles that help most of the people most of the time. But I know these principles are fallible. I see the students seize on the principles and hold on to them as markers in otherwise unmapped terrain.

I interviewed one very successful student who went on to become a successful writer and editor. She told me "the technical direction" in the course "served as an anchor; the writing technology meant I was en route to something besides the swirl of thoughts in my mind." The point is that the lectures, disguised as solid course content that give students a partly illusory sense of security and solidity about writing, are actually a part of the course frame. The lectures are part of the frame because they, like the rules and procedures, serve to insulate course activity from the chaotic world around it. The real content for the course is not in the lectures; the students provide the real content in their writing. When students become autonomous writers—the successful outcome of this teaching —they move naturally to an appreciation of the nerve-racking complexity of writing. The frame, even as illusion, provides necessary security for the personal development that it takes to produce a good writer. The frame offers a time-out from the world as it is; students use this time-out to gather their strength.

9. Conclusion

Other instructors with quite different personalities from mine have applied "expressive writing" pedagogy with results that confirm the outcomes of my trials. And just as Winnicott's theories about infant development illuminate other kinds of development at other times of life, "expressive writing" pedagogy has been adapted successfully to various situations. I and others have applied this pedagogy in community literacy workshops, in elementary school and high school, in the communications segment of a high-powered MBA program, and in seminars for university professors. A colleague at Queens University uses a form of this pedagogy to teach professional ethics at the Queens University Law School. The Department of Psychiatry at the University of Toronto has arranged for a "narrative competency" (another name for this pedagogy) workshop for faculty members that may lead to trials to assess its value in medical education. Winnicott was a psychoanalyst, and his theories grow out of his work as a clinician. Most psychoanalytic theorists focus on pathology. Winnicott's emphasis on healthy development makes his work particularly appropriate to understanding health-giving learning. However, my reliance on a psychoanalytic theory to illuminate this pedagogy does not suggest that teachers should in any way act as therapists with their students. The good-enough teacher must know and respect this boundary, an important part of the securing frame. When students, as rarely happens, present non-writing issues that call for professional help, I refer them to the university health service. Learning, because it may be therapeutic, must not to be confounded with therapy.

Winnicott, like Lacan, assumes "that the subject comes into be(ing) in the field of the Other" (Flax, 1990, p. 126). Yet unlike Lacan, who argues that the presence of the other produces alienation from self and other, Winnicott sees the good-enough other who offers the good-enough environment as setting the minimal conditions for the subject's development of capacities for both autonomy and connection. To the extent that my observations of university students learning to write may be considered a form of clinical observation, Winnicott's predictions about the impact of environmental factors on development appear to be confirmed, especially in a writing course where communication, a form of connection between self and others, lies at the heart of the enterprise. Lacan's portrayal of the self estranged by culture and by the presence of the other seems to describe students' relationship to academic life so long as they perceive this environment as an unsafe place for their authentic selves. The discourse of students who present artificial constructed selves to their professors is alienated, defensive discourse designed to protect the True Self from the threat presented by the other.

While the argument I have presented here applies most directly to university writing courses, Winnicott's theories of development offer rich theory for teachers at all levels who are ready to consider the psychological and nonrational factors that condition development and learning. If the teacher is "one who ought to know," the nonrational dimension of teaching and learning is something the teacher ought to know about.

Psychoanalytic theories, because they address the underlying complex of factors that cause people to do what they do, offer teachers a way of understanding the learning, or the lack of it, that takes place in their classrooms. In particular, psychoanalytic theories show us how the performance of learners may depend on factors that seem remote from the material or the skill being learned.

Winnicott presents an understanding of interpersonal dynamics that applies directly to the interaction of teacher and student. Winnicott's "facilitating environment" describes conditions that a conscientious and knowledgeable teacher can reproduce. These conditions make a safe space for the student's authentic self, see the teacher become a collaborative partner in learning, and set a well-defined frame to secure the "play" that enables development of the authentic self. Winnicott has given us a theory of development that applies well beyond the writing class to all learning situations. The specifics will vary.

The "good-enough" teacher will experiment to discover how these principles apply to specific courses. Courses usually repeat from year to year with many variables held constant. This repetition creates a good framework for experimentation. I have found that by the fourth repetition of a course my experiments begin to yield good information about the factors that produce a "facilitating environment" for learners in that setting. The cumulative impact of experiment and observation can yield a highly effective learning environment—as well as insight into human nature.

Whatever we teach we deal in human relationships. We reward our students and ourselves when we make these relationships as effective as possible. To do this, we need to understand a great deal more than our subject matter.

Works Cited

Allen, Guy. (2000) "Language, Power and Consciousness: A Writing Experiment at the University of Toronto." In Charles Anderson and Marian MacCurdy, eds., *Writing and Healing: Toward an Informed Practice*. Urbana, Ill.: NCTE. Pp. 249-290.

Allen, Guy., ed. (1989) *No More Masterpieces: Short Prose by New Writers*. Toronto: Canadian Scholars' Press.

Bollas, Christopher. (1993) "The Aesthetic Moment and the Search for Transformation." In *Transitional Objects and Potential Spaces: Literary Uses of D.W. Winnicott*. Ed.

P. L. Rudnytsky. New York: Columbia University Press. Pp. 40-49.

Britton, James N. (1970) *Language and Learning.* London: Penguin.

Chong, Nancy, Martha Kofie, and Kwanza Msingwana. (1993) *Only Mountains Never Meet: A Collection of Stories by Three New Writers.* Toronto: Well Versed Publications.

DeBassige, Mary Lou. (1989) "Lakeview Indian Day School." In Allen, ed. *No More Masterpieces: Short Prose by New Writers.* Pp. 41-44.

Flax, Jane. (1990) *Thinking Fragments: Psychoanalysis, Feminism, and Postmodernism in the Contemporary West.* Berkeley: University of California Press.

Garrison, Roger H. (1981) *One-to-One: Making Writing Instruction Effective: Instructor's Manual to Accompany Garrison's How a Writer Works.* New York: Harper & Row.

Lacan, Jacques. (1953-1954) *Le Séminaire: Livre 1: Les Écrits techniques de Freud, 1953-1954.* Paris: Éditions de Seuil.

Lee, Jennifer. (1996) "Going to Chinese School." In *The Totally Unknown Writers Festival: 1996; Stories.* Toronto: Life Rattle Press. Pp. 8-21.

Rudnytsky, Peter L., ed. (1993) *Transitional Objects and Potential Spaces: Literary Uses of D. W. Winnicott.* New York: Columbia University Press.

Rudnytsky, Peter L (1993a) "Introduction." In Rudnytsky, ed. (1993), *Transitional Objects and Potential Spaces: Literary Uses of D.W. Winnicott,* pp. xi-xxii.

Tirrell, Mary Kay, Gordon M. Pradl, John Warnock, and James Britton. (1990) "Re-presenting James Britton: A Symposium," *College Composition and Communication.* 41, pp. 166-186. Quoted in Wyatt-Brown (1993).

Usuelli, Alamatea Kluzer. (1992) "The Significance of Illusion in the Work of Freud and Winnicott: A Controversial Issue," *International Review of Psychoanalysis,* 19. Pp. 179-187.

Winnicott, D.W. (1958) "The Capacity to Be Alone." In Winnicott (1965), *The Maturational Processes and the Facilitating Environment: Studies in the Theory of Emotional Development,* pp. 29-36.

_____. (1960) "Ego Distortion in Terms of True and False Self." In Winnicott (1965), *The Maturational Processes and the Facilitating Environment,* pp. 140-152.

_____. (1962) "Ego Integration in Child Development." In Winnicott (1965), *The Maturational Processes and the Facilitating Environment*, pp. 56-63.

_____. (1963) "Communicating and Not Communicating Leading to a Study of Certain Opposites." In Winnicott (1965), *The Maturational Processes and the Facilitating Environment*, pp. 179-192.

_____ (1965) *The Maturational Processes and the Facilitating Environment: Studies in the Theory of Emotional Development*. London: Hogarth Press.

_____. (1967) "The Location of Cultural Experience." In Winnicott, *Playing and Reality* (1971), pp. 95-103.

_____. (1969) "The Use of an Object and Relating Through Identifications." In Winnicott, *Playing and Reality* (1971), pp. 86-94.

_____. (1971) *Playing and Reality*. London: Tavistock Publications.

_____. (1971a) "The Place Where We Live." In Winnicott, *Playing and Reality* (1971), pp. 104-110.

_____. (1971b) "Playing: Creative Activity and the Search for Self." In Winnicott, *Playing and Reality* (1971), pp. 53-64.

_____. (1971c) "Playing: A Theoretical Statement." In Winnicott, *Playing and Reality* (1971), pp. 38-52.

Wyatt-Brown, Anne M. (1993) "From the Clinic to the Classroom: D. W. Winnicott, James Britton, and the Revolution in Writing Theory." In Rudnytsky, ed. (1993), *Transitional Objects and Potential Spaces: Literary Uses of D.W. Winnicott*, pp. 292-303.

Seven

TEACHING THROUGH DISCUSSION

Jeffrey Tlumak

In this chapter, I will present seven interconnected sets of recommendations for promoting effective discussion in the classroom and offer some concrete ways of applying them. Much of what I suggest is supported by empirical research and the testimony of colleagues, but I have also tested each proposal repeatedly myself.[1] Teaching through discussion is a methodological approach to generating a critical, reflective, and dynamic classroom environment that is applicable to general education. While I will draw on examples from my discipline of philosophy, the organizational strategies and techniques offered here may be adapted for use in any discipline with respect to course focus and subject matter.

I begin with the first class session. My attitude toward what I do at a first class meeting has evolved over the years. Although I still take seriously my obligation to make a contract with students by previewing the overall character of the course and specifying requirements and main objectives, I have noticed the benefits of moving away from the kind of elaborate, detailed overview I used to provide. I used to construct an elegant outline of issues and their logical interrelations—largely submitting to the natural propensity to control and impress early under conditions of anxious uncertainty—but aside from the fact that such an outline means very little to students at that stage of the proceedings, it already exemplifies a certain pattern of interaction that I want to discourage and so should not dominantly exhibit; it is generally not enough to just tell the students that I want certain things but then exemplify the opposite behavior. To introduce students to my procedural aims by professing commitment to active discussion yet immediately proceed to devote the bulk of my first session to some huge outline already places students in a relatively passive position with respect to me. So I now from the start exemplify the atmosphere that I am trying to promote, and plan a first class with as pain-staking an eye to motivating involvement as to responsibly informing students of substantive course content.

If you centrally aim to help students acquire factual and non-applied conceptual knowledge, then motivating involvement through discussion is not vital, since lecture and discussion are roughly equally effective, at least with highly-motivated, high-achieving students with digital and auditory talents. And admittedly lecture is a quicker and less risky way to cover material. But discussion is superior in developing problem-solving skills, in achieving affective objectives such as changing attitudes and developing interests, in helping students to transfer knowledge to new situations, in strengthening retention, and in motivating further learning. In general, discussion is especially appropriate for higher-order cognitive objectives: application, analysis, synthesis, and evaluation. The challenge is to balance structure and openness. While I provide an outline of my procedural methodology in an appendix, I will give a detailed account of my approach to teaching through discussion in what follows.

1. Objectives for the First Day of Class

I list eight desiderata for a first class meeting to help improve a discussion-oriented course, and then elaborate on some of them. At my first meeting, I want to achieve, among other things, the following eight goals:

(1) Break the ice; reduce tensions. It seems to me a mistake to underestimate potential student anxiety. If I am nervous, and I have been doing this for over twenty-five years, then they will likely be nervous as well.

(2) Begin to diagnose background knowledge, beliefs and general cognitive tendencies. After all, people learn on the basis of what they already know or at least believe; those background dispositions provide the skeleton or anchor on which you develop new material. To the extent that early on I can have a partial fix on where these particular students are coming from, to that extent I can adapt my own presentation more effectively.

(3) Begin to form a community of inquirers. This is largely a social task. If you really want to promote interaction, then there are certain physical and social arrangements that will work better than others.

(4) Generate curiosity and a sense of anticipation. Relatedly, I am increasingly struck by how significantly a teacher's enthusiasm and excitement—emotions tend to be contagious—together with a kind of intellectual integrity and a personal concern (signified even by little things like quickly learning students' names and referring back to the student when using his or her input), contribute to joint classroom inquiry. At a recent, student-sponsored dinner for favorite faculty, I was struck by the recurring theme of optimistic concern in student testimonials.

(5) Elicit some provisional positions for subsequent analysis and evaluation. I want students right away to put something on the table that is theirs, so that in a weak sense they have something at stake and have begun to invest in the course process. But this should not be a threatening commitment; it is one of my central goals is to have a decidedly low-risk first encounter. Even so, I want them to have something which provides a starting point which they can then hark back to later when certain other issues come up. Given the limits of

memory, it is a challenge to record everyone's perspectives. But there are ready devices for meeting that challenge, such as a diagnostic questionnaire I will characterize shortly. Students submit the completed questionnaire to me, I keep copies to enable memorization of response-patterns, and then throughout the semester I can invoke their initial commitments as we explore issues more deeply. This kind of tool for fostering ongoing intellectual re-examination has repeatedly worked very effectively.

(6) Generate low risk interaction. One way I do this is to stress sincerely— and I never say anything I don't mean; it would be blameworthy to set someone up for a certain frame of mind and then do something else afterwards which beats him or her down—that this ongoing use of their early responses is overridingly a tool of intellectual house-cleaning or self-examination, not my effort to change their minds in some antecedently preferred way.

(7) Exemplify, not just describe desired procedure, as I mentioned earlier.

(8) Phrase responses in encouraging ways. I don't want to be overly nice about this sort of thing, but it seems to me to make a difference what words you use when you respond to a student's question. For example, when I started teaching my habitual, earnest, enthusiastic response to nearly every student contribution had the form, "yes, but." I would acknowledge with the "yes" then immediately withdraw the experienced affirmation with the "but." Or I used to say "look, I want you to interrupt me anytime." Interruption violates conversational etiquette, so my word-choice at least mildly discouraged interruption. Now I'll use a connotatively positive phrase like "contribute anytime." Especially compared to other, more crucial matters, I don't want to exaggerate the importance of non-inhibiting word-choices, but it seems to me that in subtle ways all of these things taken together make a difference.

Now that I have offered eight behaviors I aim to incorporate in every first class-session, here are a few effective ways to achieve these goals. The first is to have students fill out information index cards, which include basic infor- mation such as their preferred means of communicating with me outside of class (phone or email), but more importantly, information that enables me to contour my efforts to each new class. Minimally, I ask them to specify relevant back- ground and concurrent course work, convey their central goals and interests, and what the optimal class substantively would be like for them. I also ask students to provide outstanding teaching tips given their past educational experiences, and inform me at their discretion of any additional, special facts about them individually as learners or people (I urge them to include learning disabilities so that I can make special accommodations).

The first time I invited this input I did it as a kind of public nod to my concern for them, but then I filed it away in a drawer and didn't responsibly use it. Now I helpfully chart, regularly review, and use it in small but effective ways.

You obviously cannot radically transform a course in light of this guidance, but there are many ways in which, explicitly, so that the student knows that you are being responsive, you can adapt what you would do.

For example, if I have some English majors in my modern philosophy class, I will stress certain things and use certain altogether apt illustrations that I would nevertheless likely fail to highlight otherwise. Or I will use input to achieve early rapport, as when one student humorously wrote, "serve cakes and pies whenever possible," and so I came marching in next class with a bowl of cookies, jokingly bemoaning the fact that while I much wanted to be responsive, on my salary I couldn't afford cakes and pies, but hoped less expensive cookies would satisfy. This sort of early personalized exchange is especially valuable to me because I tend to be intense and earnest when I teach, so no matter how good I feel in my heart there are other aspects of my behavior which make me prone, for example, to intimidate more than I want. And since under "teaching tips" students sometimes recount their most ruinous (suffering with an uncontrolled, self-indulgent monopolizer all term, feeling humiliated by sarcasm, etc.) as well as most memorable learning situations, you are preemptively alerted to some of the most important insights as teacher. The information card, if taken seriously, can genuinely help.

A second device I have used to fulfill the early conditions for a successful, discussion-oriented class is the low-risk questionnaire. Different questionnaires would naturally be appropriate for different classes of mine and obviously for yours, but the rationale for use is transferable. Since I include a heavy component of value theory in my introductory class, I begin with an ethics questionnaire, which I have crafted over the years, and which serves several valuable functions (see Appendix 2).

First, the questionnaire provides an occasion for students to start talking in a very low-risk environment. I stress that my current concern is not to have them mount a strong defense or even elaborate explanation of their positions—there will be plenty of time and enhanced skills to defend things later—for now I just solicit their opinions, reflective or unreflective, tutored or untutored. And people generally enjoy giving their cost-free opinions. So right away virtually everybody has opened their mouth by the end of the first period.

Second, the questionnaire is really very carefully crafted in a few ways. Statements are arranged so as to exhibit a pattern. Many students have inconsistent views, so you don't get a clear pattern, but that's important to know too. But after I see a certain pattern of responses I might say to myself, "this person is an act utilitarian who is confidently liberal on most social issues," and so on for different patterns and different views. I know what their antecedent position is. Since I want this exercise to be low-risk, I don't expose these kinds of tensions yet, but in fact, there are mine fields throughout this questionnaire.

For example, the first statement says, "what is right is what society says is right." The second says, "what is right is what God wills." Several students agree to both of these. Now eventually I'll be able to show them some tensions between these views, in a constructive, non-damaging way. Or one later item affirms that everyone always ultimately acts out of self-interest, while another asserts that everyone should always act out of self-interest. Probing and relating these two claims will later offer opportunity to discuss some important relations between human nature and psychology on the one hand, and moral theory on the other.

I will shortly urge use of a kind of modified debate format, and it is important for this format to work well that I get roughly a fifty-fifty disagreement among class members on the issue to be debated, and the questionnaire provides me that sort of information as well. For example, I often effectively focus on psychological egoism, the claim of universal self-interest. Usually the majority think it is true, but a hefty minority disagree. So now I know that later on I can use the issue of egoism as an example for some other technique. Again, it gives me a lot of information about student backgrounds.

2. Organizational Suggestions for the First Week

A few additional points about the first week. When you have a lot of discussion, you are often accused of being less well-organized, and indeed on my own early course evaluations, my lowest ratings, relatively speaking, were always on "course organization" (as well as "promotes imagination"). Now if there is one feature of my personality that is incontestable it is that I am a very organized guy; the point is, given their implicit definition of pedagogical organization, I may have seemed ill-organized to the extent that I was always having spontaneous discussion. So I learned that I have to employ a very explicit ongoing framework, of which I recurrently remind them, so that they know what I knew all along, that our inquiries really are well-organized.

The same with the issue of imagination. I always got very high ratings on promotion of critical thinking, but noticeably lower ratings on promotion of imagination. It turns out that students tend to understand imagination in a certain way, paradigmatically like what they exercise in certain kinds of literature courses, but I want to show them that many of the same things that I am honing in developing critical thinking are also instances of nurturing imagination. I have discovered that it is never enough to just say this. For example, I often point out to them that if I am teaching how to give counter-examples to generalizations, that is a method of imagining scenarios, constructing thought-experiments, an effort of the imagination. But you can't just say it. What you have got to do is constantly model the skill, the relations between the skills, explicitly talk about what they are in relation to one another, have them practice it, and so on.

There are two final organizational mechanisms that I introduce in the first week, but not the first class because I don't want to overwhelm them, and both with an eye to enabling maximally productive discussion. First, I distribute a single sheet which includes every good and bad mode of reasoning that I am going to use the whole semester. There are many rules, bad and good, that you learn in a logic class that are virtually never used in real life at all; you can get all the ones that people really use on one sheet. I can generate a sense of expectation of mastery when I vouch for the power of these rules, assuring them right up front, "we will recurrently use this, but I want you to know now that when you master these skills of logic you will master all the ones you need to do a wonderful job in this course." It is something that they can use over and over again, at home and in class. It is a cohering device; it in itself provides a kind of additional organization that might not have existed otherwise.

A second orienting, guiding and coherence-preserving tool is a manageable list of critical questions (and distinctions) to ask about course materials that will be used in homework and classroom activities. Here are some general questions: (1) What's the main point?; (2) Is there unclarity or ambiguity?; (3) What are the reasons for the position?; (4) Are the reasons good?; (5) Is there missing evidence or hidden assumptions?; and (6) Does the position have desirable or worrisome implications or consequences? This is a recurrent procedural demand that they know is another element which helps organize the course, substantive foci aside.

Whatever topics I choose to stress in a given semester, I am always committed to empowering my students by helping develop their critical thinking skills, and such development is largely a matter of orchestrating activities to continuously stimulate students to express as explicitly and articulately as possible, and to take seriously, their own and others' thinking: what is at issue, what it assumes, what it implies, what it includes, excludes, highlights, and foreshadows, what are its alternatives, etc.; and to help the student do this with intellectual humility, courage, empathy, perseverance, and fairmindedness.

Without weighing the class down with concentrated doses of lexicon, I think it good to gradually habituate students to make their thinking explicit by using and having them use analytic terms such as "claims," "assumes," "implies," "infers," "concludes," "is supported by," "is consistent with," "is relevant to," "is irrelevant to," "is credible," "is plausible," "is clear," "is in need of analysis," "is in need of verification," "is well-confirmed," "is empirical," "is conceptual," "is a judgment of value," "is a matter of opinion," "is a matter of fact," "is theoretical," "is hypothetical," "is settled," "is at issue," "is problematic," "is analogous," "is biased," "is loaded," "is a point of view," "is a frame of reference," etc.[2]

3. Recommendations for Promoting Effective Discussion: Having an Object of Joint Focus

I now leave strategies especially tied to the very beginning of the semester to present my other six sets of recommendations for promoting effective discussion. The second set can be subsumed under the advice to have an object of joint focus. I have found that the following five practices well-serve this goal.

First, a public blackboard (or object such as a painting, film clip, enactment of a role, experiment, etc.) seems to work better than a private handout, and I say this as a committed devotee of handouts for various other purposes (including even conscience-soothing, so that when I think I did something inadequately, I can discharge my guilt by distributing the remedying handout; here the less self-indulgent benefit is that students see you struggling to improve as well, and take the in-process nature of inquiry, of which discussion is a natural component, more to heart). But for promoting discussion, I find that using a handout (with a different sheet in each person's hands) tends to generate greater passivity and diffusion of effort than having a focal, public object of attention on the board.

Second, read (or have someone else—not too quickly—read) the text out loud. I have always done this, but I have become increasingly impressed at how powerful it can be to read slowly through a manageable portion of text with students. Then stop and talk about each sentence. This not only helps students learn to read a text better, but allows the kind of focus which invites good and relevant discussion. To hark back to an earlier desideratum, it too helps form a community of inquirers.

Third, use an explicitly exhibited, *prima facie* tempting but multiply challengeable (in terms of logic, missing premises, contestable, stated premises, potentially unwelcome implications, masked presuppositions, etc.) argument, considered step by step, to structure an entire class-session. Besides directly obliging their questions and objections, students are more relaxed about pursuing even more tangential confusions and curiosities when they have a vital core of material securely recorded. Some such structuring or initial setup is necessary to have the most profitable discussions. I first learned this when several years ago, intoxicated by my perceived increased success in leading discussion, I went whole hog and decided to have the ideal, pure discussion class. Using "the more the merrier" maxim, I would come into my intro class, say something important and provocative, and then expect fireworks. For example: "Everyone has a right to do whatever he or she wants with his or her own mind and body, so long as no one else is harmed. What do you think?" This was the biggest flop of my teaching career. You can offer this sort of unbounded invitation occasionally—in the context of some recognized, ongoing, organizing project—but more often than not, there should be some preparation or groundwork for the discussion.

This is true for a variety of reasons, some of which will come out later, including the fact that most people don't think that quickly. If you do not give them an opportunity to figure out where they are going to stand, no matter how interesting the issue is, most don't want to venture an opinion, especially because, as I will point out shortly, there are lots of risks of various sorts in saying anything in a class. Also, students justifiably resent discussions in which they are expected to profit primarily from the half-baked ideas of other students.

Fourth, small group preparations often work wonders in nurturing high-quality discussion; using one early (when enhanced social cohesion is still a premium) but not at the very beginning (when many students are likely to be less trusting of more intimate, freer exchanges) of a semester seems to pay especially high dividends in spawning subsequent discussion. Many students who were not prone to say anything in my class would talk animatedly and intelligently with peers in student groups (with three to five members), and then would be sufficiently loosened up to be readier to talk in the larger, total class group as well. (The evidence indicates that brainstorming possible questions, possible solutions, etc. also works better in subgroups than in the whole group.) For example, in the second week of my modern philosophy class (average enrollment of 35), when I get to the second of Descartes's meditations I instruct students to get into groups of four or five, study the six concluding paragraphs that represent the so-called "wax passage," and answer two central questions (about Descartes's main aims and route to those aims). I tell them that each group must achieve some reportable consensus; eventually I will allow individuals to air minority views, but initially I don't want to hear anything about them, but want participants to negotiate so that they can all feel comfortable with what they report to the entire class. Yet they must negotiate under strictly imposed time constraints (generally half an hour), as if they were a corporate board obliged to make a consequential business decision by firm deadline. I casually eavesdrop on but studiously refrain from intervening in group conversations, and am frankly often amazed at how probing and cooperative the discussions are.

I also require each group to choose a spokesperson. The spokesperson will introduce the other group members and state the consensus-position. Next and importantly, I require each subsequent spokesperson to take into account what each previous group concluded. So each has to pay careful attention to (perhaps jot notes on) what colleagues have said. One of my goals, always—a goal surprisingly hard to achieve consistently—is to really get students to talk to each other and not just talk to me. On occasion I have flatly said, "Don't even look at me; I'm not here for discussion today; I am just a board monitor; I am not going to say anything." They are still apt to face toward me instead of each other. But there are ways to break this habit. One way in the present context is to oblige spokespersons to edit their presentations explicitly in light of preceding ones, specifying points of agreement and disagreement, identifying entirely new points, etc. It then becomes natural (and if not, I unobtrusively induce them) to look at their predecessors, identify them by name in prelude to reaffirming or repudiating their accounts, attend with greater precision (and so intellectual respect) to the separable components of those accounts, and so on. The benefits accrue most to those most heavily burdened, namely later and later contributors for whom there is ever deeper water under the bridge.

Fifth is the previously-mentioned, modified debate. Here is an example of how the format works. I put the statement, "everyone always ultimately acts out of self-interest," on the board, and then ask students physically to sit on different sides of the room, facing each other, depending upon whether they agree or disagree, and those who cannot decide occupy some physical middle ground. I then ask them (2) not to debate in the classical way, where the aim is to score points as quickly and as effectively as possible, come what may, but (2) to argue their position as sincerely and vigorously as they can, (3) to openly acknowledge the force of opposing considerations, (4) articulate doubts about their own evidence, and (5) generally strive to follow the weight of argument wherever it in process leads them. So if even momentarily, they have judgment-suspending doubts or a change of heart, they are to move physically to the undecided position or other side of the room. They should feel free to move more than once. Aside from its various intellectual benefits, this exercise typically generates a tremendous amount of camaraderie (unlike standard debates). I can't tell you how delightful it is when the first person gets up and walks to a changed location (especially if that person has spoken with some conviction earlier) and everybody laughs and applauds.

A final, lovely use of the modified debate is to manifestly exhibit the power of good-willed discussion and simultaneously model writing paradigms in your field by composing papers in outline from resources produced solely through their unassisted efforts. So while my students debate the truth of psychological egoism, I as silent recorder sketch, pairwise when possible, all the relevant considerations, pro and con, they offer. I end the debate so as to leave myself about fifteen minutes at the end of the session to trace out as perspicuously and unbrokenly as I can just the kind of argumentative essay I seek optimally from them. Again, I stress to them that I composed the essays by well-organizing materials that they, not I, created.

4. Types and Uses of Questions

Skilled use of various types of questions is my third, and obviously very important category of procedures for fostering educative discussion. There are lots of ways of classifying questions. The most familiar advice is to ask questions at a variety of (allegedly) increasingly sophisticated cognitive levels, eliciting recollection of fact, comprehension in the form of paraphrase or translation, application of concept or principle to a new case or circumstance, analysis of concepts or theses into component parts, organization or synthesis of elements in a new (for the student) structure, judgment based on data or evidence, etc. We are also sensibly told (for most of our fields) to ask questions of different fundamental sorts, including empirical, conceptual, normative, preferential, metaphysical or deeply presuppositional, and so on.[3] Or we might distinguish question-types as exploratory (What are the "facts"?; What went wrong?; What can be done?); challenging or testing (Is the solution adequate?; Are others possible?); contextual, designed to broaden perspective and help tie things together (How is this solution like or different from that one?; What kinds of solution do we have?); prioritizing (Which is the best solution?; Why?); concluding and conceptualizing (What have we learned?; What are the principles involved in the choices we made?); etc.

One practically valuable classification scheme that may not be so familiar organizes the dynamics of questioning according to two variables: range of permitted answers—some questions only have one right answer, others a few acceptable answers, still others indefinitely many acceptable answers—and range of addressees—one individual, a subgroup, the whole class, and so on—and then the various permutations among these two dimensions.[4] One might distinguish between (1) hot-seat questions, directed to an individual with just one or a few acceptable answers; (2) toss-up questions (as on the old GE College Bowl), directed to a group with just one or a few acceptable answers; (3) inviter questions, directed to an individual but with many acceptable answers; and (4) free-fire questions, directed to a group and having many acceptable answers.

Each of us may have moral or personal reasons for shying away from some types of questions and welcoming others. But every one of these types have an appropriate role. A hot-seat question can build confidence in a student who needs bolstering if it is at the right level. On the other hand, it risks driving a student away. I tend to avoid them as initiators of discussion (I confess to some moral discomfort with their use in that role), but do use them as follow-up probes to a student's freely volunteered and seemingly genuinely engaged contribution. But I do not aim to downgrade intrinsically this or any other type of question; I just want to point out how important or risky they might be at a certain juncture in your teaching. So, for example, it is a serious mistake to make a toss-up question either too easy or too hard. If it is too easy, people who readily know the answer are nevertheless understandably reluctant to give it, since they fear condemnation by peers as a nerd or a brown-nose. This is not surmise, ask students! Obviously, if it is too hard it's no good either. It's even better if the teacher lacks a definitive answer to a toss-up. Since if the teacher knows the answer then there is the danger of the undesirable setup in which the instructor's implicit, inhibiting message is, "I have something in mind, can you guess what's right? No, you're wrong. No, you're wrong too. No." But if it's something you don't know how to answer yourself, that generates much better discussion. Then they won't get slapped down.

Inviters impose some pressure, but there is safety in their open-endedness. And free-fires tend to instigate the most discussion. It is worthwhile to note that posing questions in certain orders tend to be counterproductive. For example, it is a bad idea to follow an easy toss-up question with a difficult hot-seat question, because you penalize the contributor. Suppose that you ask, "Who did so-and-so?", and someone helps out and volunteers the answer, and then instead of rewarding you penalize that person by saying, "If you can answer that, how about this one (that you're unlikely to handle)?" You can imagine the volunteer silently resolving, "I will never do that again!" I am just hinting at such pitfalls, but it is striking when you read the empirical research how such little things make big differences.

5. Taking Account of Cognitive and Motivational Psychology

A fourth set of recommendations for promoting effective discussion requires taking account of cognitive and motivational psychology. Reconsider questioning for a moment. When a student asks a question, there are several stages to the process: (1) identifying the need to ask; (2) deciding whether it is legitimate to ask; (3) getting the attention and permission to ask; (4) asking; and (5) dealing with potentially unpredictable responses. There are dangers and opportunities for doing good for your students at each stage. Remember that as the student pauses to determine the need to ask, things are moving on. Usually, you have to take some time to think about what you want to ask. Then by the time you figure out whether or not you want to ask something, you may wonder if it is legitimate to ask. Are you too late? Was it answered earlier and you forgot? And so on.

Most advice about teacher response is obvious enough. Make clear you've heard and appreciated the question (but not by regularly paraphrasing it, as if the student can never satisfactorily formulate it on his or her own—though you can constructively specify that you are adapting the question for your own purposes); don't deflate by brusquely saying things like, "As I said earlier" (if you had only been listening), etc. Perhaps less obvious is that any verbal response by you slows down an up-and-running class discussion (I have seen great teachers sustain and direct discussions by subtle body language, especially gentle head and eye gestures), and that in order to build momentum sometimes the less said early in discussion the better. Less obvious still, in my judgment, is the prudence to honor the depth of a penetrating question by *not* attempting an answer, but leaving perplexity, or revealing puzzlement about a similar question.

I suspect that my psychologically-grounded view about the use of devil's advocacy is controversial. I used to play devil's advocate often; indeed, generally, one thing I try to do during the course of a semester is to exhibit clearly every role that is part of the integrated activity that constitutes doing philosophy. Sometimes I try to exhibit vividly sympathetic understanding, careful and caring understanding; sometimes sustained criticism; sometimes integration or synthesis of seemingly disparate ideas, and so on. We know that all these get joined together in actual intellectual exploration, but I try to isolate these activities as well, to show them how to perform them. As part of my effort to hone critical skills, I would play the devil's advocate, but I wouldn't identify my role as such. I would just do it. Only afterwards I would point out, if the need arose, that I was playing devil's advocate. I now think this is a mistake, even a kind of moral mistake. That is, I think that if you are going to play devil's advocate you should specify your intentions in advance. Otherwise, you in effect immunize yourself from being wrong, and you thereby cheapen the process and cheapen the truth. You leave yourself the excuse to say, "I don't have to defend anymore because I was only making-believe; I was just toying with you and now I'm just going to retract." On the other hand, if you are up front about your role, devil's advocacy is an excellent educational technique.

Application of other psychological truths serves to expand and enrich discussion. Learning occurs best when immediate usefulness exists, and people tend to acquire stably only the knowledge they seek and value. One example of how I have adapted those insights to my own teaching is that I've shifted heavily away from my initial teaching strategy of presenting the full array of alternative theories and then trying to apply them to concrete worries and cases, to more often going in the other direction. I now try to generate a felt need for theory through confrontation with a problem that does not seem resolvable otherwise. Then one can bring theory in on the white horse, to save the day; the student has an immediate, felt incentive for mastering theory.

Some other sound advice based on cognitive or motivational psychology includes these: Link the familiar with the new, current interests with interests to be created. Give students a feeling of accomplishment. Say when you think material is more difficult, but express confidence that the group can benefit and succeed anyway. Achievement motivation is highest when one's estimated chance of success is approximately fifty-fifty.

The impact on motivating discussion by placing oneself squarely and with intellectual integrity within the community of inquirers is far greater than I once expected. Two practices that I have found particularly meaningful are acknowledging and explaining changes of mind, especially if student-induced, and admitting one doesn't know something, that the search for knowledge sometimes proceeds haltingly, etc. One of the most beautiful moments in my teaching career—and similar things have happened over the years—occurred when I was arguing about John Locke's account of freedom in my Modern Philosophy class. I was arguing a point I had developed over the years, which I firmly thought was correct. One especially persistent student was resisting and arguing in a different position. It was a good-natured dispute, valuable in its own right. But I left the session and thought hard about the issue again that night, and like a moment of epiphany, I realized, this student is right! It was very exciting because it systematically and positively affected other components of my understanding of Locke. And so with genuine, not calculated enthusiasm, I came to the next class meeting and said, "I thought about this some more, and you were right, and let me explain why." I had other plans for that day but spent the whole day just explaining in great detail why I was wrong, exactly how I now came to see that I was wrong, and why this was right, and its significant implications.

I learned later that the students took this to be one of the high points not only of my course, but of any course they had ever taken. Pivotal was the fact that I was part of this community of inquiries, and not only acknowledged that I had made a mistake, but gave due credit, devoting a whole class to the student's valued contribution. Similar benefits accrue to admitting when you don't know something (but will take steps to come to know).

A final suggestion for employing psychological theory, but in this instance I have not adequately tested it myself. Test the benefits of using influential cognitive development schemes to better understand the possibly varying perspectives of your students. One often-touted scheme is Perry's, on which the student matures from (1) learn true-false from the teacher, to (2) authorities disagree relativism (everyone has a right to his or her own opinion), to (3) learn criteria for better and worse opinions, to (4) rational commitment in spite of uncertainty. For that matter, there are a host of schemes that fascinate, some focusing on non-cognitive instead of or in addition to cognitive styles (Myers-Briggs; visual vs. auditory vs. kinesthetic vs. digital dominant learning styles; etc.) My own resistance here is not to the theories, but with their feasible application. For suppose I know that my class is evenly divided among learning styles. That would perhaps dictate, on considerations of fairness, allowing each group the opportunity to operate from their special strength, so my use of a variety of teaching tactics. But I would do this anyway. And given my obligation to teach a certain kind of subject-matter, I would stress and aim to improve capacity in the cognitive activities central to that subject-matter even if I knew it frustrated the antecedent psychological dispositions of my audience.

6. Assignments and Class Sessions

The fifth through seventh sets of recommendation require little elaboration. The fifth advises taking advantage of discussion-promoting relations between assignments and class sessions. Here there are several practices that are educationally beneficial in their own right, but also funnel into class interaction. Use particular study questions to help focus thoughtful effort. Use questions for reflection to be raised at the conclusions of readings. Allow revisions in papers, giving input on how to revise. Among other things, substantive revision requires responsiveness to pertinent materials which have emerged since the original, so provides determinate incentive to grapple with that new material. Provide steady feedback to students, so that your class will be more like an ongoing conversation, in which their input is more natural and your evaluation of their performances is less momentous.

In many fields, requiring students to keep low-risk, low-burden journals not only palpably prepares them with questions for discussion, but often provides the seeds for their more polished essays. I require two components to their journal entries. The first sketches the reading's main line of thought, and is graded for adequacy. The second wholly aims to encourage them to let their inquisitive and creative juices flow, and receives full credit regardless of content so long as it represents serious effort. To underscore for them that this is not like a well-crafted paper, but a personal opportunity to let their thoughts soar, probe, play, etc., I convey my preference for handwritten entries, better still in ink with cross-outs rather than erasures and refined substitutes. A penultimate proposal for connecting assignments to more interactive class meetings prescribes that students closely read a certain kind of handout in preparation for discussion. The kind of handout I have in mind charts alternative theories in a given area, the ways to generate specific versions of the theories, and key interrelations among the theories.

For example, I use one crowded sheet of paper divided into thirds, with one section articulating alternative normative theories of obligation (designed to answer the question, "What ought we to do?"), the second section presenting alternative normative theories of value (designed to answer the question, "What is valuable for its own sake?"), and the third section outlining alternative metaethical theories (designed to determine the meaning and logic of fundamental moral notions, and how moral theories are evaluated. The key to its special value is that by tracing out (as in a flow chart—the stress on process and not just results is important to enabling their thinking here) the sequence of commitments one needs to make in order to arrive at a fully determinate version of a theory, you are wonderfully sensitizing students to the joints of the (sometimes otherwise overwhelming) theoretical beast, guiding them to points of potential vulnerability, rendering more perspicuous the definitive differences among alternatives, and generally arming them with increased capacity (and to that extent, propensity) for high-level discussion.

Last, let me put in a good word for role-playing, and I'll stick with an application in ethics as an example. Suppose you are teaching several important figures, and so cannot assign extensive readings for each. Consider requiring students to select (at least a few weeks before the end of the semester) one of the figures to read more extensively and prepare to represent in an end-of-semester discussion. More than one student should pick the same figure if enrollment dictates, and the entire activity only seems feasible in relatively small classes. When discussion day arrives, students submit the notes they have taken on their supplemental reading, you introduce each student as the character he or she portrays, and each is strictly obliged to stay in character. Each makes a brief, initial presentation of outlook. Then cross-questioning occurs (with the aim of establishing the superiority of one's own outlook). Each student aims to elaborate his or her position more fully and convincingly as discussion progresses. During this time, you intervene by asking directed questions only if some students are not saying enough to pass the assignment. Near the end (but only then), you may allow yourself one or two important questions for each character, especially in order to correct major misrepresentations, highlight crucial oversights, or create in students' minds further questions, which lead to further thought. Most students like the fact that they have specially mastered one thinker. At the event itself they usually do their part and have lots of fun.

7. Clarifying, Sustaining, and Refreshing Through Examples

Examples can clarify, sustain, and refresh discussions, and deserve a category of their own. I do think that people are interested in other people, so to the extent that, without saying anything inappropriate, you can reveal a little bit of yourself, to that extent you likely stimulate discussion. This does not include prematurely announcing your own view on a controversial issue—that often chills discussion, or makes it less cooperative. When I talk about the fact that my father, though he didn't do this for a living, was interested and so got a professional degree in hypnosis, and then use some examples of hypnosis, including occasions in which I was the subject, to make certain points about freedom, students seem unusually fascinated and ask me more questions, even questions that go well beyond the current issue about my non-professorial life.

Very brief (so long as appropriate) indulgences of students' personal curiosity refreshes their attention, as well-transitioned shifts in focus generally do.

Shared experiences make exceptional examples. To illustrate a point about the roles of habit and will in human conduct I was once talking about the social anxieties I had when I was in junior high school. It was an experience many of them shared, so they had incentive to discuss the philosophical point I was proposing; similarly with examples that directly affect the students.

For example, if I am talking about justice or fairness, instead of coming up with some concocted, very abstract case, I will say something like, "What factors are relevant in deciding on a fair grade for a student; what should count?", and after I elicit from them a policy on grading, I can then ask whether it can be extrapolated to social justice, such as distributions of benefit and burdens to the whole society. Or is there an important disanalogy? A danger here is to use a provocative but offensive example. Sternly telling a student who has just insisted that there are no defensible, objective standards, but that what is right is what each person believes to be right, that you the instructor believe that all subjectivists should fail the course, drives home a logical point, but likely with too great a cost to good will. On the other hand, to assign even known libertarians the task of legislating salaries for the fulfillment of various social roles while preserving a veil of ignorance as to which role they will ultimately fill can be a non-abrasive, powerful inducement to care about the needy and greater equality.

The use of pithy case studies enjoyably provokes as well. Instead of exploring abstractly the kinds and rankings of evils, tell a story about the need to replace Satan as prince of darkness, give a profile of the vying candidates (embodying different paradigms of evil), and invite their adjudication. Or instead of straightaway asking which of two competing moral values is overriding, begin with a story of a concrete moral quandary someone faced.

A final idea, presumably applicable only in certain forms of inquiry, is to prepare a chart of examples to test all anticipatable intuitions on a given topic. I have one on the topic of personal identity and responsibility which allows me to challenge any account thrown my way, a surefire way to keep lively discussion going. In general, vivid examples can be used to substitute for experience. And again, examples provide objects to focus attention jointly.

8. The Role of Discussion: The Overall Picture

I close by reinforcing the need for a plan to incorporate discussion in overall course structure, and with a seventh and final theme about the instructor's roles in discussion. I am wedded to the idea that my classes should be largely discussion-oriented, but as I mentioned earlier, unless I do certain things to make clear the role of the discussion in the overall scheme—for example, using the board occasionally to show where the group has been, where it has arrived at, and where it is going—all aspects of the course are less effective. Planning is often done badly on a large scale even when it is done well on a small scale. A general guideline worth highlighting is that if you aspire to nurture both intellectual and social growth through regular discussion, structure at least most of the course for cooperation, not competition.

And what about your own role in discussions? You can play many legitimate roles—moderator, equal participant, source of direction, invisible board monitor, etc.—but for the most part stick to a role when you adopt it on a particular occasion. It is perhaps fitting to conclude on an exhortation like this that instantiates the general plea to keep commitments. In the art and craft of teaching, whether the issue is intellectual, emotional, practical, or moral, this impresses as centrally sound advice.

Appendix 1
Teaching Through Discussion

I. First Class
   1. Break the ice
   2. Begin to diagnose background knowledge and belief
   3. Begin to form a community of inquirers
   4. Generate curiosity and a sense of anticipation
   5. Elicit some provisional positions for subsequent analysis and evaluation
   6. Generate low-risk interaction
   7. Exemplify, not just describe, desired procedure
   8. Phrase responses in encouraging ways
      A. Background and interests information cards
      B. Carefully constructed questionnaire (most of class time)

First
week:
      C. List of critical questions to ask about course materials, to be used in work at home, classroom activities, tests and papers
      D. Single sheet with needed rules of good and bad reasoning

II. Having an Object of Joint Focus
   1. Public board better than private handout
   2. Reading text aloud
   3. Small group preparations with specific goals and guidelines
   4. Modified debate format (philosophical chairs)
   5. Fully structured argument to be considered step by step

III. Types and Uses of Questions
  1. Ask questions at a variety of cognitive activity levels:
       (i) recollection,
       (ii) restatement (comprehension),
       (iii) application,
       (iv) analysis,
       (v) organization,
       (vi) evaluative judgment
  2. Ask questions of various fundamental sorts:
       (i) empirical,
       (ii) analytic,
       (iii) normative,
       (iv) preferential,
       (v) metaphysical and presuppositional
  3. Dynamics of using different types of questions, classified according to:

		Individual	Group
(i) Address			
(ii) Range of answers		few acceptable permitted answers	hot-seat toss-up
		many acceptable answers	inviter free-fire
(iii) time for answers			
(iv) follow-up to answers			

IV. Taking Account of Cognitive and Motivational Psychology
  1. Process of student questioning involves:
       (i) identifying need to ask,
       (ii) deciding it is legitimate to ask,
       (iii) getting attention and permission to ask,
       (iv) dealing with potentially unpredictable response
  2. Advance notice of devil's advocacy
  3. Best learning occurs when immediate usefulness exists
  4. Model, articulate, and promote practice of skills, in isolation, re-integrated (profession of interconnections is not enough)
  5. Personal interest: learn names; show knowledge of individual interests, talents, contributions made
  6. Link familiar with new, current interests with interests to be created
  7. Give students feeling of accomplishment, empowerment
  8. Earmark more difficult tasks but express confidence in success
  9. Don't erode sense of adequacy by regular paraphrase of comments
  10. Achievement motivation highest when estimated chance of success approximately 50-50
  11. Acknowledge and explain change of mind, especially if student-induced
  12. Admit if don't know, that search sometimes proceeds haltingly
  13. Test benefits of using cognitive development schemes: *e.g.*, Perry's
       (i) learn true-false from teacher,
       (ii) authorities disagree relativism,

(iii) learn criteria for better opinions,

(iv) rational commitment in spite of uncertainty

V. Taking Advantage of Relations Between Assignments and Class Sessions
 1. Use study questions
 2. Use questions for subsequent reflection
 3. Require low-risk, low-burden journals
 4. Use discussion worksheets
 5. Allow revisions
 6. Provide steady feedback
 7. Use handout exhibiting steps in theory-construction
 8. Use role-playing

VI. Clarifying, Sustaining, and Refreshing Through Examples
 1. Use pithy case studies
 2. Use personal examples
 3. Use examples which directly affect students
 4. Prepare with chart of examples and counterexamples to test all anticipatable intuitions on a topic

VII. Role of Discussion in Overall Course Structure
 1. Reinforce scaffolding in which spontaneous pursuits occur. Place discussion. If it doesn't fit, identify its character as such.
 2. Occasionally pause to convey explicitly pedagogical plan
 3. Interact informally at beginning and end of class to convey natural character of "official" discussions
 4. Structure course for cooperation, not competition
 5. Remember small-scale planning is insufficient, and large-scale planning is difficult to do well

Your Role in Discussion:

Make it clear and (almost always) stick to it:

(i) equal participant,

(ii) source of direction,

(iii) moderator,

(iv) silent board monitor,

(v) transcriber of minutes, etc.

Appendix 2
Ethics Questionnaire

Please respond to each question using the following scale: SA (strongly agree), A (agree), C (can't answer or unsure), D (disagree), or SD (strongly disagree).

1. What is right is what society's members believe to be right.

2. What is right is what God wills or commands. To know your obligations you need to know what God wills.

3. What is right is what leads to the greatest good for the greatest number (of people; of sentient beings; of living things; of all things). Motives are irrelevant.

4. The only thing that counts in determining whether someone did the right thing or not is the motive. The results of the action are irrelevant.

5. What is right is neither more nor less than following the Ten Commandments.

6. What is right is what maximizes one's self-interest.

7. People have no moral obligations to themselves.

8. Lots of factors rightly enter into our moral rules, such as the amount of good produced, and such special relations as friendship, the repayment of debts, and the keeping of promises. To figure out what is right you have to weigh all the positive and negative applications of these rules.

9. No one knows what is right or wrong, or good or bad.

10. Moral judgments are expressions of personal taste, neither true nor false.

11. The only motive people have in doing anything is to get something for themselves. Even when they help others, it is only because it makes them feel good.

12. Some people think that love has value by itself, but its value is just the pleasure one derives from being in love and loving. The same holds true for peace, beauty, knowledge, etc.

13. Things of value in our society should be distributed only to those who can afford them as a result of their success in competing in our economic system.

14. Things of value should be distributed to each individual according to need (and we should receive from each individual according to that person's abilities).

15. Things of value in our society should be distributed on the basis of merit.

16. Things generally desired should be distributed equally, numerically when possible, and on the basis of each waiting a turn if numerical equality is not possible.

17. Whenever one does something morally wrong, one deserves to be punished.

18. We should only punish as a means to prevent wrongdoing or improve people.

19. We should compensate for past injustices by discriminating in favor of minorities now.

20. Abortion is sometimes permissible even when the woman's life is not at risk.

21. Parents have a right to terminate the life of a severely defective newborn.

22. A family has a right to terminate the life of one of its much-suffering, terminally ill members.

23. Insofar as others are not adversely affected, a person has a right to commit suicide.

24. Society has a right to kill those who commit certain crimes.

25. Any kind of sexual activity is permissible between mutually consenting adults.

26. It may have been that slavery in the United States led to more good than bad overall. But it was still wrong to keep slaves.

27. Only a rational being can have obligations.

28. Only a rational being can have rights ("claim" obligations from others).

Notes

1. Cf. Wilbert J. McKeachie, *Teaching Tips: Strategies, Research, and Theory for College and University Teachers*, 9th ed. (Lexington, Mass: D.C. Heath, 1994).

2. See Richard Paul, *Critical Thinking* (Rohnert Park, Cal.: Sonoma State University: Center for Critical Thinking and Moral Critique, 1990).

3. See Rodney P. Riegle, in K.A. Strike, ed., *Philosophy of Education* (Urbana, Ill.: Philosophy of Education Society, 1976), reproduced with enrichment in Ronald T. Hyman, "Questioning in the College Classroom," Idea Paper No. 8 (Manhattan, Kan.: Kansas State University: Center for Faculty Evaluation & Development, August 1982). Also see William E. Cashin and Philip C. McKnight, "Improving Discussions," Idea

Paper No. 15 (January 1986).

4. *Cf.* John Immerwahr, "Asking Questions: Ways to Promote (or Destroy) Class Discussion," *Metaphilosophy* 22:4 (October 1991), pp, 364-377. Also see "Formulating Discussion Questions to Increase Student Participation,' in *The TA at UCLA* (Los Angeles: UCLA, Office of Instructional Development, 1990).

Eight

THE CLASSROOM EXPERIENCE AS A LABORATORY FOR SELF-UNDERSTANDING

Marc Lubin

The importance of immediate student experience in the process of higher education has long been an established pedagogical goal. This premise has been especially emphasized in the social sciences and the humanities where the deeper understanding and appreciation of human experience is a foundational orienting principle. Since selected course objectives in these areas enhance the development of the self, the active inclusion and direct participation of the student in the learning experience itself is intrinsic to this approach.

In deepening student appreciation of course concepts, experientially oriented instructors have devised multiple methods to evoke, observe, and guide student participation in the classroom. Experiential components to learning that view self-exploration as an essential aspect to personal growth and development become even more meaningful when they are directed toward uncovering the connections between personal, self-related material that is sharply defined and relevant to students' lives and course topics. The exploration of personal meaning creates an additional and fundamental source of data for students to integrate with the course materials being formally presented. This approach thus allows for the active and direct interplay between the lessons being presented and the students' sense of selves, so that self-understanding is more directly a part of the understanding of the lesson itself.

While the classroom experience is frequently designed to engage student learning in the cognitive areas, the relevance of learning that emphasizes personal growth can be further enlivened by the process of self-recognition in relation to the lessons being taught. In fact, such recognitions may already exist by way of muted student associations to particular readings or theories that resonate with their personal experience. The potential utility of such associations in the personalized understanding and interpreting of classroom material is often ignored in the traditional classroom, even though such associations may play an important role in how the material is understood and processed by students. Whether or not a direct focus exists, such experiences still color and may even define how students understand the concepts being presented to them. Therefore, they affect the more personal lessons students take away from the classroom.

1. The Primacy of Self-Understanding

Self-knowledge is a primary goal for the making of a good psychologist, but it is also a standard we often impose in higher education. While this chapter will explore the ways in which a range of classroom experiences can be meaningfully connected to the immediate "lesson of the day" in clinical psychology training, there is a wider premise for general education: selective knowledge connected to personal experience and self-observation may be actively and meaningfully pursued in a wide range of educational arenas. Such an approach is not required for learning to take place or to be effective in general education, but the particular advantages of experiential learning are an increase in student motivation, and a stronger investment in the connection of course concepts with overall comprehension, reflectiveness, and self-understanding.

The emphasis on the role of personal growth and development is most relevant to the education of individuals who are being trained in the human helping professions, for they are most likely to draw upon their personal experiences, reactions, and dispositions during direct service delivery. In summarizing one of Freud's major psychoanalytic principles, Erik Erikson (1964) notes that "you will not see in another what you have not learned to recognize in yourself" (p. 29). The human service professions are founded on the primacy of self-observation and the critical analysis of behavioral, emotional, and phenomenological manifestations of human experience. Ignorance of one's own internal processes that contribute to the interpersonal and intersubjective dynamics of the therapeutic encounter severely limits the vision and potential effectiveness of the helping professional. As a consequence, the emphasis on self-understanding becomes a cornerstone in the education of such professionals. Within the constraints of a lesson objective that addresses fundamental issues in working directly with serving others, a focus on the intrapsychic events within the self is a critical element in the applied classroom setting. This is especially important in the education of psychologists.

Most teaching in the area of clinical psychology has relied upon traditional teaching methods, including lecture, discussion, role-playing activities, and the use of audio and video materials for observation and modeling purposes. There are also group courses with a strong experiential component, in which students participate as group members and then observe the group process in relation to critical group concepts.

However, the use of the immediate classroom experience itself as a resource for learning clinical psychology is less common, despite the fact that powerful psychological currents run through every classroom. Several publications have addressed the classroom experience as a critical mine for understanding and teaching psychology (Lubin, 1984-1985, 1987; Lubin and Stricker, 1991; Yalof,

1996). These works stress the extensive richness in the classroom with respect both to the direct and indirect learning of clinical concepts and ways of practicing as a clinician.

My personal experience as a graduate student provided me with few opportunities to witness or experience in emotionally immediate ways the actual meanings of psychology concepts, or to significantly alter a personal attitude toward a client within a classroom context. Typically, such psychology classes were characterized by the above formats which, while interesting and evocative, left little imprint or memory after the class time ended. All that remained of class time were extensive notes to be reviewed for examinations. Once the course ended, I usually could remember nothing specific about what transpired between the instructor and myself or other students.

However, one dramatic exception profoundly affected my approach to teaching. As a graduate student at the University of Chicago, I vividly recall many classroom experiences with the distinguished psychologist, Dr. Bruno Bettelheim. He emphasized the significance of self-observation and empathy in working with troubled children. His confrontative and provocative teaching style captured and held the attention of most students who attended his courses.

As a teacher of psychology graduate students over the past 21 years, I determined that I needed to find my own way to repeat the impact of Bettelheim's teaching, without the confrontational and provocative qualities that were uniquely part of his character as a teacher. I needed to give comparable attention to the classroom process, and create experiences that would assure my students would leave with class time memories that could be applied in their future careers, just as I had done with my memories of Bettelheim's courses.

In my teaching, I have attempted to repeat Dr. Bettelheim's focus on self-observation and the development of empathy. I believe these emphases have been fundamental to my students' growth and training. They have constituted a major part of my course objectives and class time activities since the first class I taught in psychopathology.

In my teaching style, however, I have attempted to model myself as a clinical instructor who blends the qualities of a good clinician—attentive, receptive, encouraging, and facilitative of student learning, while creating a structure that will result in the development of clinical knowledge and clinical skills.

To illustrate the impact of Bettelheim's teaching and its ultimate expression in terms of my own teaching, I will describe several moments in my own graduate learning that captured the essence of what I now try to communicate in each class to my students.

This following occurred in a small doctoral seminar on psychoanalysis with Dr. Bettelheim. I was presenting a case in which I was attempting to describe schizophrenic processes in a severely disturbed adolescent boy (Ralph) with whom I was working as a very new child care counselor in a residential facility. I had eagerly and anxiously begun my account in describing what I believed were this boy's unreasonable demands that I purchase him an ice cream bar following a trip to the doctor. I reported to the seminar that I had refused his request and that the boy had become highly agitated and quite angry with me, a further sign of his emotional disturbance. Dr. Bettelheim abruptly interrupted me, and asked why I had refused the request.

Up to that point, I had been intent on pursuing a diagnostic presentation of this disturbed boy, focusing on presenting the severity of his psychopathology to the seminar and Dr. Bettelheim. I had no investment in further describing or exploring my relationship with Ralph, nor did I regard his agitation as being more than a sign of his severe self-control problems. Therefore, Bettelheim's interruption startled me. These moments were the beginning of a critical and paradigmatic learning experience for me.

At first I thought that my refusal was perfectly understandable and actually irrelevant to my presentation of the case of Ralph. In my mind, Ralph's response was a product of his pathology, not my behavior. I then noticed that I did not wish to answer Bettelheim's question. I began to realize that I did not have an immediate or comfortable answer to his question, and I was growing embarrassed that I did not, especially in front of the other students.

However, I did begin to remember that other counselors had forewarned me of Ralph's entitled, demanding, and "manipulative" ways. They predicted that he would probably ask for ice cream and that I should not give into his manipulativeness. In recalling their advice, I then became aware of how important it was for me to gain their approval during those first few weeks in the facility, and not appear to be "weak" and gullible in their eyes. I started to realize that when Ralph asked for the ice cream, my stern and irritated response was an effort to communicate to him that he was not going to "push me around" and make me look foolish to my new peers.

With this new information, Dr. Bettelheim now was able to help me understand that Ralph's angry and agitated reaction had more meaning than I had immediately recognized. After I had articulated my self-protective and dismissive stance toward Ralph's request, I had begun to see his reaction toward me in a new light. Bettelheim then was able to observe that since my "no" to the boy was motivated primarily out of my anxious concern for my self-image in the eyes of my co-workers, the boy's agitated reaction was more understandable. Ralph was responding not only to my frustrating his wishes, but was also reacting to his perception that my primary motive for refusing him was self-protective rather than related to him and his therapeutic needs.

Bettelheim stressed that I might have been more successful had my reaction been informed by my direct observation and knowledge of Ralph. Ralph then would have trusted my investment in him, and might have been more therapeutically responsive to my reaction. A refusal under those conditions would have flowed more genuinely from my therapeutic concern for Ralph, and less from my concern over my self-image.

As the years have passed, I have returned to this anecdote in my thoughts about teaching. Those exchanges provided experiential templates for my thinking about what matters in the classroom. Those perspectives have formed the core of my approach to classroom teaching experience.

2. The Importance of Focus in the Classroom Experience: The Inception of Self-Observation

Bettelheim's powerful attention to that one interaction helped me to focus my reflections and to uncover a range of hidden motives that lay behind what appeared to be a trivial intervention. That circumscribed attention generated a series of reflections that re-organized the way in which I observed certain clinical and academic challenges. Such focal activity convinced me that detailed attention to such exchanges was critical toward establishing a rich learning focus.

Prior to this time, I had found most class time discussions to be characterized by students and instructors constantly shifting topics and speaking in global terms. Such discussions, while interesting, did not galvanize my attention nor leave me with a clear memory that I could draw on in future readings or clinical encounters.

In this context, his question had introduced a new element into my introspective processing that had not existed before. He had sharply defined the area of my experience that required focused attention. What was originally a passing and insignificant moment in a descriptive process was now highlighted for the purpose of further exploration. His question provoked me to pause and begin to recognize barely discernible reactions to that part of my exchange with Ralph. As a response, I had begun a process of focused and disturbing self-observation that surfaced information critical to understanding Ralph's reactions to me.

I recognized that persistent instructional focus and a delimiting of the observational field could stimulate information critical to re-framing a problematic interaction and open up extended speculations regarding additional observations. This process relied totally upon the extension of a type of self-processing that included memory, thought, and feeling that re-contextualized the originally indecipherable problem. There was now a new backdrop against which that original information might be placed, with an entirely new perspective available for application.

3. Self-Observation and the Emergence of Motives

Once Bettelheim's question had been asked, I was able to learn about the value of immediate self-observation that was focused on a specific event. In those moments immediately following Bettelheim's query, "Why did you say no?," I first became uncomfortably aware of my need to objectify and distance myself from Ralph and from Bettelheim's question. This emerging self-image was disturbing since I was attempting to present myself as a developing psychologist with concern about disturbed individuals and their psychopathology. In my first account, I had been looking to Dr. Bettelheim and my seminar peers for approval of my diagnostic assessment of this adolescent boy.

In reflecting further, I became painfully aware of motives related to my refusal that had formerly been barely discernible to me. As noted above, I began to recognize my primary need to gain peer acceptance in this new setting. In addition, I became aware of my discomfort with Ralph's demandingness, and my anxiety that he might become even more insistent if I did not say no.

I then could observe that my process of asking myself such questions led to the emergence of motives that played a very significant role in my actions. I then realized that I partly wished to hide these unflattering motives from myself, the seminar, and Dr. Bettelheim.

4. Awareness and Appreciation of the Concept of Dynamic Psychology

In those moments, I began to get a more vivid sense of the actuality of a major conceptual premise of dynamic psychology as it related to my clinical work, in which unpleasant motives may be blocked out or suppressed in order to maintain self-regard. While I had generally known about motives and defenses personally and intellectually, my clinical understanding was now based on a direct self-observation achieved in a classroom and a clinically applied setting.

In focusing on this one event, I experienced a strong reluctance to acknowledge such motives to myself and even less to the seminar and Dr. Bettelheim. This very reluctance, however, was an essential element in observing my learning process. It also brought forth the actual experience of "defending" myself against my sense of embarrassment about my self-protective motives. While my beginning status as a child care worker made such concerns quite understandable and expected, it was difficult for me to feel comfortable with these insecurities.

5. Experience of Insight and the Dawning of Empathy

As I experienced this first public acknowledgment of personal motives flowing into a professional relationship, I observed that my new understanding and beginning acceptance of my motives helped to explain one part of Ralph's agitated and defiant reaction to me. With my recognition that I was actually antagonistic toward Ralph's request, and that his request in some way threatened me as a worker, I could reach a broader understanding of his response.

My new understanding started to shift my view of Ralph's reaction from that of a frustrated, manipulative, entitled "brat," who felt defeated trying to convince me to buy the ice cream, to that of an individual who felt peremptorily dismissed and a source of danger to his caretaker. In that fleeting moment, his sense of personal failure with me added to his intolerance of hearing "no" to such a request. His agitated reaction, then, was designed to undo his sense of defeat and humiliation as he observed his negative impact on me. With this new information and perspective, I could then empathize more fully with his upset at feeling dismissed by my immediate refusal of his request. I would also begin to re-consider the underlying purposes of this request.

6. Central Teaching Insights Derived from the Experience

Apart from the specific insights gained about my own story, I more fully appreciated that an intense examination of a well selected single event that at first seemed tangential could actually be rich in yielding an array of powerful and underlying meanings. These meanings then could lead to an unfolding series of personal and conceptual understandings, and finally to a greater empathy with another person now based upon a broader vision of the particular exchange.

I was captured by this process. In retrospect, I recognize it formed the core of my own teaching philosophy and ways of employing class time. As a consequence of this type of experience, I am convinced that learning is most possible with personal engagement that is focused and guided. Such a focus can yield a heightened capacity for self-observation, and for the collection of critical information about oneself that can deepen the student's knowledge about relevant concepts and the disturbing behavior of other human beings.

7. The Application of Teaching Insights in Classroom Structure: General Description of Basic Classroom Processes

Because self-observation is intimately linked to personal and professional growth, my classes contain elements of the above experiences related to the emotional and conceptual understanding of course material.

Each class includes a focus on a discrete experience or set of experiences relevant to a central clinical concept and type of interaction. In the ensuing examinations of those narratives, I hope to demonstrate to the students the value of intensive self-observation around well described events. If the process unfolds as designed, I then expect students to achieve a greater sense of self-understanding and empathy for their clients around the memory of a meaningful narrative as I gained with Ralph.

In order to reach the above goals, I gather several narratives, frequently asking for the elaboration of student thoughts and feelings as they describe their experiences. Once I locate a particular description that will provide the richest and most vivid linkages to the classroom focus, I "freeze frame" that description.

At those moments when the sequence is sharply defined, the deeper meanings of the event and the student's reactions begin to evolve. The students' initially casual attitudes toward a particular experience become more focused. The formerly unobserved moment is now observed, magnified, and examined. A new and emotionally charged learning opportunity is now available that has galvanized student interest and can be recalled through remembering the narrative imagery of the episodes presented.

The stage is now set for students to begin learning more extensively just how these self-observations can ignite further self understanding and the understanding of critical concepts. Students become aware of the connections between their experiences and the relevant readings, interactions, and clients to be studied during that class.

Once these connections begin to be established between self-experience and clinical concepts, it is then possible to reconsider how that self-experience may then provide a template for their understanding of the client's experience. In that same way, the meanings of the client's experience begin to shift from a detached, intellectual, and distant portrait to an immediate empathy toward specifically troubling communications from the client. Dr. Bettelheim had stimulated an increased interest in Ralph, an impact that was ultimately of enormous help in my subsequent work with him. I wish to evoke the same intensified investment in clinical work among my students through this process.

8. The Meaning and Significance of Class Time

In my view, students consciously and unconsciously use class time to monitor instructor attitudes toward their revelations and ideas. They are acutely sensitive as to my stance toward their comments, their difficulties in learning, and the presentation of their own examples of experiences relevant to the class topic. The classroom, in this context, is a laboratory in which such instructor attitudes are expressed in multiple ways, and in which the instructor's honesty, comportment, sensitivities, and interactional skills may be directly observed by students.

Instructor openness to the students' observing and exploratory processes is critical to student learning. These attitudes are clearly what students observe most intensively in the classroom, and so it is where learning is most immediate, observable, and available for internalization. By building and elaborating on these observations of receptivity, curiosity, and respect, students may be more effective practitioners, with more genuine and informed understanding toward their own clientele.

9. Organizing Principles: Conceptual and Empathic Connections

One major organizing principle for class time is that each student reaction or narrative selected for full discussion must be connected to a critical concept or theory discussed during that class. Such material is selected for focus based on its relative fit for such an integration. By tying easily understandable student experience to highly relevant clinical concepts, I am able to help students appreciate the value of their experience as a critical reservoir for learning, so that they can understand in a more intimate way the underlying human experience upon which the concept is based.

A second significant principle is that those student reactions chosen for intensive observation and reflection must also be tied to a troubling client experience. My goal is to demonstrate that by observing, understanding, and accepting less flattering aspects of their own underlying reactions and behaviors, students will be less threatened by parallel troubling elements of a client's behavior. They will understand that under certain conditions, they too well might behave as a client they had first thought was "unreasonable."

These organizing principles are even more important in teaching students who will work directly in human services, and for whom the understanding and integration of their emotional and cognitive experience is essential. Thus, the major cornerstone of my class time planning is to provide a guided process focused on immediate experiences of students that will exemplify the critical concept or clinical dilemma of the week.

After completion of such a process, I expect that students will then possess a self-awareness and empathic readiness to both grasp the clinical concept and the case material in greater depth and with deeper appreciation for the realities of their practice.

10. Capturing the Experience:
Creating a Safe Environment for Self-Observation

In order to elicit such experiences from students, I have to create a safe environment so that they are freer to mention their "everyday" reactions to specific life or classroom events without excessive self-consciousness or inhibition. I do so by actively inviting and encouraging their stories about selected daily life events, class readings, or unexpected but evocative events that occur in the classroom.

These selections are organized around experiences that both myself and my students can easily share. I may contribute examples from my experiences as a student, practitioner, teacher, or administrator, and I will speak directly of personal lapses in these areas. In all these ways, I seek to inform students that I can truly accept and empathize with their reported experiences of personal lapses, resistances, and confusion.

When I make such contributions, or indirectly communicate that I fully understand and appreciate their experience, students are usually encouraged and emboldened. Their fears of a harsh or punitive judgement coming from me as both administrator and instructor are diminished. They are more forthcoming in describing their reactions. I, in turn, am sincerely gratified and pleased by their increased participation. As I listen, I connect their relevant comments and reactions with the class focus. By doing so, I am explicitly recognizing the learning value of their participatory efforts, which then further facilitates their openness in the classroom.

One relevant classroom exchange occurred when I asked students one evening to discuss their reticence to raise questions or observations. I attempted to indicate that my interest was in the service of understanding and reflecting upon the experience of reluctance to speak in the classroom. It was clear they felt some danger in speaking up. With that information, students spoke of their critical attitudes toward the readings and their fears of openly acknowledging that they had not understood the readings. One even disclosed she had not completed the assignment. Since my purpose at this time was in understanding student reticence rather than in evaluating student participation (I left my evaluation activities for papers and assignments), students were responsive to my questions and were surprisingly honest and direct in their comments. One consequence was that students were then able to surface questions which they had been embarrassed to ask prior to this discussion, and to provide experiences that built a foundation for understanding more about the interactional meanings of a silence in clinical situations.

11. Capturing the Experience: Establishing a Common Focus

In order to engage the immediate connection between student interest and the learning needs of the class, I identify a common experience that is immediate to all students, irregardless of their age or level of sophistication. I link that experience with the critical concepts or topics of the week. As noted earlier, these experiences are drawn from students' reactions to class assignments, to everyday events, and to actual and sometimes unplanned classroom exchanges that take place between the instructor and the student.

All students can quite easily identify with another student's anxious reactions to particular assignments or exams, to being kept waiting for an appointment, or to wanting to get a good grade and gain the instructor's approval. Since such reactions are common and shared informally among most students, rather than being highly privatized, they are more comfortable discussing them in a class-room context. There are also clear boundaries around the degree to which a student may reveal aspects of their personal life in such a setting.

12. Capturing the Experience: Establishing a Selected Experiential Focus

As noted above, I attempt to identify and highlight with my students a circumscribed human experience that is frequently unobserved and dismissed as having any psychological significance. Just as Bettelheim stopped me to ask why I would say "no" to Ralph, I attempt to create a situation in which students are asked what is passing through their minds when they made a personal or clinical observation. I then ask them to sustain their focus on that observation. That first task was to teach the value of sustained attention to, and exploration of, the "little things" that unfold into rich and meaningful events.

It is critical that in establishing this focus, I also sustain the focus by returning to it in the course of discussion, redirecting student comments to the topical area or the event being studied, and concluding the discussion with a summary of observations and comments and their relationship to the learning task for the class. Such efforts require both a tolerance for the occasional tangential comment and the continuing search for its connection to the central theme of the exploration of the class.

13. Experiential Topics: Reactions to Class Assignments

Students occasionally find it hard to understand a concept in the readings. Such difficulties are expected because students may not have an available clinical or personal referent, or be familiar with a new type of theoretical language. In addition, such learning difficulties can be compounded as a consequence of individual histories with reading and learning, as well as interactions with past teachers and parents. Students may also react to the personal meanings embedded in psychological readings, and such reactions may further complicate their understanding.

It is at those times that students' deeper reactions to class assignments can be rich in meaning. Usually, such emotional reactions are never exposed or examined in a classroom setting. Students more frequently discharge such feelings in the company of their classmates without self-awareness or self-scrutiny. By focusing on these experiences in the service of developing self-observational skills and conceptual learning, students are able to find new understanding and relevance in their own immediate experience.

For the above reasons, I invite students to report their problems in completing assignments in detail. I do so in order to identify a clear and specific portrait of a significant human interaction with another figure—be it the writer or myself (who assigned the writer).

In addition, I have responded to student questions or critiques about particular readings with further questions of my own in an effort to locate the nature of their psychological reaction to the readings.

In one class, a student seemed perplexed about Freud's comments regarding the "taboo on touching," saying that he could not understand the concept. It seemed very removed and distant from him. He found it had little real meaning or relevance. I asked if he himself could identify any touching taboos he had observed in himself or others in general terms that were not necessarily overly personal or embarrassing. He began to realize that he actually could begin to associate to areas of his own development related to bodily areas that were highly charged and connected to prohibition and inner criticality and shame. Other students echoed similar memories. All could then begin to relate vividly to the concept. The discussion then led to why such a universal experience was not immediately apparent to most students.

Aside from the quality of Freud's prose, I suggested that the topic itself might be emotionally charged so that the immediate associations to the conflicts around bodily touching would be difficult to immediately recall or to acknowledge. Students were then able to observe that a process involved in obsessive compulsive functioning—intellectualization—was actually a process apparent in their response to the concept.

I have, for example, focused on the student's reactions to their failure to understand a particular set of concepts. In a course on psychopathology, I asked who in the class had not finished the readings for a particular week. One brave student raised her hand. I inquired as to how this occurred in terms of planning and processing the readings. Quite quickly the student became aware of her anxieties and strong disagreements with the reading, as well as her lack of familiarity with some of the concepts. What at first appeared as legitimate tasks taking her away from her reading could now be seen as avoidant and protective. These observations allowed the class to recognize that concepts related to defense mechanisms were operant as they read their assignments on defense mechanisms.

The discussion brought home concepts such as suppression, denial, avoidance, and rationalization. Such detailed descriptions also contained more immediate ways to comprehend theoretical concepts such as "bad object" (the writer or instructor who is persecuting them and threatens to humiliate and shame them), or aggressive drives (toward the writer or instructor for inflicting this anguish on them), or defensive operations against that aggression (turning against the self, denial, undoing, reaction formation, rationalization), and defensively tinged behaviors (delays, distractions, obsessive ruminations, etc.).

Once students could observe these connections to the theoretical concepts, their understanding then provided a foundation for appreciating parallel emotional and behavioral responses in clients. Such understanding helped to cut through some students' efforts to distance themselves through intellectualization from the parallel experience of their clients. In another example, I had noticed that one student had not fully completed his first written class assignment in preparation for a class discussion about one of his clients. In his subsequent discussion of his client, he voiced his criticism of her lack of motivation for psychotherapy, and her avoidance of conflictual emotional issues in the psychotherapy hour under review. I realized that he was struggling with his own avoidance of disclosure just as he was portraying his client. I then noted to him that he had not fully completed his written assignment for that class which had been to describe his client and the therapy interaction in more detail. I then inquired about his own observations as to why he had not fully completed the assignment.

Following an extensive and mutual inquiry about his anxieties about acknowledging his uncertainties and self-doubts in completing this assignment and making a first presentation to me and his peers, he was able to more fully recognize that both he and his client shared the experience of fear and avoidance regarding early exposure. As a consequence of this discussion, he was able to take a far less judgmental and far more empathic stance toward his client's avoidant behavior, since he could now recognize the same mechanism within himself.

14. Observing Student Reactions to the Instructor

I find that explicitly observing student reactions to aspects of my instructional presentation has been highly productive in terms of engaging students in the classroom process. Students have the opportunity to express their observations of me, and explicate an internal process normally hidden from the classroom process. By doing so, they receive practice in articulating such experiences, which are the core of important learning experiences.

An example: on occasion, assignments listed in my syllabus have been ambiguous or confusing to students. After I inquire about which areas need further explication, I have then asked students about their fleeting impressions of me in light of their comments about my syllabus. By doing so, I have provided students with an opportunity to voice critical observations about me by first acknowledging such observations myself. I then asked what happened to those thoughts as the class went on. Students then have reported how uncomfortable they were with their negative impressions of me in light of the confusing parts of my syllabus. They have commented that such observations were conflictual for them in terms of their wishes to idealize me. They also spoke about their fears that in expressing such observations directly to me, I might retaliate and give them lower grades at the end of the course. They said they began to notice that they preferred not to reflect further on such observations, and had dismissed them from their awareness prior to my bringing this topic to their attention in class.

Such discussions provided me with opportunities to draw parallels to the psychotherapy situation, in which clients also hide troubling perceptions of the therapist which are threatening to their concept of a secure and non-conflictual relationship. In response, I had the opportunity to correct my syllabus, which also served to reinforce students' directness in making observations of my instructional work.

Another example: I had noticed a deadness in the classroom following a request for questions, comments, observations, and reactions to the week's readings. After I inquired about the silence, a student described her reasons for not speaking, saying she was upset with the reading for the week, in which the authors did not make themselves totally clear. She spoke angrily about the authors, accusing them of being inconsiderate and self-preoccupied. Following these comments, she and others confessed to their worries about my response to their critical feelings toward the readings. This discussion provided students with a foundation for considering the meanings of classroom inhibition in relation to fears of attacking or being counterattacked by the instructor. In doing so, they could openly reflect upon their attitudes toward the instructor with respect to concepts related to transference and authority. Such attitudes once again were easily applied to the therapeutic or counseling situation.

In a formerly noted example, I spontaneously observed a dynamic in the class's relation to me as instructor, administrator, and authority figure, which tied well into the major concept being reviewed for the evening. The topic was "projective identification," an elusive and complex term that, for purposes of this paper, will be defined as the effort of an individual to attempt to evoke an internally painful experience in another individual through interactional pressure.

In the first segment of that particular class, students enthusiastically had volunteered personal experiences in which they were vaguely aware that a certain behavior of theirs was designed to upset another party. However, later on, when encouraged to raise any further questions or observations regarding the readings, they were silent. As I waited, I noticed a pressure on myself to speak, as well as some frustration at their reticence. In keeping with the evening's topic, I decided to raise these observations by asking what their reluctance was to speak up. Several students indicated they were afraid to expose their confusion to me.

As several students expressed their reasons, which also included a sense of shame over not having completed the readings for class that night, or of having intensely negative reactions to the article itself, we could also focus on their thoughts regarding the impact of their silence on myself and their peers. As we discussed this topic, students became aware that their silence in this context could be viewed as an example of a "projective identification" in which they hoped that either myself or their peers would experience their distress and frustration, and "do the talking for them." Their fears of severe punishment for harboring or expressing critical thoughts toward particular readings could then be related to the concept of "projection" of their anger toward the writer onto myself, an administrator/instructor. This projective then magnified their expectation of my retaliatory response, and thus intensified their inhibition.

I focused on this experience in class to demonstrate the immediate utility and relevance of the concept. I also wanted to observe nuances in the learning environment in such a way as to make the students' anxieties a topic of interest and deeper understanding rather than one characterized only by shame and withholding. In addition, I wished to show students that I was indeed somewhat different from their "projected" or anticipated imago of a hypercritical authority.

The cross-cultural value of these exercises was also demonstrated in the following week when the class was discussing concepts related to self-esteem. I had encouraged students to explicitly discuss their desires for my approval in the classroom context as a way of further considering the psychological need for "mirroring" (attentive and affirming responses from others). One foreign student spoke directly about his difficulties in achieving a sense of being understood and gaining approval from English speaking students. He described how such experiences led to a feeling of inferiority, despite the fact he had only been in this country for five months at the time and could not realistically be expected to have gained further mastery.

Another foreign student described her struggles in knowing whether she had achieved affirmation from her peers and the instructor when our non-verbal affirming responses were subtlety different than those in her native country. I was then able to connect such experiences in cross-cultural dialogue with concepts related to self-esteem and needs for affirmation.

This discussion helped to encourage a female student then to speak up about her feeling embarrassed about the prior week's discussion when she had volunteered a comment and, at the time, I had encouraged her to raise it later when the topic would be discussed in more detail. Her self-disclosure was extremely helpful as it focused the class on the pervasiveness of the phenomena of psychological vulnerability, the experience of narcissistic injury and the subsequent feelings of mild fragmentation and loss of cohesiveness that follow a perception of disapproval, no matter how reasonable it might appear to an outside observer. I could also point out to the class that her resiliency in articulating her painful experience was a distinguishing element in assessing the relative sturdiness of an individual's self-observing capacities in terms of recovery and articulation of the hurtful experience.

I pointed out that not only was her revelation personally important, but that such revelations in a therapist-client context could also be highly therapeutic for the client.

15. Using Classroom Experiences as Foundations for Understanding

I have used other classroom exchanges to demonstrate their psychological significance and relevance to students. These exchanges can be especially vivid and meaningful because of their immediacy and the instructional tact required to facilitate open student participation. Students learn immediately about the value of articulating an immediate series of thoughts and feelings. They observe how such reactions can be elicited by the instructor in a way that is neither judgmental or evaluative, but primarily supportive.

In this context, the instructor's attitudes toward student commentaries are critical models for students learning to identify with a less evaluative and more facilitative therapist model. Students observe how the instructor deals with hearing observations that may be critical of the instructor's performance. Once again, such observations provide a demonstration of therapist attitudes toward encouraging open communication from clients.

I make observations that I believe carry clinical and conceptual significance for both classroom and psychotherapy. For example, in the first or second class in one course, I observed that some students were returning several minutes after the break time was over. I decided that for multiple reasons I would focus on the issue of lateness that would address psychological aspects of lateness, perceptions of myself and other instructors in establishing firm time boundaries, and the interactional meanings of lateness. Students observed that they had not been aware of the multiple implications of the experience of their late return to class. They were then able to more immediately observe the relevance of concepts such as "transition times," "testing the limits," "separation" and the meaning of the therapeutic ground rules related to maintenance of the time framework. I also became cognizant of my role in demonstrating the importance of observing these behaviors in an exploratory fashion and, at the same time, actually hold to the time boundaries established for the class as a model for punctuality and consistency.

16. Using Outside Experiences for Classroom Learning

In employing experience relevant to most students, I have sometimes asked students to report a story from their daily lives that will help to illustrate a significant psychological concept. As one way to help students understand the concept of hidden motives, I asked students to recall the experience of being late. One student described her chronic lateness to gatherings, first saying others were always upset with her. Still, she somehow had a problem in getting places on time. By focusing on her imagined discomfort about being on time, she began to discover that her initial unhappiness about lateness hid her fears of actually being on time. This type of *in vivo* classroom discovery helped demonstrate the concept of hidden motives in a way that was highly relevant to all students.

In attempting to clarify concepts related to interactional pressures, I have asked students to identify times when they felt "sulky" or demonstrably "unhappy," and wanted their significant other to know about it, without describing how they were feeling in words. One student noted how, in response to her friend's canceling an engagement, she had subtlety questioned the entire relationship, hoping he too might feel fearful of her "canceling" her engagement with him. Other students could easily identify with this situation, which then provided a vivid way to illustrate particular concepts related to interactional dynamics.

This approach also made the point that all of us may frequently engage in provocative behaviors designed to upset others when we are confused, overwhelmed, or conflicted about our emotional reactions to certain interactions. Because such psychological reactions are most quickly denied in oneself and observed in others, I help students to understand that they, like certain defined clinical populations, could project, disrupt, and agitate others in ways that are

identical to the preferred interactional patterns of individuals described as
"borderline," "depressed," "psychotic," or "acting out."

17. Written Reflections on Conflictual Interactions

In order to reinforce the in-class experiences and evaluate student development
in terms of self-observing and conceptualizing applications, I required one
written assignment that asked students to report a particularly agitating
experience with another party, and observe their own sequence of thoughts, self-
images, and feelings through the experience in terms of the other party's impact
on them. I then asked them to consider how they might have impacted the other
party in terms of their behavior and interactions. As a final part of the
assignment, I request they then connect those observations to the relevant
interactional concepts in the psychotherapeutic relationship such as transference
and countertransference.

Typically such students have reported disturbing exchanges with intimates,
salespeople, instructors, workmates, classmates, children, siblings, parents,
clients, supervisors, and others. These events are described in detail and for the
most part are very charged for the students.

This assignment basically includes all the components stressed in the in-class
activities, and essentially guides the students in their movement from an
antagonistic to an empathic attitude toward the partner in the dialogue.

Students report that this assignment is most helpful in reinforcing the
reflective classroom processes, in developing a dramatically heightened self-
awareness, achieving a better grasp of the relevant course concepts, and
understanding another person in more depth. I am also able to assess the
students' capacities to self-observe, develop an empathic position with respect
to understanding their impact on the other party, and to do the conceptually
integrative work.

18. Summary

Each of the classroom experiences presented in this chapter contain a number
of critical lessons for the students in my classes. These lessons are fundamental
for the personal and professional development of individuals planning to be
human service professionals. The repetition of these lessons in different formats
throughout each class period and each course was part of an effort to reinforce
student learning and depth of understanding.

In order for such learning to take place, students were provided with focused
self-observing exercises. Such exercises were designed to access internal
experience, so as to bring previously hidden thoughts and feelings to their

awareness that could be connected to central course objectives. The emergence of heightened self-awareness was also designed to lead to a reorientation toward client experience and behavior, culminating in a stronger sense of empathy.

The structured and improvised use of class time was foundational in providing the central experiences upon which the class could build conceptual understanding. Basic principles that governed the direction of student processing of their experience were organized around connections to core concepts and the development of empathy.

In order to gather necessary student participation, it was critical that I establish a safe environment in which students might directly describe their self-observations. In this context, the tone and quality of my requests and responses to student stories were carefully monitored by students in terms of my acceptance and respect for their participation.

To further encourage wide student involvement, I attempted to identify and focus upon experience that was common to most students, so that all could relate to a central, clearly defined, and relevant presentation. By providing observations and concepts, I attempted to prevent a dilution of focus, and allow for the elaboration of two to three central ideas that could be "taken" from each class. Such was my experience with Dr. Bettelheim. I observed that my own learning was much enhanced when I had a central story or theme than when I was inundated with a broad range of global ideas. By having central and dramatic stories that would be drawn from students and/or clients, a narrative structure would then be available upon which conceptual understanding could be developed. Student reactions to course assignments, instructor behavior, classroom experiences, and typical life events formed a basic experiential core to all classes. To buttress the learning from these classroom discussions, I asked students to produce a written assignment that required them to perform the types of self-observing processes that echoed the classroom methodology.

My efforts in these contexts were to do in structured and less threatening ways what Dr. Bettelheim had done to me through his questioning of my motives in the interaction with Ralph. By asking students to provide self-observations in a context of encouragement and interest, I was able to turn students' attention to their own experiences, and to do so with an approving and respectful attitude. By the end of these courses, many students achieved a greater measure of self-acceptance. I measure this outcome, in part, from their interest in taking subsequent courses from me, and from specific positive comments addressing this particular approach in their course evaluations. In addition, many students demonstrated this enhanced capacity to self-reflect and to conceptualize their experience in both their classroom and written self-observing activities and in clinically applied examinations.

In retrospect, I believe that the potential significance and value of these immediate classroom exchanges cannot be overestimated for students capable of appreciating their implications. That belief is founded on my own experience with Bettelheim, in which his particular teaching focus deeply affected my further professional development and choice of subsequent instructors, who echoed a similar emphasis.

When students-as-professionals come across critical concepts in their readings, or when they would encounter a troubling reaction in a client or themselves, I hope they would recall a vivid classroom experience or discussion associated with those observations. Such recall might allow them a greater measure of conceptual understanding, a greater tolerance for self-observation, and enhanced self-awareness. These memories would provide the emotional and cognitive foundations for subsequent empathically informed interventions that would yield considerable benefits for their clientele and themselves.

Works Cited

Erikson, Erik H. (1964) *Insight and Responsibility*. New York: W.W. Norton.

Lubin, Marc. (1984-1985) "Another Source of Danger for Psychotherapists: the Supervisory Introject," *International Journal of Psychoanalytic Psychotherapy*, 11, ed. R. Langs. New York: Jason Aronson. Pp. 25-45.

_____. (1987) "Teaching Clinical Skills in Professional Psychology." In *Standards and Evaluation in the Education and Training of Professional Psychologists*, eds. E. Bourg, R. Bent, J. Callan, N. Jones, J. McHolland, and G. Stricker. Norman, Okla.: Transcript Press. Distributed by the American Psychological Association. Pp. 99-106.

Lubin, Marc and George Stricker. (1991) "Teaching the Core Curriculum." In *The Core Curriculum in Professional Psychology*, ed. R. Peterson, J. McHolland, R. Bent, *et al.* Washington: American Psychological Association and National Schools of Professional Psychology. Pp. 43-47.

Yalof, Jed A. (1996) *Training and Teaching the Mental Health Professional*. Northvale, N.J.: Jason Aronson.

Nine

EDUCATION IN THE TWENTY-FIRST CENTURY

John Lachs and Shirley M. Lachs

The fast pace of the modern world has at last defeated the risk-aversive conservatism of the human soul. We have come to accept, to expect, and even to welcome change. For a while, sound business practice was described as "management of change" and periodic alterations in product line, advertising, and the appearance of things have become standard, though by no means always effective, marketing techniques.

Surprisingly, the conversion of universities to primarily business institutions has not imbued them with this veneration of change. The marketing efforts of institutions of higher education have moved in line with the state of the art in the promotion of business, but the product line has remained largely unimproved. This may reflect the imperfect control administrations exert over slow-moving, recalcitrant faculties. The faculty's jealously guarded power over educational programs has made curricular innovation difficult to achieve, especially in traditional degree offerings. Administrations can start new programs here and there, but when it comes to the all-important bachelor's degree, for example, they are selling nineteenth-century lipstick to smear on twenty-first century lips.

The rapid development of the information industry may force major changes in the quiet hamlets of the academic world. At the very least, it is beginning to raise the question of what, if anything, the genteel and cumbersome residential university can offer beyond what is or will soon be available in information from the Internet. The question is likely to become more immediate with each annual increase of tuition. It will become pressingly urgent with the next major expansion of the Internet and once ordinary Americans begin to feel comfortable seeking information by electronic means.

At that point, the monopoly colleges and universities enjoy over credentialing young people may no longer be enough to justify and sustain their existence. They may face the fate of industries built on outmoded technologies. Just as email and the fax machine have displaced the telegraph, so learning at one's personal computer at home may squeeze out the lecture hall. Universities may go the way of Western Union.

Those who see college education with unclouded eyes readily admit that it is a tedious and inefficient process. Dull teachers, uninterested students, fragmented disciplines, and forced study unmotivated by real-life concerns make progress slow and the long-term retention of knowledge improbable. But what good would retention accomplish, in any case? The volume of information conveyed in the undergraduate classroom is a tribute to the cognitive achievements of the human race, but very little of it is of any direct value to young people trying to make their way in the world. Hoarding it is like stockpiling old bottles, shopping bags, and pieces of string with the justification that one never knows when they might come in handy.

Even the packaging of college level courses reveals the essential unconcern of faculty for the natural beat of intelligence. Curiosity is fed by problems we encounter and respects no disciplinary bounds. It takes us wherever we must go to get the answers we need. The results are memorable even without the attempt to memorize them. The typical college course, by contrast, covers a mound of loosely connected facts and theories in disciplinary isolation. The selection of topics rests in the hands of instructors who rarely bother offering a rationale for what they require or teach. The emphasis is on covering material, as if salvation or insight into the hidden recesses of reality depended on learning no less than the approved quantity of calculus or Chaucer.

Should it surprise us, then, that students show little interest in their work and that possibly as many as three in four cheat in writing papers and in taking exams? The fact that students admit to this level of dishonesty is a sign not of remorse but of open contempt of the system whose interest is in evaluating and not in educating them. If they must pass tests, they will pass them in whatever way is easiest or most effective; they see faculty talk of the dignity of learning and of the intrinsic value of knowledge as self-justification by funny little people who could never hold down regular jobs.

There is another side to faculty-student relations. Some young people come to admire some of their teachers and become their lifelong friends. A few find their lives changed or at least their purposes redefined as a result of meeting thoughtful adults who care. And more perhaps than we suspect carry away with them a small part of their teachers in happy memories, endearing habits, or a distant enthusiasm for the life of mind. But these are unplanned by-products of the system, not its primary goals.

Do such occasional fortuitous outcomes justify the expenditure of vast amounts of money and effort? The continued existence of colleges and universities is due as much to their power and position as to a vital need for their services. If the social inertia that allowed them to establish and maintain their power is swept aside by the electronic revolution, perhaps we should greet their decline as well-deserved. No one grieves over the fate of the dinosaurs; why should we shed tears at the death of state universities?

Traditional defenses of liberal education are beside the point in the face of the electronic challenge. No one, after all, suggests that we abolish liberal arts colleges and send the next generation to engineering school. Reading good literature and having some idea of how the physical world operates may well be of great personal value to people, but they need not be connected with spending four years in a dorm. At question is not what good reflection and learning might do, but how best we can get people interested in and competent at pursuing them. Will schools of liberal education still provide something special when the sum of human knowledge is at the fingertips of anyone with modem and monitor?

The answer is clearly yes and exploring it points us in the direction of what computers cannot give and what is, at least in one of its forms, the most neglected service of universities. Human immediacy in the form of new friends and the lasting companionship of peers constitutes one of the warmest and most worthwhile features of the residential experience.

Cynical outsiders among the students charge that many young people go to college to make contacts and to find mates, and they suppose that this is a devastating objection. But there is nothing wrong with making preparations for life at any time and in any context. And, in any case, the benefits of the campus are significantly broader: the mixing of students of differing values and lifestyles from varied family backgrounds, divergent social classes, and different parts of the world broadens their horizons and enriches their sympathies. They remember involvement in student organizations and adventures in the dorms with a fondness reserved for the best days of one's life.

Although such immediacy could be achieved by other means as well, the residential university is a convenient instrument for getting young people to-gether under civilizing conditions. The educational value of this togetherness has never been fully utilized. Colleges and universities make occasional, half-hearted attempts to integrate what students do and learn in the residences with the intricacies of the curriculum, but faculty visits and dorm seminars fall far short of what could be done. Better coordination of practical life on campus with the abstract materials of the classroom offers a splendid opportunity for improving education and providing a more attractive alternative to the Internet.

Important as student camaraderie is, it does not constitute the most valuable contribution of the residential college to the growth of young people. Another sort of togetherness, inter-generational immediacy, defines the work of education. Surprisingly, this vital interaction between teachers and students is poorly understood and therefore inadequately supported by institutions of higher education.

Small colleges used to pride themselves on the close connection between professors and those enrolled in their classes. There were legendary figures in many schools whose devotion to young people structured or took over their lives: they were friends, advisers, savvy mentors, older brothers, loving uncles, and patient confidants to generations of students. They were available to listen and to help, to comfort and to make small loans at anytime of the day or year. Their students were their children or their grateful family, and the wells of their generosity seemed never to run dry.

This is an ideal that cannot be imposed on people. It was freely chosen by a few who viewed teaching as a calling and instinctively understood its profound, even sacred, significance. Though this may seem an absurdly romantic ideal to professional teacher-researchers today, there were and there continue to be some individuals who conduct their lives in its light. Nearly everything pulls against it: the busy-ness of the modern world, family obligations, the demands of the profession, even the physical distance at which faculty live from campus make it difficult to spend a great deal of time with students.

Colleges and universities, of course, acknowledge the significance of contact with students. They oblige faculty to hold office hours. They also operate advising systems and some of them organize hopelessly artificial "fireside chats" to encourage faculty to invite students into their homes. Such formal initiatives never amount to much. Many faculty members think of the mandated contact as a nuisance and an interruption; students quickly detect faculty displeasure or lack of interest and learn to stay away. The most effective student-faculty relationships may well occur in the labs when researchers take a promising student or two under their wings. But even there, the contact is limited and professional, and tends to lack depth of human encounter and of caring.

What makes extensive student-faculty immediacy so important? To understand this, we must get a clear grasp of what faculty, at their best, represent. In addition to being accomplished professionals, they are also expected to be mature human beings. The rigorous standards that govern hiring, retention, and promotion in a market where jobs are relatively scarce, yield assurance of professional competence. Age, experience, and service in a humane and responsible institution make the expectation of maturity reasonable. The obvious fact that this demand frequently goes unmet is of no significance when we speak of what faculty do *at their best* or what they ought to be and do. That cars may not start and that mechanics may be unable to fix them present no threat to our knowledge of what they ought to or ought to be able to do.

In one respect, faculty are no different from other mature adults, contact with whom is of genuine value to young persons in the process of defining themselves. From another perspective, they are special, and especially useful for purposes of self-formation, because they have devoted their lives to intellectual pursuits that involve criticism and reflection. Persons of that sort will, of course, make their share of mistakes. But even their relations to their failures are likely to be, or at any rate ought to be, more intelligent than average. They tend to want to understand why they failed in order to prevent the same mistake from overtaking them again. Such reflection establishes habits that not only reduce costly errors in the conduct of life, but also provide a sweet sense of assurance that we can deal with problems.

Perhaps it is best to make the point we wish by calling attention to two different ways of storing knowledge. We safeguard the information we develop by writing it down, publishing it in books, or putting it on the Internet. We also stockpile knowledge in living human beings in the form of experience and the products of reflection. The information contained in books is inert; it does not reorganize itself as does knowledge in persons. It remains safe, unchanged and accessible, always ready to be added to but never growing deeper or more complex than we made it.

What is stored in persons, by contrast, is living knowledge constantly in the process of transformation. Perhaps because much of it does not exist in the form of sentences, its depth is indeterminate; people questioned about what they know can surprise even themselves. This is because a single well-formed query can add to living knowledge by causing a reorganization of existing materials, the way a spark of electricity fuses hydrogen and oxygen to create water or in the fashion that tapping the side of a kaleidoscope rearranges colors into a new picture.

In more familiar language, asking people questions gives them an opportunity to think, draw on their experience and come up with something new. The demands of communication are such, moreover, that participants in the conversation may have to reformulate their questions and their answers in terms they have not used before and thereby contribute to the creation of novel ideas and insights.

Nothing like this is available in today's machines. We can learn new things by surfing the Net and those who are inventive about where to look can uncover a great deal. But often the information runs out before the questions do, and machines don't improvise. They are incapable, moreover, of particularizing their answers, that is, of adapting their information to the needs and situations of the people who want to know and presenting it in terms suited to their level of understanding and state of mind.

The simple way to say this is that we cannot have a conversation with Websites. The more complete and more accurate way of putting it is that human beings are, among other things, vast collections of experience, organic systems of storing and using the living past. This is why talking with reflective older people can be so rewarding; their years of experience, crystallized into ideas, can give us stunningly rich perspectives on life. And this is also why it would be a great privilege to be able to question Plato or Napoleon one evening over a glass of wine. We have the words and know the exploits of the famous dead but, as a wonderful student used to say, we have a few more questions. No one can answer those questions but the people concerned and, alas, they took their share of knowledge with them to the grave.

What colleges and universities can offer that is unavailable from the PC is what they have always offered at their best: firsthand contact with remarkable people whose knowledge of their fields and whose experience of life have been integrated into the unity of a person. Such conversation is of benefit to both students and teachers. Students gain access to the accumulated wisdom of the human race through a dynamic medium that rewards searching and novel questions with thoughtful and often surprising answers. Teachers, in turn, find stimulation under the scrutiny of inquisitive young minds. Much human knowledge is unfocussed or tacit; the opportunities and irritations of dialogue force the articulation of thought and bring indistinct ideas to the clarity of explicit consciousness.

Sustained communication between mature scholars with a measure of life experience and young people in the early stages of charting their course meets the most exacting requirement of education: it results in the transmission of knowledge to a new generation. In assessing its value, we should not overlook the role it plays in creating new insights and in keeping established truths vibrant in the minds of those long familiar with them. Nor must we underrate the importance for the future of society of the inter-generational faith engendered by such nurturing contact.

Lectures on videotape, on audiotape and, if delivered from detailed, antique notes, even in the lecture hall come closer to the way knowledge is stored in books or on the Internet than to the manner in which it can be created and obtained through open questioning and collaboration. As a method of conveying information, lectures lack the speed and the free-ranging exploration typical of computer access to data. The information they present is rarely the reason for our interest in them; the source of their fascination is the eloquence and angle of vision of the lecturer. What makes such presentations worthwhile is the opportunity they afford of seeing and asking questions about how another human being perceives the world or some intriguing portion of it.

Laboratories have for centuries provided a setting for cooperative enterprises in which intellectual sparks can fly. But in scientific work, as in every activity in which persons meet, the central variable is the quality of the interaction. In spite of the claims of people who disguise nasty imperiousness as the defense of high standards, benevolent mentoring is not incompatible with the demand for top performance. To the contrary, high expectations in a friendly, supportive environment are more likely to bring results than the terror imposed by moody tyrants.

Hands-on education in scientific inquiry and laboratory investigation in which faculty adopt students as their junior partners are, therefore, permanently valuable services electronic media cannot supplant. Their benefit derives from the same source as that of face-to-face work in the humanities and the social sciences. Searching, unimpeded inter-generational communication informs the young and stimulates their elders. The unpredictably rich results of questioning can make students the teachers of their teachers and their interchange a source of exhilaration and delight.

We are in greater need of what the residential college experience offers than perhaps any prior generation. Our world is disablingly busy. The demands of their jobs and of their complex lives make it difficult for parents to devote extensive attention to their children. Childcare workers and teachers, whose professional services are supposed to assure the moral growth and intellectual development of the young, are overwhelmed with people they must benefit. They cannot spend much time in direct personal contact with any of them. As a result, a significant number of individuals grow up without getting to know older, more experienced persons and without the benefit of feeling their sustained love.

This loss can be devastating. Inter-generational friendship is the sole method of handing down the habits of caring without which human life remains empty and often turns bitter. As any skill of the heart, this cannot be taught through words or through exercises devised by counselors. It is the grateful response of people to a happy childhood in a nurturing community, the desire to pay the next generation for what was received from the last.

Even at their best, residential institutions of higher education are poor substitutes for loving families. But they are among the few alternatives available today. College students are old enough to appreciate the deeper reaches of inter-generational friendship, yet not so jaded as to have ceased looking for warmth and guidance. Under the right circumstances, they can develop rich and caring relationships with their teachers. Though most of these remain temporary partnerships, some grow into lifelong commitments to intense mutual support.

The windstorm of the electronic revolution feels like a zephyr in the sheltered valleys of the academic world. Colleges and universities have not even started to assess the changes they will have to undergo to survive in the new world of the twenty-first century. They appear to trust in their credentialing power to stave off disaster. But before long, some reputable institutions are bound to recognize the windfall of offering legitimate degrees through electronic distance learning. This will set off a competitive stampede, resulting in a squeeze on prices. Will students short on money and time not prefer the cheaper and faster electronic degree to spending years at marginal institutions?

A painful consolidation of residential colleges and universities is as near a certainty as anything in the future can be. Rich schools are likely to survive, but even they will find their missions and their curricula transformed. To move in the direction of providing closer and more extensive contact with faculty, they will have to revamp their educational strategy. The imaginative use of new technologies that alone makes this possible will, in the process, altogether transform the undergraduate program.

Full recognition that books and the classroom do not constitute effective ways of teaching facts is likely to revolutionize what teachers and students do. Electronic access to all the cut-and-dried material of education will liberate faculty from lengthy exposition and boring drill. Students will have all the facts they need at their fingertips, with easy machine checks that they got them right. Since they will uncover the facts as needed for the solution of problems, they will master them in their context and remember them better.

This should enable faculty members to attend to the tasks of education proper: to teaching skills of investigation, theory formation and hypothesis testing, and to enhancing critical judgment and the scope and depth of appreciation. The resulting growth involves expansion of both the rigor of thought and the sweep of imagination, conferring on students some of the same pleasures critics, scientific investigators, and creative artists enjoy. We hardly dare say it: education might, in this way, become as joyous for students as it has always been for the best of their teachers.

We do not mean to suggest that utopia is just around the corner. It never is. But the ingenuity of human beings has now put tools at our disposal that enable us to do what prior generations could not even dream. Transmission to the young of important portions of the accumulated knowledge of the human race need no longer exact the pain of dozens of years of rote memory. Much more material than any one person could ever remember is now available in response to simple commands typed into or spoken to machines.

Before long, we will find ourselves tied to our computers as we are tied to our cars; they will become integral elements of the self. The critical question is how we will learn to use this external memory for the purpose of improving human minds and, through them, human lives.

The effects of externalizing memory are likely to replicate the effects of finding a machine solution to providing the conditions of any important practice. The ease with which the activity can be performed makes for a vast increase in its frequency and a decline in the value we place on performing it the old way. So, for example, when writing was invented and accounts of past events could be stored in libraries or on walls, oral histories, passed from bard to bard, were nearly eliminated. And the advent of the typewriter brought with it a flood of writing, along with decreased appreciation of fine calligraphy.

Our veneration of the power of memory is also likely to evaporate as we learn to replace factual information stored in individual brains with communal data banks. Contests such as "The College Bowl" may come to look like freak shows without a point, much like the performances of people who try to play eight instruments at once to imitate an orchestra. Forcing students to remember large bodies of information and rewarding them for feats of recalling disconnected facts may appear sad or even bizarre to subsequent generations.

This is the context in which we must understand the impact computerized storage will likely exert on educational practices. Even a cursory assessment of how much time is spent on memory work suffices to indicate the extent of the changes we face. The optimistic interpretation of these impending events is that the development of technology is at last lifting from humans the burden of brute or unfitting activities. Dishwashers have liberated us from the daily imperatives of the sink and backhoes have taken over the hard work of digging. Why should the task of carrying with us the irrelevant details of the world not pass from us, as well? Thought and appreciation constitute more worthy uses of our time and capacity than storage of dead facts.

Such an optimistic account of developments is clearly better than the alternatives. But to make it acceptable, we must dispel a possible misunderstanding and call attention to a peril. When we speak of handing over the work of memory to machine substitutes of the human brain, we do not mean to imply that we will walk around with empty heads, unable to recall anything that happened to us. On the contrary, investigation and appreciation are themselves impossible without mastery, and that means storage and integration, of skills. Thought requires a subject matter held fast in memory and we cannot decide on the direction of inquiry without sustained knowledge of the shape of facts and of what about them needs to be explained.

Evidently, such contextualized ordinary memories are not what computers are in the process of replacing. Human minds, particularly the interested intellects of the young, are like flypaper: everything they come in contact with sticks to them. Such effortless remembering is a condition of operating in the world, and it enriches life in incalculable ways. Without it, we cannot know whether tires go on the car or as decorations around the neck. And we fail as friends if we are unable to distinguish strangers from those we love.

We have in mind, instead, the forced ingestion and periodic regurgitation in educational institutions of vast quantities of unrelated facts. At times when information is difficult to come by, such privately stored knowledge is invaluable, in just the way a flashlight comes in handy when the lights go out. But it is a mistake to organize education as if we perpetually faced the dark.

The danger confronting us is that our success has become our problem: the wonderful aids we have devised for mastering facts and understanding the world may diminish the felt seriousness of education. Traditionally, the discipline of compulsory memory work has carried the burden of conveying the momentousness of learning. The cry for a return to basics in education may, in fact, be simply the desire for effort and earnest respect to infuse the enterprise. Prosperity has supposedly made young people soft or unambitious. Since human nature, at least in its current incarnation, has no respect for the easy, eliminating the pressure of rote memory may make education painless or even fun, and thereby sap the energy with which we tackle it.

The long-term challenge facing educators at all levels is to find ways to sustain the motivation of students and to convey to them the life-creating power of appropriating the culture of the past. Fortunately, early indications point to success. Access to vast reaches of the Internet keeps young people riveted to their seats in front of monitors for hours. Such natural curiosity combined with desire for the companionship of caring adults should give teachers everything they need. In any case, simple as access to information has become, there is nothing easy about interpreting and explaining the facts. Learning more about the world, therefore, will always be a challenge that the contagious excitement of good teachers can convert into the work of personal and intellectual growth.

ABOUT THE CONTRIBUTORS

GUY ALLEN is Professor of Writing in the Professional Writing Program at the University of Toronto. He was the Coordinator of the Psychoanalytic Thought Program for several years and was awarded a national teaching honor for higher education in Canada. He is the managing editor of a small literary press for new writers, co-hosts a community radio program that broadcasts autobiographical narratives, and is the founder of the popular *Totally Unknown Writers Festival* in Toronto. He has numerous publications in teaching and pedagogy and is the editor of *No More Masterpieces: Short Prose by New Writers*.

FRANK GRUBA-McCALLISTER is Professor and Associate Dean of the Illinois School of Professional Psychology-Chicago. He specializes in existential and phenomenological psychology, health psychology, and the psychology of spirituality. He has contributed several publications to the professional literature on these topics and has been the recipient of multiple awards for teaching excellence at the Illinois School.

DAVID A. JOPLING is Associate Professor of Philosophy at York University. He was a Mellon Fellow in psychology at Emory University, has authored numerous articles in Continental philosophy and philosophical psychology, and is the author of *Self-Knowledge and the Self*. He is currently a consultant and representative for the Ontario Ministry of Education and Training.

JOHN LACHS is Centennial Professor of Philosophy at Vanderbilt University. He is one of the leading interpreters of the American philosophical tradition and has received numerous awards for teaching excellence and the advancement of scholarship, including the Herbert Schneider Award for Lifetime Contributions to American Philosophy. His recent books include, *In Love with Life*, *The Cost of Comfort*, *Thinking in the Ruins*, and *The Relevance of Philosophy to Life*.

SHIRLEY M. LACHS is a classicist and has taught Latin for many years. She writes with her husband on issues of education and is the co-editor of George Santayana, *Physical Order and Moral Liberty*.

MARC LUBIN is Professor and Dean of the Illinois School of Professional Psychology-Chicago. He is a Diplomate on the American Board of Administrative Psychology and currently teaches and supervises graduate students in clinical psychology. He has been a consultant to child-care teachers and social workers and was a developmental teacher of disturbed children at the University of Chicago Orthogenic School. He has several publications on graduate teaching in psychology, specializes in psychoanalytic theory and practice, and maintains a private practice in psychotherapy in Chicago.

GEORGE DAVID MILLER is Professor of Philosophy, Graduate Director, and Director of the Scholars Program at Lewis University. He is the recipient of several awards for teaching excellence including the Carnegie Illinois Professor of the Year. He specializes in the philosophy of education, serves as Associate Editor of the Value Inquiry Book Series (VIBS), and is the author of several books, including *Negotiating Toward Truth, On Ethics and Values,* and *An Idiosyncratic Ethics.*

JON MILLS is a psychologist and a philosopher. He received his Psy.D. in clinical psychology from the Illinois School of Professional Psychology, Chicago, his Ph.D. in philosophy from Vanderbilt University, and was a Fulbright scholar of philosophy at the University of Toronto and York University. He is currently Internship Coordinator and Clinical Supervisor in the Mental Health Program at Lakeridge Health Corporation Oshawa, an Associate with the Research Institute at Lakeridge Health, and a member of the Core Faculty at the Adler School of Professional Psychology in Toronto. He serves as Associate Editor of the Value Inquiry Book Series (VIBS), has numerous publications in philosophy, psychology, psychoanalysis, and education, and is co-author of *The Ontology of Prejudice.* He maintains a private practice in Ajax, Ontario.

JANUSZ A. POLANOWSKI is a full-time faculty member in the Arts and Humanities Department at Nashville Technical Institute and teaches in the Department of Philosophy at Vanderbilt University where he is a Ph.D. candidate in philosophy. He specializes in process philosophy and ethics and is the co-author of *The Ontology of Prejudice.*

JEFFREY TLUMAK is Associate Professor of Philosophy at Vanderbilt University. He was Director of Vanderbilt's Graduate Program for several years, founding editor of the American Philosophical Association's *Newsletter on Teaching Philosophy,* member of the APA's Committee on Teaching, and recipient of the Outstanding Graduate Teacher Award at Vanderbilt. He also serves as an advisor for the university's Center for Teaching. He has published numerous contributions on modern philosophy and epistemology and authored an educational audiotape script, *Descartes, Bacon, and the Rise of Modern Philosophy.*

INDEX

VIBS

The **Value Inquiry Book Series** is co-sponsored by:

Adler School of Professional Psychology
American Indian Philosophy Association
American Maritain Association
American Society for Value Inquiry
Association for Process Philosophy of Education
Canadian Society for Philosophical Practice
Center for Bioethics, University of Turku
Center for International Partnerships, Rochester Institute of Technology
Center for Professional and Applied Ethics, University of North Carolina at
Charlotte
Centre for Applied Ethics, Hong Kong Baptist University
Centre for Cultural Research, Aarhus University
Centre for the Study of Philosophy and Religion, College of Cape Breton
College of Education and Allied Professions, Bowling Green State University
Concerned Philosophers for Peace
Conference of Philosophical Societies
Department of Moral and Social Philosophy, University of Helsinki
Gannon University
Gilson Society
Global Association for the Study of Persons
Ikeda University
Institute of Philosophy of the High Council of Scientific Research, Spain
International Academy of Philosophy of the Principality of Liechtenstein
International Center for the Arts, Humanities, and Value Inquiry
International Society for Universal Dialogue
Natural Law Society

Philosophical Society of Finland
Philosophy Born of Struggle Association
Philosophy Seminar, University of Mainz
Pragmatism Archive
R.S. Hartman Institute for Formal and Applied Axiology
Research Institute, Lakeridge Health Corporation
Russian Philosophical Society
Society for Iberian and Latin-American Thought
Society for the Philosophic Study of Genocide and the Holocaust
Society for the Philosophy of Sex and Love
Yves R. Simon Institute.

Titles Published

1.   Noel Balzer, *The Human Being as a Logical Thinker.*

2.   Archie J. Bahm, *Axiology: The Science of Values.*

3.   H. P. P. (Hennie) Lötter, *Justice for an Unjust Society.*

4.   H. G. Callaway, *Context for Meaning and Analysis: A Critical Study in the Philosophy of Language.*

5.   Benjamin S. Llamzon, *A Humane Case for Moral Intuition.*

6.   James R. Watson, *Between Auschwitz and Tradition: Postmodern Reflections on the Task of Thinking.* A volume in **Holocaust and Genocide Studies.**

7.   Robert S. Hartman, *Freedom to Live: The Robert Hartman Story,* edited by Arthur R. Ellis. A volume in **Hartman Institute Axiology Studies.**

8.   Archie J. Bahm, *Ethics: The Science of Oughtness.*

9.   George David Miller, *An Idiosyncratic Ethics; Or, the Lauramachean Ethics.*

10. Joseph P. DeMarco, *A Coherence Theory in Ethics.*

11. Frank G. Forrest, *Valuemetrics^N: The Science of Personal and Professional Ethics.* A volume in **Hartman Institute Axiology Studies.**

12. William Gerber, *The Meaning of Life: Insights of the World's Great Thinkers.*

13. Richard T. Hull, Editor, *A Quarter Century of Value Inquiry: Presidential Addresses of the American Society for Value Inquiry.* A volume in **Histories and Addresses of Philosophical Societies.**

14. William Gerber, *Nuggets of Wisdom from Great Jewish Thinkers: From Biblical Times to the Present.*

15. Sidney Axinn, *The Logic of Hope: Extensions of Kant's View of Religion.*

16. Messay Kebede, *Meaning and Development.*

17. Amihud Gilead, *The Platonic Odyssey: A Philosophical-Literary Inquiry into the* Phaedo.

18. Necip Fikri Alican, *Mill's Principle of Utility: A Defense of John Stuart Mill's Notorious Proof.* A volume in **Universal Justice.**

19. Michael H. Mitias, Editor, *Philosophy and Architecture.*

20. Roger T. Simonds, *Rational Individualism: The Perennial Philosophy of Legal Interpretation.* A volume in **Natural Law Studies.**

21. William Pencak, *The Conflict of Law and Justice in the Icelandic Sagas.*

22. Samuel M. Natale and Brian M. Rothschild, Editors, *Values, Work, Education: The Meanings of Work.*

23. N. Georgopoulos and Michael Heim, Editors, *Being Human in the Ultimate: Studies in the Thought of John M. Anderson.*

24. Robert Wesson and Patricia A. Williams, Editors, *Evolution and Human Values.*

25. Wim J. van der Steen, *Facts, Values, and Methodology: A New Approach to Ethics.*

26. Avi Sagi and Daniel Statman, *Religion and Morality.*

27. Albert William Levi, *The High Road of Humanity: The Seven Ethical Ages of Western Man,* edited by Donald Phillip Verene and Molly Black Verene.

28. Samuel M. Natale and Brian M. Rothschild, Editors, *Work Values: Education, Organization, and Religious Concerns.*

29. Laurence F. Bove and Laura Duhan Kaplan, Editors, *From the Eye of the Storm: Regional Conflicts and the Philosophy of Peace.* A volume in **Philosophy of Peace.**

30. Robin Attfield, *Value, Obligation, and Meta-Ethics.*

31. William Gerber, *The Deepest Questions You Can Ask About God: As Answered by the World's Great Thinkers.*

32. Daniel Statman, *Moral Dilemmas.*

33. Rem B. Edwards, Editor, *Formal Axiology and Its Critics.* A volume in **Hartman Institute Axiology Studies.**

34. George David Miller and Conrad P. Pritscher, *On Education and Values: In Praise of Pariahs and Nomads.* A volume in **Philosophy of Education.**

35. Paul S. Penner, *Altruistic Behavior: An Inquiry into Motivation.*

36. Corbin Fowler, *Morality for Moderns.*

37. Giambattista Vico, *The Art of Rhetoric (Institutiones Oratoriae,* 1711-1741), from the definitive Latin text and notes, Italian commentary and introduction by Giuliano Crifò, translated and edited by Giorgio A. Pinton and Arthur W. Shippee. A volume in **Values in Italian Philosophy.**

38. W. H. Werkmeister, *Martin Heidegger on the Way,* edited by Richard T. Hull. A volume in **Werkmeister Studies.**

39. Phillip Stambovsky, *Myth and the Limits of Reason.*

40. Samantha Brennan, Tracy Isaacs, and Michael Milde, Editors, *A Question of Values: New Canadian Perspectives in Ethics and Political Philosophy.*

41. Peter A. Redpath, *Cartesian Nightmare: An Introduction to Transcendental Sophistry.* A volume in **Studies in the History of Western Philosophy.**

42. Clark Butler, *History as the Story of Freedom: Philosophy in Intercultural Context,* with Responses by sixteen scholars.

43. Dennis Rohatyn, *Philosophy History Sophistry.*

44. Leon Shaskolsky Sheleff, *Social Cohesion and Legal Coercion: A Critique of Weber, Durkheim, and Marx.* Afterword by Virginia Black.

45. Alan Soble, Editor, *Sex, Love, and Friendship: Studies of the Society for the Philosophy of Sex and Love, 1977-1992.* A volume in **Histories and Addresses of Philosophical Societies.**

46. Peter A. Redpath, *Wisdom's Odyssey: From Philosophy to Transcendental Sophistry.* A volume in **Studies in the History of Western Philosophy.**

47. Albert A. Anderson, *Universal Justice: A Dialectical Approach.* A volume in **Universal Justice.**

48. Pio Colonnello, *The Philosophy of José Gaos.* Translated from Italian by Peter Cocozzella. Edited by Myra Moss. Introduction by Giovanni Gullace. A volume in **Values in Italian Philosophy.**

49. Laura Duhan Kaplan and Laurence F. Bove, Editors, *Philosophical Perspectives on Power and Domination: Theories and Practices.* A volume in **Philosophy of Peace.**

50. Gregory F. Mellema, *Collective Responsibility.*

51. Josef Seifert, *What Is Life? The Originality, Irreducibility, and Value of Life.* A volume in **Central-European Value Studies.**

52. William Gerber, *Anatomy of What We Value Most.*

53. Armando Molina, *Our Ways: Values and Character,* edited by Rem B. Edwards. A volume in **Hartman Institute Axiology Studies.**

54. Kathleen J. Wininger, *Nietzsche's Reclamation of Philosophy.* A volume in **Central-European Value Studies.**

55. Thomas Magnell, Editor, *Explorations of Value.*

56. HPP (Hennie) Lötter, *Injustice, Violence, and Peace: The Case of South Africa.* A volume in **Philosophy of Peace.**

57. Lennart Nordenfelt, *Talking About Health: A Philosophical Dialogue.* A volume in **Nordic Value Studies.**

58. Jon Mills and Janusz A. Polanowski, *The Ontology of Prejudice.* A volume in **Philosophy and Psychology.**

59. Leena Vilkka, *The Intrinsic Value of Nature.*

60. Palmer Talbutt, Jr., *Rough Dialectics: Sorokin's Philosophy of Value,* with Contributions by Lawrence T. Nichols and Pitirim A. Sorokin.

61. C. L. Sheng, *A Utilitarian General Theory of Value.*

62. George David Miller, *Negotiating Toward Truth: The Extinction of Teachers and Students.* Epilogue by Mark Roelof Eleveld. A volume in **Philosophy of Education.**

63. William Gerber, *Love, Poetry, and Immortality: Luminous Insights of the World's Great Thinkers.*

64. Dane R. Gordon, Editor, *Philosophy in Post-Communist Europe.* A volume in **Post-Communist European Thought.**

65. Dane R. Gordon and Józef Niznik, Editors, *Criticism and Defense of Rationality in Contemporary Philosophy.* A volume in **Post-Communist European Thought.**

66. John R. Shook, *Pragmatism: An Annotated Bibliography, 1898-1940.* With Contributions by E. Paul Colella, Lesley Friedman, Frank X. Ryan, and Ignas K. Skrupskelis.

67. Lansana Keita, *The Human Project and the Temptations of Science.*

68. Michael M. Kazanjian, *Phenomenology and Education: Cosmology, Co-Being, and Core Curriculum.* A volume in **Philosophy of Education.**

97. Roxanne Claire Farrar, *Sartrean Dialectics: A Method for Critical Discourse on Aesthetic Experience.*

98. Ugo Spirito, *Memoirs of the Twentieth Century.* Translated from Italian and edited by Anthony G. Costantini. A volume in **Values in Italian Philosophy.**

99. Steven Schroeder, *Between Freedom and Necessity: An Essay on the Place of Value.*

100. Foster N. Walker, *Enjoyment and the Activity of Mind: Dialogues on Whitehead and Education.* A volume in **Philosophy of Education.**

101. Avi Sagi, *Kierkegaard, Religion, and Existence: The Voyage of the Self.* Translated from Hebrew by Batya Stein.

102. Bennie R. Crockett, Jr., Editor, *Addresses of the Mississippi Philosophical Association.* A volume in **Histories and Addresses of Philosophical Societies.**

103. Paul van Dijk, *Anthropology in the Age of Technology: The Philosophical Contribution of Günther Anders.*

104. Giambattista Vico, *Universal Right.* Translated from Latin and edited by Giorgio Pinton and Margaret Diehl. A volume in **Values in Italian Philosophy.**

105. Judith Presler and Sally J. Scholz, Editors, *Peacemaking: Lessons from the Past, Visions for the Future.* A volume in **Philosophy of Peace.**

106. Dennis Bonnette, *Origin of the Human Species.* A volume in **Studies in the History of Western Philosophy.**

107. Phyllis Chiasson, *Peirce's Pragmatism: The Design for Thinking.* A volume in **Studies in Pragmatism and Values.**

108. Dan Stone, Editor, *Theoretical Interpretations of the Holocaust.* A volume in **Holocaust and Genocide Studies.**

109. Raymond Angelo Belliotti, *What Is the Meaning of Human Life?*

110. Lennart Nordenfelt, *Health, Science, and Ordinary Language*, with Contributions by George Khushf and K. W. M. Fulford.

111. Daryl Koehn, *Local Insights, Global Ethics for Business*. A volume in **Studies in Applied Ethics.**

112. Matti Häyry and Tuija Takala, Editors, *The Future of Value Inquiry*. A volume in **Nordic Value Studies.**

113. Conrad P. Pritscher, *Quantum Learning: Beyond Duality.*

114. Thomas M. Dicken and Rem B. Edwards, *Dialogues on Values and Centers of Value: Old Friends, New Thoughts.* A volume in **Hartman Institute Axiology Studies.**

115. Rem B. Edwards, *What Caused the Big Bang?* A volume in **Philosophy and Religion.**

116. Jon Mills, Editor, *A Pedagogy of Becoming.* A volume in **Philosophy of Education.**